Isak Dinesen

. . . his poetic temperament which, we might say, is not rich enough, or, perhaps, not poor enough, to distinguish poetry and reality from one another. The poetical was the *more* he himself brought with him. This *more* was the poetical he enjoyed in the poetic situation of reality; he withdrew this again in the form of poetic reflection. This offered him a second enjoyment, and his whole life was motivated by enjoyment. In the first instance he enjoyed the aesthetic personally, in the second instance he enjoyed his own aesthetic personality. In the first instance the point was that he enjoyed egoistically and personally what in part was that with which he himself had impregnated reality; in the second instance his personality was effaced, and he enjoyed the situation, and himself in the situation. In the first instance he constantly needed reality as occasion, as factor; in the second instance, reality was submerged in the poetic. (Kierkegaard, "Diary of a Seducer," *Either/Or,* 301.)

You call an artist a seducer and are not aware that you are paying him the highest of compliments. The whole attitude of the artist towards the Universe is that of a seducer.

For what does seduction mean but the ability to make, with infinite trouble, patience and perseverance, the object upon which you concentrate your mind give forth, voluntarily and enraptured, its very core and essence? Aye, and to reach, in the process, a higher beauty than it could ever, under any other circumstances, have attained. (Isak Dinesen, *Ehrengard,* 12.)

ISAK DINESEN

THE LIFE AND IMAGINATION OF A SEDUCER

Olga Anastasia Pelensky

OHIO UNIVERSITY PRESS / ATHENS

partly funded by the National Endowment for the Humanities
and the Rowland Foundation

© Copyright 1991 by Olga Anastasia Pelensky
Printed in the United States of America
All rights reserved

Ohio University Press books are printed on acid-free paper ∞

Library of Congress Cataloging-in-Publication Data

Pelensky, Olga Anastasia.
  Isak Dinesen : the life and imagination of a seducer / Olga Anastasia
Pelensky.
    p.   cm.
  Includes bibliographical references and index.
  ISBN 0-8214-0968-9
  1. Dinesen, Isak, 1885–1962—Biography.   2. Authors, Danish—20th
century—Biography.   I. Title.
PT8175.B545Z79   1991
839.8'1372—dc20   90-45735
  [B]   CIP

❦ *For Anastasia Lepak, Kris Poli, Jeff Snyder, and, in memory, Panko Marshalok*

"When the design of my life is completed, shall I, shall other people see a stork?"

(ISAK DINESEN, *Out of Africa*, 253.)

CONTENTS

I. THE ARISTOCRAT

II. THE ADVENTURER

III. THE AUTHOR

List of Illustrations

Acknowledgments

This book was made possible to a large extent by a grant from the Rowland Foundation, which through the good graces of Edwin Land made my research trip to Africa possible. His support has been an important beacon during the construction of this volume.

This book is the result of the generous spirit of many people, both here in America, and abroad, in Denmark, Africa, and England.

My research began in Denmark, where I made two trips, drawn by the kind invitation of people who knew Isak Dinesen, the atmosphere of her family home, and the substantial collection of papers on Isak Dinesen at the Royal Library in Copenhagen. In Denmark, I would like to thank: Hendrik Rosenmeier for helping me launch my research there; both he and his wife graciously made me feel at home. Thorkild Bjørnvig for providing much encouragement and support for this project, and for relating his impressions of the baroness, her paradoxical (and implicit) call for all writers to eliminate all identity; both he and his wife Birgit with warm spirit opened their home to me on the island of Samsø, and, with the sea all around, talked to me about the baroness; without hesitation they passed along a then unpublished English translation of *The Pact*. Aage Henriksen for spending many hours speaking to me about his relationship to Isak Dinesen in between walks and pastries, giving me access to his private papers (where the Kierkegaard link was made clear), adding an important dimension to my understanding of her; he and his wife made me most welcome in their home in Humlebæk. Clara Selborn (formerly Svendsen) for hosting me at the small fishing village of Dragør and recalling her days as secretary to Isak Dinesen, as well as taking me on a tour of Rungstedlund, showing me the author's study overlooking the sailboats along the Strandvej; she tirelessly answered my questions through the mail, and sent along copies of *Blixeniana* to me. Jonna Dinesen for her grace and entertaining me at Leerbæk, where she spoke to me about her sister-in-law from her unique perspective, and her daughter Anne Kopp for her observations. Ole Wivel for receiving me with good humor, and taking time from a busy work schedule at Glydendal to meet with me, relaying his views of Isak Dinesen from his vantage point as her publisher; he made clear the tenets of the Heretica literary movement in Denmark of which Isak Dinesen was a part. Knud Jensen for taking time from his position as director of the Louisiana Museum to help clarify the Pierrot figure Isak Dinesen played out; his observations on her relationship to the Heretics were particularly helpful. Viggo Kjær Petersen for sharing his personal insights into Isak Dinesen at the end of her life, revealing a glimpse of her thinking then. Bent Mohn for reading from his diaries of his relationship to Isak Dinesen. And Frans Lasson for agreeing to meet with me and answering questions about Isak Dinesen's authorship.

For providing a deeper understanding of the Danish culture, I would like to thank Allan Frederiche, the Danish ballet historian for so kindly meeting with me, giving me an understanding of the role of the ballet and theater in Denmark during World War II, and the importance of the *commedia dell'arte* to Danish life; Niels Larson, the director of the Pantomime Theatre at Tivoli Gardens, for sketching in details on the history of the pantomime and *commedia dell'arte*; P. O. Olesen of the Hunting Museum in Rungsted, who rather unexpectedly and on short notice illuminated the history of the surrounding area of Rungstedlund; and Karen Neiiendam, the director of the Royal Court Theatre, and Kristian Vang, for adding to my knowledge of the importance of masquerade and the theatrical to Danish history. Steen Eiler Rasmussen for providing the crucial information that Isak Dinesen saw herself as living on a stage, recalling her delight at the stagelike expanse leading to her home along the Strandvej; he kindly met with me at a difficult personal time and spoke of his relationship to Isak Dinesen during World War II. Nils Davidsen-Nielsen for pointing me in the direction of background material on Denmark during the war, and for arranging for my quarters in the heart of Copenhagen, near Tivoli; he and his wife Marianne made my stay during my return visit to Copenhagen a particularly fruitful one.

While I have a rudimentary knowledge of Danish, several people in Denmark helped me with translation, including Metta Pors. Helle Bering-Jensen provided a major shortcut in my research and helped me avoid translation errors by translating the major portion of the Danish writings; her observations about Danish life and history, as well as the literature, were very helpful.

In Africa, I was fortunate enough to meet people who knew Isak Dinesen when she lived on her coffee plantation at the foot of the Ngong Hills. In Africa, I would like to thank: Errol Trzebinski for being a vital link in Kenya, meeting me in Mombasa and outlining the issues in Isak Dinesen and Denys Finch Hatton's life as she saw them. It was because of her advice that I was able to meet the late Ingrid Lindstrom, and her undauntedness driving through rough areas with no roads that I came to see Denys Finch Hatton's home on the sea, not far from the Arab ruins Isak Dinesen mentions in *Out of Africa*. Ingrid Lindstrom was most warm in her welcome and shared her special understanding into Isak Dinesen's life in Kenya; the late Rose Cartwright reinforced the adventurer theme in Isak Dinesen's life and clarified aspects of her last years in Africa; both Rose Cartwright and Ingrid Lindstrom, through their gentle and indomitable spirit made that time in Isak Dinesen's life take on reality. Jennie Lee Richert for putting me in touch with Kirby McCaffrey, and helping me maneuver my way through my research in Nairobi. Kirby McCaffrey, for bringing me out to see Peter Beard on his hog farm, not far from the Ngong Hills, who met my unexpected visit with good grace and hospitality. There I met the late Kamande Gatura (Kamante in *Out of Africa*), who spoke movingly of his relationship to Isak Dinesen; Vanessa McCaffrey kindly translated the interview. Ulf Aschan, the godson of Bror Blixen, for giving the world of the white hunters definite shape, as did Peter Beard and David Allan. Ulf Aschan shared his impressions of Bror Blixen and how they differed from the prevailing perceptions. Lady Erskine for introducing me to Mbaire Mutuguti, making a friendship possible that continued here in the United States. Mbaire Mutuguti and Kahoya Mbugua for giving me important insight into contemporary Kenya; their observations helped me to understand the life of the Gikuyu and Masai during colonial times. A festival of dancers held in Nairobi with students from all over Kenya made it possible to understand the nature of the *ngoma* and the splendor of the dances. A safari to Masai land added to filling in the outline of Isak Dinesen's life in Africa.

In England, I would like to thank: Elspeth Huxley for sharing a historian's perspective on Kenya; through her kindness I was able to meet Lady Altrincham and Cockie Birkbeck (Hoogterp). Lady Altrincham for graciously adding her views on Isak Dinesen; as the wife of the governor of the colony in the 1920s, she offered insights into what was a difficult time for Isak Dinesen in Africa. Cockie Birkbeck for kindly and unhesitatingly sharing her understanding of her ex-husband, Bror Blixen.

In the United States, Parmenia Migel Ekstrom generously gave me access to all of her papers, spending many hours offering her observations from her unique perspective as official biographer. Eugene Haynes for preparing a special gathering of welcome, and sharing his papers and reminiscences, giving me an American perspective on Isak Dinesen. Judith Thurman for meeting with me near the beginning of this project and kindly extending her advice. Robert Langbaum for giving me his own experience as a pioneering American critic working on Isak Dinesen.

For taking the time to answer questions, I would like to thank Iris Murdoch, John Gielgud, and Jan Wahl. The late Beryl Markham, in her own way, added to this biography.

In 1985, at the University of Minnesota, an international conference on Isak Dinesen, directed by Paul Houe, was held which drew together scholars, critics, and writers from around the world. Aage Henriksen, Robert Langbaum, William Jay Smith, Viggo Kjær Petersen, Anders Westenholz, Sara Stambaugh, Marianne Juhl, and Bo Hakon Jørgensen were among those in attendance, all adding their voices to moving the parameters of understanding further. It was here that I was able to test some critical ideas on Isak Dinesen, as well as at the University of Wisconsin (Madison), with the kind invitation of the Scandinavian department. Excerpts from the manuscript appeared in the *Washington Post, Boston Globe, Christian Science Monitor, Philadelphia Inquirer,* and *Miami Herald;* readers responded by sending along their own personal experiences in Kenya, confirming my own.

The staffs of many libraries patiently and repeatedly aided in my research. I would like to thank: Pat Iagnuzzi for her help at Tufts University Library, along with Margaret Gooch and the staff there, Paul Depta and the reference staff at Cambridge Public Library, Steve Olderr and his former staff at the Riverside Library in Illinois, the staffs of the Royal Library in Copenhagen, the British Library, Nairobi Library, Columbia University Library, the Boston Public Library, Boston University Library, Yale University Library, Harvard University Library, Vanderbilt University Library, New York Library, the Library of Congress, and the University of Texas Library. Through a travel grant, the National Endowment for the Humanities made a trip to the University of Texas Library possible.

This project was originally suggested by Martin Green as a dissertation at Tufts University, and his observations and suggestions inform much of the book; Bernard McCabe was a second reader who provided valuable support and encouragement; Susan Gubar was a third reader. Gloria Ascher asked pertinent and incisive questions. Ian Jack read early drafts of the manuscript, making detailed comments for which I am most grateful; the revised version here owes much to his generous time and comments.

For their patience, encouragement, and good will I would like to thank Holly Panich and Duane Schneider, as well as the staff at Ohio University Press.

Frederick Hetzel kindly came forward with advice, Suzanne Comer offered enthusiasm, Austin Olney graciously responded to questions, Colin Jones gave support, as did Roger Straus.

Friends and family were unfailing in their enthusiasm and encouragement: Anesta Rapoport helped at critical times, as did Gale Rapoport; Alan Rapoport also provided encouraging words. Barbara Harrison supported the project unstintingly, passing along important books. Diane Wynne Carmody helped make an extended visit possible at the Isak Dinesen conference in Minnesota. Ted Vrettos gave sage advice when needed, as did Vas Vrettos. Nancy Davies with humor and wit saved many a frustrating day. Mary Castelli and Gary Palmer offered hospitality and help, as did Ann Hablanian, Cindy Stone, and David Kronberg. Hernan Milan unhesitatingly offered support. Also, for their good cheer, I would like to thank Mary Schulman, Jerry Schulman, Manual Navia, Jim Schuele, Cas Giampaolo, Susan Auerbach, Bill Canning, Ethel Githii, Habib Malik, Ronna Johnson, Mark Cianciolo, Barb Ramsey, Hector Cornejo, Elizabeth Robson, Joan Meskin, Lubko Fedan, Orest Fedan, and Nancy Fedan.

Pam Haley offered important insights and extended my understanding of language. Marie Halun Bloch passing along her own inspiring experiences. Anastasia Lepak and Michael Lepak offered their heartening advice. Pat Olderr listened sympathetically, as did Steve Olderr and Billy Olderr. My sister Kris Poli read through the manuscript, offering her unwavering enthusiasm and observations. Jeff Snyder spent many patient hours discussing Isak Dinesen, sharing my quandaries, and offering his suggestions.

Permissions

Permission for the use of photographs is kindly granted by Thorkild Bjørnvig, Bente Christiansen at Tivoli, Eugene Haynes, Knud Jensen, and Clara Selborn of the Rungstedlund Foundation.

Grateful acknowledgment is made to the following: Aage Henriksen and Arne Ekstrom for permission to quote from private papers. Quotes from the Random House Papers are used by permission of the Rare Book and Manuscript Library, Columbia University; quotes from the Eugene Walter papers are used by permission of the Houghton Library, Harvard University; excerpts from the introduction to Hans Christian Andersen's *Thumbelina and Other Fairy Tales*, copyright 1962, are used by permission of the Macmillan Publishing Company.

❦ *The art of writing a biography is the act of being presumptuous: of presuming that a pattern exists to the human self when what exists instead is the* illusion *of pattern; of presuming that essence emanates from the human soul when what emanates instead is the* aura *of essence; of presuming that the boundaries of truth will emerge from a human life when what emerges instead are the* blurred *outlines of truth, of definition.*

A Note on Critical Sources and Themes

There are two main biographies which have been published in English on Isak Dinesen: Parmenia Migel's pioneering study, *Titania*, in 1967, and Judith Thurman's fine work, *Isak Dinesen, The Life of a Storyteller*, in 1982. Aside from that, there have been three or four memoirs by family and friends which appeared in the 1970s. Recently, Anders Westenholz's *The Power of Aries* has added important correspondence to the Dinesen African letters, Thorkild Bjørnvig's *The Pact* has revealed his relationship to Dinesen and correspondence from her last years, and the English translation of Aage Henriksen's *Isak Dinesen/Karen Blixen*, containing his influential essays appearing in Denmark over the last twenty-four years, have contributed to the critical discourse. Until quite recently, in fact, only four critical books had appeared in English on Dinesen, the most important one being Robert Langbaum's study *Isak Dinesen's Art; The Gayety of Vision*, which was published over twenty-five years ago; adding to this is the feminist reading of Dinesen's tales by a Canadian, Sara Stambaugh, which has just appeared, *The Witch and the Goddess* (a complement to the translation of Marianne Juhl's feminist reading in *Diana's Revenge*) and Susan Aiken's post-structuralist study, *Isak Dinesen and the Engendering of Narrative*. But despite the critical activity (most of it in the form of articles) stimulated by current popular interest, as well as by an international conference at the University of Minnesota in 1985, no other critical books have appeared in English.

Adding to the critical discourse, a selected list of new information appearing in this biography of Isak Dinesen follows.

Collections and Interview Sources

1. Newly discovered collections of rare manuscripts at the libraries of Harvard, Yale, Columbia, the University of Texas, and the Library of Congress were used, as well as peripheral discoveries at Vanderbilt University Library and the Boston Public Library.
2. For the first time the private collections of Parmenia Migel (Dinesen's official biographer) were made available, including a letter from Thomas Dinesen which made clear where he thought Migel's biography had erred and been correct. The private collec-

tions of Eugene Haynes, and Aage Henriksen were particularly important to discovering the informing influences on Dinesen during the last decade of her life.

3. Of the new interview sources, Aage Henriksen (teacher, critic, and scholar in Denmark) was the most important. For the first time it became clear that in the last decade of Dinesen's life and writings Henriksen's influence was substantial, rivaled only by her protégé, Thorkild Bjørnvig.

4. Information on the history of Denmark from interview sources, including the directors of the pantomime theater in Tivoli, the Royal Court Theater, the Hunting Museum, and the Danish ballet, revealed information which illuminated such works as *The Angelic Avengers* and *Last Tales*.

5. Over 200 files on Isak Dinesen's life and work, including correspondence and literary manuscripts, at the Royal Library in Copenhagen have as yet not been integrated into scholarship on her. Most of the material quoted from those files are used here for the first time.

6. Newspapers in the British Museum and the Nairobi Library provided crucial links to similarities and differences between the development of British East Africa and South Africa, as well as providing a contemporary view of early life in Kenya, and the thinking of the colonists during World War I.

7. The newly discovered collection of correspondence at Columbia University (containing over 500 letters) provided answers to many unanswered (and frequently asked) questions about Dinesen's authorship. One of the most striking revelations was that *Out of Africa* had over 8,000 editorial corrections made on the original manuscript by her American publisher; her British publisher worked with her on nearly a daily basis for several months until the manuscript was ready for publication.

8. The collection at Harvard University Library (supplemented by the private papers of Parmenia Migel) provided additional information on Dinesen's visit to Rome near the end of her life.

9. Aage Henriksen's private papers made clear the strong connection between Dinesen and Kierkegaard (since published in *Blixeniana*).

10. The private papers of Eugene Haynes added another dimension to Isak Dinesen's American visit shortly before she died.

Major New Themes Informing the Biography

1. The tradition of adventure, of militarism, and of the military class shaped Isak Dinesen's life and imagination.

2. The psychic split between the Dinesen men and the Westenholz women was repeated in Isak Dinesen's life; the strong Westenholz women and their feminist inclinations found a receptive Dinesen.

(Up to now the Westenholz women have been seen largely as retiring or overbearing.)

3. The personality of Isak Dinesen's father currently available in English. Her father was the single biggest force upon her imagination, and the effects of his internal disturbances as a failed adventurer were far reaching.

4. The history of English colonialism in Africa, and Dinesen's participation in it; *Out of Africa* was written out of that experience, a record of colonialism as myth.

5. The Danish history of romance and masquerade, of the dramatic and theatrical, inspired Dinesen's personality and writings.

6. The strong hold on Dinesen's imagination of the feudal society that was part of Danish history until fairly recently (seen in the life of Dinesen's grandfather particularly) manifests itself in her thematic concerns.

7. The *commedia dell'arte* and the tradition of pantomime in Denmark appears in Dinesen's tales, as well as in one of the roles she played.

8. The idea of Darwin and the effects of the machine upon the conception of the self affected Dinesen's childhood and life in Africa; the link of Darwin to Nietzsche and Isak Dinesen, and the idea of nihilism suggested by her gestures (and at times, in her writings), is an important one.

9. The studied self-creation of Isak Dinesen was remarked upon by friends and relatives, her insistence upon creating herself as an aesthetic object. Later in her life, the Danish influences became so pronounced that she was viewed as a cultural phenomenon.

Isak Dinesen was born Karen Christentze Dinesen on April 17, 1885, her handsome father ignoring his disappointment that she was not the boy he had hoped for and marching past his wife Ingeborg and the other Westenholz women surrounding the cradle to claim her as his own, his favorite child. Inger (Ea) was two years old when Karen (later nicknamed Tanne after her first childish attempts to pronounce her name) was born, and Ellen (Elle) was born a year later. Through a trick of fate it would not be until 1892, Thomas's birth, and 1894, Anders's birth, that the family could feel reassured its name would continue for another generation with the military distinction it had won fighting wars. Of the daughters, at least it could be said that each was pretty and would be able to marry some wealthy young Danish son of a landed estate owner.

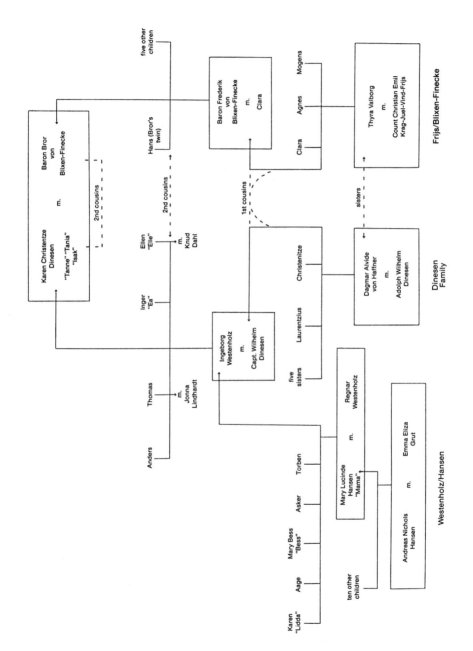

five other
children

Baron Bror
von
Blixen-Finecke

m.

Karen Christentze
Dinesen

"Tanne" "Tania"
"Isak"

2nd cousins

Hans (Bror's
twin)

Baron Frederik
von
Blixen-Finecke

m.

Clara

Mogens

Inger
"Ea"

Ellen
"Elle"

m.
Knud
Dahl

2nd cousins

Agnes

Thyra Valborg

m.

Count Christian Emil
Krag-Juel-Vind-Frijs

Clara

Frijs/Blixen-Finecke

Anders

Thomas

m.
Jonna
Lindhardt

Ingeborg
Westenholz

m.

Capt. Wilhelm
Dinesen

five
sisters

Laurentzius

Christenitze

1st cousins

Dagmar Alvide
von Haffner

m.

Adolph Wilhelm
Dinesen

sisters

Dinesen
Family

Regnar
Westenholz

m.

Karen
"Lidda"

Aage

Mary Bess
"Bess"

Asker

Torben

Mary Lucinde
Hansen
"Mama"

ten other
children

Andreas Nichols
Hansen

m.

Emma Eliza
Grut

Westenholz/Hansen

Family chart by Jeff Snyder

I

THE ARISTOCRAT

1.

Nairobi, 1914

1914: *"Wie kommen nie wieder so jung—*
so undisciplined and rapacious—
zusammen."[1]

❦ *When Baron Bror von Blixen-Finecke arrived in Nairobi in 1913 to prepare for his marriage to his curly headed, elegant fiancée Tanne Dinesen (with her marvelous dark eyes to match the soft curls), the town looked to him "like an empty old anchovy tin."*[2] *It was, said Tanne, later, "A motley place, with some fine new stone buildings, and whole quarters of old corrugated iron shops, offices and bungalows, laid out with long rows of eucalyptus trees along the bare dusty streets."*[3] *Barefooted boys reeking with sweat pulled rickshaws carrying Europeans whose talk drifted through the air as they wheeled by, lifting up the fine red dust behind them into a thin cover over the African tribesmen walking along the roads. After the long rains, the roads became muddy and impassable, and disease festered in the nearby bogs and swamps. There was an uncanny desolation to the young town, which had grown up to accommodate the railroad. Elspeth Huxley wrote that the "tin sheds which appeared . . . as vultures materialise out of clear sky when life leaves a body, had clustered over the site of Kenya's future capital."*[4] *The railroad had come into being at one end of the town, the Norfolk Hotel, the other.*

The first sight which had greeted Dr. Donaldson-Smith, the first man to enter British-ruled East Africa from the northern border, fore-shadowed the dramatic social contradictions which the Europeans would bring with them to Nairobi. The good doctor was greeted by a man—a missionary—floating along in the shade of a pink umbrella, searching from his canoe for a place to build his new Methodist mission.[5]

Lord Delamere, who Tanne would later be happy to claim as her friend, was presumably the second man to enter Africa through the north, setting the fashion for flamboyant appearance and unconventional action.[6] Wearing a large pith helmet, "Big D," his red hair spreading wildly down round his shoulders, could be seen passing out oranges from baskets on the streets of that "cow-town," Nakuru.[7] A barrage of those oranges smashed all the windows of a hotel built by Delamere, the manager standing by helplessly as the owner, "Big D," led the firing line. He had little patience with petty rules, once hanging up the manager of the Norfolk for announcing that the party had ended—he hung him gallantly in the meat freezer alongside several dead sheep.[8]

One Nairobi evening, "Big D," denied dinner at the Norfolk because he was not in his finest dress, caused a stir among the diners as he entered, chicly wrapped in the scarlet cloth of the hotel's window drapes.[9] He made it clear that he preferred the company of the tall warrior tribe of Masai who kept their strength by drinking milk and blood, holding talks with them in the long evenings around the fire at his Equator Ranch as they squatted on the buggy seat brought into the sitting room for them.

He lost his wife early on, to the tropical disease and loneliness which ruined many settlers; he did not remarry until fourteen years after. He was, in the Darwinian sense, a survivor: despite his neck snapping twice, the bad heart left by malaria and colonial stresses, and a leg cut by the teeth of a devouring lion. As the newly arrived settlers sat around their evening meals in silk pajamas at their farms outside Nairobi—in the immensity of stark, open plains below the purple haze of a vast tin-grazed sky, the drumming song of Africans chanting in the air, while the *siafu* swarmed, the black ants which in a frenzy attacked men and dogs alive in glistening columns that were as long as 200 feet—they were conscious of Darwin, feeling the force of his ideas in themselves, feeling themselves to in some way be the fittest.[10] They felt exalted, both as a reaction to and a consequence of Darwin, and reveled in a heightened sense of self-superiority as they felt their understanding of life and the systems they had created to be on the one hand divinely inspired and on the other hand scientifically supported.

Accepting Darwin's hierarchical view of the world along with the other settlers, Tanne nevertheless recoiled against him when she wrote from Africa how much it pleased her "that [George Bernard] Shaw hates Darwin, something I have always done, and thinks that it is amazing that the advocate of such a *depressing* view of life was not burned but on the contrary proclaimed as a prophet!" Rather hopefully, she added: "Incidentally, as far as I understand, science as a whole is turning more and more away from Darwin nowadays."[11] By the time she wrote "The Monkey" her contentiousness had dissolved into a playful poke at Darwin, as her prioress "evolved" instantaneously from a pet monkey within a reality whose boundaries shifted dangerously; at the same time she even took a grudging liking to him when she used his support to describe the "order of precedence therein" of Closter Seven's menagerie.[12]

While the golden *El Dorado* hovered in the background, the settlers felt free to impose their "superior" will on Africa—a supremacy ensured by their possession of the rifle. In their high-collared Victorian dresses and straight trousers, they preened, stopping for tea from the silver tea sets they had brought with them, creating an aura of heightened incongruity in the midst of burnt brush and barren thorn trees where black-maned lions stalked their prey among the stamping wildebeest. Berkeley Cole, brother-in-law to "Big D," would insist that he and Tanne have champagne served in the finest glasses out in the 11:00 A.M. African forest; causing people to think her a bit strange, Tanne stepped further out when she fed her guests a hearty breakfast, herself preferring red wine and meat.[13]

As early as the 1880s "the British Government [had] found imperialism . . . difficult to avoid" and rights were granted to the Imperial British East Africa Company to conduct trade "in all the country between Uganda and the coast," giving the spur to "white settlement."[14] With the railway, started for trade and strategic reasons, England was able to control and transform Africa's political and social structure, holding together a multiplicity of different peoples with opposing interests.[15] On a visit in 1907, Winston Churchill already noticed the potential for future tensions among the various cultural groups, noting that the undetermined political status of the Indians was "the sphinx's riddle in its newest form." By 1913 the railway had made Nairobi the center of British East Africa, and Lord Delamere was the epitome of the emerging feudal system. One settler described him as having the "feudal system . . . in his bones and blood, . . . [believing] all his life in its fundamental rightness," adding that he "became an imperialist and, in particular, an admirer of Cecil Rhodes."[16] Baron Bror von Blixen-Finecke and his young fiancée moved into the feudal world Delamere exemplified when they chose to become part of the slow stream of Europeans following him into British East Africa.

While Bror was making final arrangements on the farm he had bought (and making plans to take his bride out on a "lion gallop"), handing out presents to the African chiefs to make sure he had enough Somali, Kivorondi, and Gikuyu men to work the land and complaining of the difficulty of making sure workers showed up, Tanne was writing her first letter home to her mother from the German liner the *Admiral*, steaming on its way toward East Africa.[17] A paralyzing malaise had gripped her after her mother and younger sister Elle had left her in Naples where they had helped buy blouses for her trousseau. The swaying of the huge ship as she walked on deck with nothing to meet the eye except unending expanses of blue sun-mirrored sea had made Tanne fear for her balance, and terrified, she had managed to convince the captain of the ship to let his stewardess go with her as maid until she adapted to her new life. It was, she wrote her mother, a grave mistake, and "stupid not to have brought a maid with me. It would not have mattered," she continued, "if I had been fit and strong, but you know how pampered and unaccustomed I was to exertion when I came on board. I kept thinking about the woman in 'Dombey & Son' who is always saying that *an effort must be done*, for everything was an effort for me, getting up, dressing, the whole business of living, and time after time—now you must not mind if I write honestly,—I was so tired and depressed that I felt that I would not survive until I arrived in Mombasa."[18]

There had been a brief interlude from the tedium ashore at Port Said—they were sailing in the Mediterranean sun down through the Red Sea on the way to the African seaport of Mombasa—where Tanne had found that "everything was for sale: silks and scimitars, opium, whiskey and small children."[19] A further diversion had been provided by the passengers gathered on board. One of them, a German, was on his twenty-third trip to Africa in search of the cure for sleeping sickness.[20] But a chance meeting with another German passenger was the most exciting, "A German officer, von Lettow, who belongs to a very old Mechlenburger family, who has been such a friend to me."[21] To cool themselves after the hot tropical days they sat on deck in the long evenings watching the stars and chatting, the German commander in full military regalia with his dark eye patch quite taken by the soft vulnerability of the young Danish woman sailing in trepidation to a new life.[22]

Von Lettow's appeal, Tanne proudly wrote to her family, was that he "belonged to the olden days and I have never met another German who has given me so strong an impression of what Imperial Germany was and stood for."[23] Five months later Tanne would be looking for some fine horses to ship to the forces Colonel von Lettow Vorbeck had been sent out to command in German East Africa, and hoping that he would send her a carpet from Dar-es-Salaam in appreciation. He had been charged with keeping "order in the entire colony. In the case of a European war, the plan was to wage war passively in East Africa."[24] As a memento of their meeting, von Lettow gave her a photograph of himself, signed in German. They promised each other to try to meet again, on an African safari that summer. "Try to come," he said to the pretty dark-haired woman who spoke German and English to him in a deep, seductive voice tinged with a Danish accent, *"Wir kommen nicht wider so jung zusammen"*—"We will not meet again so young."[25] Twisting the meaning, Tanne later used the phrase to remember Nairobi by: "Nairobi said to you: 'Make the most of me and of time. *Wir kommen nie wieder so jung*—so undisciplined and rapacious—*zusammen.'* "[26]

Her uneasiness grew when they left the ship at Aden. Bror, in a careless slight, was not there to meet his young bride to be.[27] He sent a Somali servant instead, with a letter. She was met by a man in a turban and embroidered gold thread waistcoat over his flowing white robes, who with many smiles touched his forehead repeatedly in a gesture of welcome, greeting her in a broken, heavily accented English, his stammer so strong that it seemed as if he would give up the ghost with each spoken word. Farah helped her with her baggage and wedding presents, staying away from one gift, her deerhound Dusk, but helping with the others, including the two small red and gold leather-bound volumes of Hans Christian Andersen which Malla, the family nanny, had given her. The only hint of her disappointment at Bror's absence was her comment to her mother that "I will not be able to send you any news of your beloved Bror."[28] Bror would meet them at Mombasa.

Out in Africa the baron would cause gossip and scandal by carrying forth the battle cry of the Dinesen men, shifting tone to an erotic cry of possession that failed to stop with hunting only the wild animals; it was an irony ignored by his protective family, who had resisted the marriage because of scandal attaching to Tanne's father.[29]

2.

The Dinesen Men

1839: "that one or nothing . . .
her or no one"

🌑 *More is known about the Dinesen men than the daughters they had or the women they married. The men began as peasant farmers who came from the area of Holbæk in Denmark, moving upward socially through shrewd marriages and financial deals made easier by their bold, romantic looks. This upward movement almost reached the aristocracy when Isak Dinesen's great-grandfather Anders, a man known for his remarkable power over others, bought land with a barony attached. But Anders died before he could be knighted Baron "Golden Eagle."[1] Throughout the generations, their women hovered in the background, lovely decorative shadows, "angels of the hearth" whose influence stopped at the fireside and cradle.[2] Dagmar Alvilde was not much different, except that a bit of scandal lingered round her. It did not keep Adolph Wilhelm Dinesen from marrying her.*

The Dinesen family moved in the heady atmosphere of a military elite, with its shining medals and decorations won from bold action on the battlefield: the Dinesen children were steeped in the heart of it.[3] It excited them and made them believe war was the place where an ideal heroism was to be found.[4] Throughout their lives they would respond to war as an aesthetic experience.[5] Their father believed nothing was more pleasing than a landscape of fighting soldiers; his daughter Tanne, denied the military conquests of the battlefield, found war acceptable on the pure clean page of literature, disliking its bloodletting aspect in real life.[6] She drew a direct line between herself and her father when she described his passion for war:

> My father was an officer in the Danish and French army, and as a very young lieutenant at Düppel he wrote home: "Back in Düppel I was officer to a long column. It was hard work, but it was splendid. The love of war is a passion like another, you love soldiers as you love young womenfolk,—to madness, and the one love does not exclude the other, as the girls know. But the love of women can include only one at a time, and the love for your soldiers comprehends the whole regiment, which you would like enlarged if it were possible." It was the same thing with the [African] Natives and me.[7]

Adolph Wilhelm Dinesen, the Dinesen children's paternal grandfather, himself became absorbed in military life, entering a military academy by the time he was twelve. The second youngest of eight children, he was forced into the military to compensate for being born too late to receive an inheritance. He became a bored young officer, his variously stamped passport attesting to his desire to seek excitement in foreign countries. (The sensitive and high-strung Hans Christian Andersen, his traveling companion for a while in Italy, scribbled in his diary about "D:" "How very much I have learned from this young, determined person, who has so often hurt me in my affection for him.—If only I had his character, even with its flaws!") He finally found it in active fighting by joining on the side of France against Algiers, winning the rank of captain and the award of the Legion of Honor. He wrote a small book about his war experiences, *Abd-el-kadar*, praising the Arab leader he had fought against, while castigating the army he had fought with.

In the first recorded spark of poeticism in the Dinesen family, he wrote: "It is all in all characteristic that overall where the French have shown themselves in Africa the trees disappear, the streams dry up, the inhabitants of the native population disappear and only desert is left. The French could conquer but they could not maintain."[8] Despite his reservations about French imperialism, he would always feel pride when remembering his role in colonizing African land for France. His granddaughter followed him (and his son Wilhelm) into Africa when she married there in 1914. She was not entirely unconscious of her participation in a tradition of adventure which had sent the British Empire rapaciously sprawling the globe for over 300 years. She was exhilarated by being able, here at least, to participate in the bold impulses of the men in her family.

Adolph Wilhelm liked to tell that after leaving the Danish army in 1839, when he first saw the massive red stone of Katholm Castle set in among "moors and marshes . . . with wind-blown trees,"[9] he cried out "that one or nothing"; when he saw his future wife, her braided and curled hair framing an innocent face made even more ethereal by delicate drop earrings, the same instincts were aroused and he thought secretly, "her or no one."[10]

It was less than one hundred years since Denmark had seen the reign of the mad King Christian VII which had led to the abolition of serfs—Denmark followed behind the rest of Europe in banning serfdom, as it had followed late in ridding its shores of paganism, Christianity coming late to the cold Viking shores. A shadowy, pike-filled moat had been built to protect Katholm Castle from an uprising among the serfs. Adolph Wilhelm himself continued to hold allegiance to the past, ruling the vast villages on his lands with the iron grip of a feudal lord. Through the sun-glazed windows he could be heard castigating some errant worker in the fields; any man who caused his anger was immediately dismissed. His family he ruled with the same strict vigilance. In "Sorrow-acre," his granddaughter would imitate this unrelenting feudal posture, aesthetically sympathizing with the ruling lord whose aristocratic principles—and belief in the "feudal right to punish"—result in the death of a peasant woman.[11] Taken from a Danish folktale, "Sorrow-acre" was an ode to the Danish aristocracy as it moved toward extinction, a lyrical act of possession meant to extend the right of aristocracy. A friend of Tanne's reminisced that "She came in her youth to live during and through the last phase of the heyday of the Danish nobility."[12] "I also experienced its close," she told him, "when the law commuting entailed estates was finally passed in 1919, it was all over. The idea had gone, though there was no reason why the old life might not continue for some years yet."[13]

The purchase of the Katholm estate with its vast lands and forests was a great financial risk, but Adolph Wilhelm gambled well and it would bring him great wealth; despite its poor soil he would make it yield enough to leave an inheritance for two sons and six daughters.

The young Dagmar Alvilde von Haffner could be proud of marrying the owner of Katholm, a man who with his granite face, drooping moustaches, bold forehead, and military uniform looked as if he had ridden straight down from the steppes of Russia. But she was marrying an arrogant man who believed that all traces of his bad temper had long ago disappeared. He ignored the scandal touching Dagmar Alvilde.[14] The marriage tied the Dinesen line to the temperamental Countess Frijs and "the great noble families of the Danish aristocracy," an aristocratic proximity which teased Tanne without sating her.[15] Everything was in the name. In "Copenhagen Season," so many delicate spheres are set to circling, forming a cycloid whose motion locates a steady line in the aristocratic locus: "A hundred spinning wheels whirred for the [noble] name in thatched cottages"—an example of the linguistic coding that emerges in Isak Dinesen's tales.[16]

In 1843, shortly before the signing of a democratic constitution, when Tanne's grandfather had barely settled down to begin his family at Katholm, Copenhagen was a city of 120,000, still surrounded by moats and ramparts as protection against possible enemy attack. To enter Copenhagen a tax had to be paid, and to prevent smuggling, searches were made of all carriages and carts clattering across the bridge into "Merchant's Haven."[17] Four gates locked the town in at night, and King Christian VIII, whose reign had brought about Denmark's Golden Age, kept the keys until morning.[18] The surrounding bare green lands dotted with pools of water could easily be viewed from all points.

Preparations for a visit to "Merchant's Haven" were those for a major journey, and in the bustle of leaving Katholm there would be much clattering of horses and raising of ducks into gusts against the sky as the carriage and four were brought out, the lake marshes and sand dunes swept bare by the cold winds. The life, like the air and soil at Katholm, would prove too thin for Adolph Wilhelm, and he would eventually purchase a winter home in Copenhagen.

From the moment Wilhelm Dinesen was born to Dagmar and Adolph Wilhelm, he was preordained for the military: officer friends of the family were present at his birth on December 19, 1845, which took place in his grandmother Anne Margrethe's home. Such an occasion called for a "few von's and de's,"[19] and his godfathers were all officers with the names of von Haffner, de Krieger, and von Fabricius—a snobbery his favorite daughter would insist on, determined that her nieces and nephews should only marry into those families listed in the Danish red book.[20]

His older brother Laurentzius would grow up to run Katholm (not with any great deal of competence), while Wilhelm was named Adolph Wilhelm after his father and expected to imitate him in a military career. It was this uncle, Uncle Lars, who was chosen—because, rumor had it, he was the most beautiful man in Denmark—to accompany Princess Dagmar as she rode to Russia on her way to marry Czar Alexander III. His journey along side the princess, the high point of his career as an officer, had, Tanne wrote in "Copenhagen Season," twisted his head, keeping him in a world of dream, "a world of bear hunts, champagne, gypsy music, and gypsy girls."[21]

To his friends Lars came to be known as "Lying Charlie," as they poked fun at him by inventing anecdotes which they attributed to him. One such tale said to have come from "Lying Charlie" was of his stumbling upon a bear while out walking without a rifle.

What did you do? he was asked.

"Why, I et him," he replied.

But despite his reputation as an old blusterer, his tales of his brush with royalty and courtly extravagance impressed his nieces and nephews as they sat around him, fascinated.[22] His niece Tanne never forgot the glimpses she caught of the unknown world into which his stories delivered them.

When Wilhelm was two years old, his father left home to defend Denmark's honor by fighting in the Three Years War against Germany. Family tradition made him a flawless hero, although he was court-martialed after the war (as a formality, it was said). An artillery officer, he had assumed command of a part of the army not under his jurisdiction. Hearing that their cannons had fallen silent, the Danes thought everything was lost and started retreating from the Germans. Adolph Wilhelm immediately ordered his own cannons fired, and against great odds the men again advanced, winning the battle. He was greatly praised for his bravery; when his horse was cannonballed from under him he leaped down and continued to lead his men. The medals of victory he wore home gave him the glamour of heroism; the recognition he received for his daring exploits sustained his self-importance. In three paintings he later commissioned of the battles he had fought in he would be at the center of the action, painted taller than any of the other fighting soldiers.

Adolph Wilhelm unwittingly prepared for a sense of the incongruous in his son by the scenes he created out of his own insistence upon comfort and self-aggrandizement. The evenings he spent with his children would always be remembered by them as they and the servants crowded around a large table where one candle burned, while their father sat alone at his writing desk, one candle burning at each end. Attention focused on the drama surrounding the father, the silence of their mother negating her presence; only late in life did Dagmar Alvide finally rebel against her husband, developing epilepsy and controlling the household for the two or three years before she died.

Wilhelm early on took from his father his iron will. When his father was away at war, Wilhelm, at home with his sisters, mother, nurses, and only brother, set himself hard against the overriding feminine influence, imitating the father he had seen rule in masculine rage. He became an unruly boy and, by the time his father returned home from the war, had developed a willful and unbending character that was softened by a compassionate turn. His sister Anna wrote how difficult change of any kind was for him as a young child:

> My brother has always from quite small been a strange character. What he once liked and got used to he did not want to give up. It was quite a torture for my mother to get him from winter into summer's clothes and vice-versa. He was very much loved by his nurses and was I think quite spoiled. He had a very very good heart but his own unbending will.[23]

Already as a small boy Wilhelm had a mind inclined toward irony: meeting visitors in the road who offered him a ride, he refused, explaining, "I am drying." When he turned round, they could see his wet trousers, crumpled down as they were about his ankles. Asked what he had said, he repeated, "I am drying, I am drying." It was this willful irony that put him in a relationship of strangeness to his family, while it gave them great amusement. As he deliberately set himself apart, he brought upon himself an inconvenience and discomfort which he bore with stoic indifference: it made him eccentric. Not only was he responsive to the ironical in an occasion, he could elicit the ironical from a situation. Wilhelm's niece wrote in her memoirs what she had heard from her mother, Thyra, Wilhelm's sister:

> He was a strange child. . . . In the winter's evening when the rest of the family was gathered around the table Wilhelm was usually standing right up in a corner in a window and then suddenly they would hear a bump. "Oh, I expect it's just Wilhelm who fell asleep," said the sisters. He would stand right up then fall asleep and fall right down on the floor.[24]

When Wilhelm showed early signs of contradicting his father's authority, Adolph Wilhelm sent the seven-year-old boy to school in distant Copenhagen. But Wilhelm was able to develop his will so that he could finally intuitively win over even his father. When his father wanted to put him into a different school, Wilhelm became ill with stomach inflammation and high fever, deliriously imagining his new surroundings as grotesque, the new boys and their teachers nightmarishly distorted. Grev Sponnech, the man in whose home he was staying, sent for the father, who relented when he saw how ill his son had become. Learning of his father's decision, Wilhelm recovered quickly and returned to Mariboe's School; the boys were delighted to have him back among them and hoisted him into the air, victoriously carrying him back into the classroom.

Wilhelm would pass on to his second oldest daughter, his favorite, a blend of vulnerability and willful persistence which was showcased by strangeness, a flair for exquisite irony.

In "Copenhagen Season," a fictional account of Tanne's father and his family, a character—an artist—expounds his theory that "the nose is the *pointe* of the whole human personality, and that the true mission of our legs, lungs and hearts is to carry about our noses."[25] And always, her father's daughter, there were the unexpected touches, as with a surrealistic eye she commented on the perfect bowels of the family, the Angels. She left out her impression that her own father's family, which she knew from her childhood visits to Katholm—the setting for "Copenhagen Season"—were "superficial,"[26] preferring to note instead "a great, wild happiness at being alive" which informed their being.[27] It was the same "exuberance of life" which in *Ehrengard* would threaten the noble family of Leuchtenstein with extinction, "like a tree through a long time blooming and blossoming to excess."[28] Almost as a casual afterthought, she observed that the Angel family was "doomed, each of them in advance marked down for ruin."[29] She was thinking of her father and herself.

3.

Captain Dinesen, Adventurer and Gentleman

1888–: "His fate cannot be otherwise . . . his blood has been poisoned."

🐦 *His daughter would have Wilhelm on her mind when, in "Copenhagen Season," she described Ib—a character she consciously modeled after him—as being like an animal with large paws, with the irresistable charm of being both tender and wild. A picture she would always keep in her study—near the angularly hung Masai spears she brought back from Africa—gives him the appearance of being hunted, as he strides boldly through the shadows of the trees, sunlight filtering down, his hunter's gun pointed before him at an angle.[1] His bearded face is caught in an intense, passionate look, the way he lived his life.*

As a scraggly looking young man, Wilhelm Dinesen had restlessly gone around Europe searching out wars to fight in and had crawled through the freezing snow among dead corpses in the war of 1864, winning the rank of captain and the honor of his men. While drinking coffee in the Paris cafés he had been witness to the Paris Commune and "sickened" by the burning of the city with petrol-soaked straw.[2] The death from typhoid of his beautiful young cousin Agnes Frijs while she was on a journey to Italy had further depressed him—superstition-crazed sailors had threatened during a storm to throw her coffin overboard.[3] Now he was seeking peace abroad, among packages and baskets wrapped tightly for the long journey to America. He was part of the first wave of Danish emigration to America after the war of 1864, when Denmark had lost 40 percent of its status as a major European power; a psychic paralysis followed in the Danes, despair offset by the lure of gold in America.[4] The women remained behind as their men left, while on street corners boys hawked sheet music about sweethearts parted by the wave of emigration.

His inner turmoil would be recalled in "Sorrow-acre" when his daughter had her character Adam thinking of seeking "harmony" in America; Tanne in some sense suggested in this minor literary detail an impulse to make easier her father's life, finally removing from Adam his restlessness and need to travel abroad, having him find meaning and significance instead in the life of home, of Denmark. In the rhythms of her own life, there emerged an instinctive need to perfect her father's life; she was in this at a natural disadvantage, not easily being able to imitate the masculine actions of her family.[5] Her brother Tommy had the same drive, and was pleased to note his ability to follow in his father's footsteps in the masculine pursuits of hunting and battle. From Africa Tanne praised Tommy's courage in World War I, calling him another "Captain Wilhelm"; she herself could only long for the birth of a "little Wilhelm."[6] Very fond of each other, both brother and sister nevertheless developed a family rivalry over who could best be like the father, perhaps even succeed in surpassing him. The tragedy of her life became the ultimate failure to achieve this perfect refinement of a life once lived separately from her own.

The trip to America for Wilhelm was relieved by icebergs, and four or five gulls following the ship and diving for its refuse. Arriving in America's Midwest after a harrowing train ride with a fire breaking out, Wilhelm saw what to him appeared as an unrelenting flat land of woods. Advertisements were everywhere, on fences made of rocks, on trees and on posts. It was not unusual to see a poor eastern family moving out west in a wagon covered with canvas, a lone cow trailing behind. With a little money a house could be sent for from Chicago, which would arrive in pieces carefully numbered and ready to build. Afterwards, in memory, Wilhelm transformed his life in America into one of idyllic solitude: "The man who has not . . . been alone—completely alone, dozens of miles from the closest human being—does not know how healing the peace of the forest is. It was up in the forest, the virgin forest of Wisconsin, where I settled for a couple of years."[7]

In reality, Wilhelm ended up constantly on the move throughout the midwestern small towns of Chicago and up into Nebraska and Wisconsin. He made his home for a while with a family in Nebraska where he lived what he called the American way by eating "white bread, pork and cranberry tarts three times a day and in general . . . [speaking] as little as possible."[8] He was admired for his knowledge of languages, and became for a time a postal clerk, then a land surveyor. In his spare time he went hunting with his "red friends," setting afire the dried grasses to frighten the animals from their lairs. It was the Indians he had been the most anxious to meet on his arrival in America, and he saw them in their red and gray blankets coming from tents along the river water near Columbus to sell their wares to passengers on the train platform. Twice he nearly met his death: once when he left a hunting party where everyone died from the freezing cold, starvation, or Indians, another time when a hunting trip he decided not to go on ended in a major massacre in what was perhaps the final significant confrontation between the Sioux and Pawnee.[9]

Dismayed by the abuse of the Indians, he wrote in disgust that "in 1872 Congress felt that the Indians should have one million dollars and that it was necessary to provide ten million dollars so that they might receive the one; nine millions were drained off enroute."[10] It was—in addition to his poetic embrace of nature—his strong affection for the Indians and sympathy at their plight, which, of all of the events on the trip, he conveyed to his daughter Tanne, inclining her towards the tribes she met in Africa:

> The first white men are generally well received by the Indians. They live with them and are eventually adopted by them. Soon more white men come and after a few years the Indians' entire existence is disturbed, his conceptual world is confused, his necessities and his desires have changed, and his religious ideas are dislocated. . . . It is not worth his time and labor to produce the old weapons, tools and foods, for the white man has everything better in this regard—and they also have whiskey: fire water. No effort is spared to possess the white man's weapons, clothing, food and most of all his fire water, and for its sake the Indian will sell everything: his precious belongings, his horses, his women, his land. Originally the government leaves them alone. The whites move in without government's blessing. The government supports them. A number of leading men are sent to Washington, where they are corrupted. There is an Indian agent. From now on they are

cheated in every way. They are killed off by disease, by loss of their means to live, the wild game. They sell their land for a small rectangular piece of land in exchange for a "reservation" that they can't leave without the agent's permission. Given barely enough to eat and a blanket a year (unless the agent cheats them out of the blanket). "His fate cannot be otherwise—even though he is a noble and a self-sacrificing race, his days are numbered, he is doomed."

When one empties a pond of its water the fish die, and one might imagine that if everyone without pure blood were to leave America and let the Indians go their own ways, the red man would still die out: his blood has been poisoned.[11]

It might be argued that Wilhelm's own blood was on the way to being "poisoned" by adventures gone bad. Unable to let go, as with many failed adventurers, Wilhelm Dinesen was always seeking the unattainable and the elusive. And like for one of the great adventurers, T. E. Lawrence (the Englishman who squatted in long white robes among Arab tribes, finally uniting them to fight the Turks during World War I), the attempt to straddle two worlds, the one of distant lands and exoticism, and the homebound, more easily understood one, resulted in an isolated sense of self. Wilhelm's adventuring and military experiences had to a certain extent "quit himself of his Danish self," until, to use T. E. Lawrence's words, there was a

resultant feeling of intense loneliness in life, and a contempt, not for other men, but for all they do. Such detachment came at times to a man exhausted by prolonged physical effort and isolation. His body plodded on mechanically, while his reasonable mind left him, and from without looked down critically on him, wondering what the futile lumber did and why. Sometimes these selves would converse in the void; and then madness was very near, as I believe would be near the man who could see things through the veils at once of two customs, two educations, two environments.[12]

This same emptying out of a sole cultural attachment to Denmark contributed to the edge of madness Wilhelm's daughter would herself eventually skirt, illness and a sense of mental displacement causing Tanne near the end of her life to pause in the middle of a conversation and howl like a wild wolf, then return to the conversation as if nothing had taken place.[13]

When Wilhelm finally settled in with his wife Ingeborg (his mother's illness had called him back to Denmark) at Rungstedlund, he was enveloped by the Westenholz women, all forty-four female cousins from his wife's family who descended at the first sign of children (no one else had yet had any), along with Mama, who would become completely absorbed in raising the Dinesen children.[14] This strong female presence called up his childhood, only now having no masculine figure to rebel against, he rebelled against the world and created a secret world away from these Victorian women who "must have made him feel hunted, surely."[15]

As a gentleman, he pursued in gentlemanly fashion his hunting at the large estates, away from the women. It was here amid the cigars and wine, the excitement of the beaters, that the split between both the feminine (steeped in embroidery circles) and masculine experience was most apparent; later, politics would provide a refuge.[16] He was, finally, unable to maintain the balance between two worlds that moved in ever greater incompatible tensions, the world where he longed for stability and quiet, and the world where danger was its own enticement.

His suffering came from this tension of two worlds in collision: the irony, desperation, and the haunted sense of a happiness and peace never quite achieved. When the two worlds collided in a final, dramatic way he hurt the person who had understood him the best from a harbor of serenity and who had accepted him the most—his wife.

4.

The Westenholz Women

"a woman is nothing but a cross between a fish and a snake"[1]

There was a peculiar twist to the Westenholz women surrounding the Dinesen children: they were resilient and at times headstrong in perpetuating the Victorian mode of thinking, tempered in turn by an intelligence and sensitivity given free reign in an unexpected streak of feminism. This did not alter the fate of the women on Tanne's mother's side, which depended invariably upon the men they were able—or unable—to attract and marry. When—and if—they married, it was often to powerful men who enjoyed wide parameters of unquestioned influence which was not always abused; in the case of Tanne's maternal great-grandfather, Andreas Nicolai Hansen, the power was too much, and it went to his head to erupt in unpredictable gasping fits of violence.

The Westenholz women are remembered as "not quite ordinary" women,[2] as being marked by having an "exclusive view of the world."[3] Earliest records locate the family name of Westenholz—Tanne's mother was Ingeborg Westenholz—back to outside a small town in Germany, north of Hanover in Celle. A sign at a crossroad still points the way to the village of Westenholz.[4]

Drawn by the possibility of a different existence, when European laws were changing to allow freer movement between countries, the Westenholzes had emigrated to Denmark at the turn of the eighteenth century. Their ancestors were English and Norwegian, with men who were drawn into the military and the church. Bred in Copenhagen, they became free thinkers and intellectuals who shunned country life, and eventually embraced Unitarianism in a country that favored Luther. The ultimate meeting of the Westenholzes and Dinesens in marriage would bring together an admixture of the grace of country life and the lure of city strangeness. It was a meeting which would eventually press against Tanne, until the two opposite sides of the families—as characterized by the movement of the Dinesen men, the stillness of the Westenholz women—coming together made her feel a sense of negation, the *horror vacui* she would write about, feeling at times as if she did not, could not, exist.[5]

It is difficult to trace the Westenholz women through the generations, marriage absorbing them into other families. What appears clear is that Tanne's maternal grandmother, Mama, after marrying into the family, crystallized the genius of the Westenholz women. A picture in the family album shows a young serene Tanne, her hair parted in the middle and braided in a bun at the nape of her neck, dressed up in imitation of Mama, a contemplative look on her face, the shawl draping from her shoulders as she studies a book on the small, wooden table before her. From Africa, Tanne would write her grandmother one Christmas: "I am . . . rather like you."[6]

Born Mary Hansen to Andreas Nicolai Hansen and Emma Eliza Grut, Mama grew up among Copenhagen's finest, the splendid houses lining up the Bredgade. The huge corner house where the Hansens lived was a reminder to the neighboring nobility that other social possibilities existed in their midst, its stoic splendor among the ornately marked houses a jarring point for the noble eye. There were eight brothers clamoring through the austere house, and they kept their three sisters on edge, delighting in their own ability to shift reality into an unexpected mode. Leaving a nest of baby snakes near the stairway, they would gloat over the shrieks of their sisters as they came across them slithering about. Naming their hens after their sister's friends, brother Gustav would announce in mock serious tones at the dinner table that "Anna Ibsen was busy roosting at the moment," while "Henriette Agier had already laid an egg." It was this youthful masculine humor that tempered the bleakness of a household ruled by a tyrant.[7]

Mama had a streak of rebellion in her that manifested itself early on as a young girl, honed and fine tuned by her relationship to her eight brothers. Asked by the Pastor Rafford (with whom she had religious lessons for eight years in preparation for confirmation, something which usually required only one year of religious instruction—she later reacted against this and did not have her own children confirmed, creating a moment of panic for her daughter Ingeborg when she confessed to her dashing suitor Captain Dinesen that she had never been confirmed) to promise not to quarrel, she stuck to a tight hold on the truth, saying that she could not promise since "I have eight brothers, you know." She accepted the tender protections of her brothers while understanding the protective power of female self-willfulness in a home where masculine power ran disturbingly unbridled.

Family memory was riveted to Tanne's great-grandfather Andreas who looked out at the world through solid features which gave him a clear and impressive appearance, the classic look of a man who enjoyed the prerogatives and privileges of the *paterfamilias*. One of Copenhagen's wealthiest men, his fortune had been made in shipping during the Napoleonic Wars and his grandson, Aage, imitated him by making his fortune in Siam, inspiring Tanne in turn to seek the golden *El Dorado* in Africa. He understood the feminine weakness for romantic display and it was said that in a grand gesture he had shipped gravel from England to place beneath the feet of his homesick English wife. But his flair for romance was mixed with a brutality which confused his wife and from which his children never recovered; few of the children in their turn managed to form happy marriages. The romantic inclinations of this great-grandfather were intensified by his boorish behavior; his antics took on a different patina with the distance of time and were passed down as family romance among the Dinesen children.

Mama along with her brothers and sisters were immersed in a family kept simmering by their father's violent unpredictability, and an irritation which stayed with them throughout their life. Their father could be frightening, his tantrums bordering on the ridiculous: arriving at the breakfast table slightly out of breath, his reverberating shouts about having broken all of his nails while rushing to button his shirt were heard throughout the house. Social decorum did not prevent him from taking his tyrannical rule outside the home—once in a train carriage, forbidden by the other passengers from opening the window, he thrust his heavy cane through the glass to get some air.

Puritanically, he pulled away from joy, seeing in it an unsettling instability. When he attended the marriage of his daughter Emily to a young Scottish merchant, he roared disapprovingly at the decorations and pulled down everything with his own hand. Mama would always remember how the family had moved swiftly to correct the damage the father had caused, trying to right the room before the young couple arrived to be married. He had a suspicion of sex as it manifested itself in its innocence, once throwing down the stairs the music teacher who had shown too much interest in his young daughter Mary—Mama. This suspicion passed on to his children. One of his sons when he became a father, noticing a son of his own looking pasty and ill asked him if he had caught an "abominable disease" which would make him unfit for decent human company.[8] The word syphilis was too offensive and prurient to mention—a finicky insistence upon sexual purity which would eventually haunt Tanne.

Mama, despite herself having seven children would convey to her grandchildren—the Dinesen children—a similar revulsion toward any suggestion of the physical and the sensual. There was deep shame for a woman, she told them, if a man even dared approach her with hints of a marriage proposal. In this she reflected her morally straitened family—laced in like the English Puritans—and the Victorian suspicion of sex.

But with her it went further. She had witnessed her mother's attachment to a difficult and emotionally brutal man and instinctively traced it back to the physical relationship. These warnings of the "dangers and pitfalls" lurking in anything sexual brought about a rebellious turn in her granddaughter, as Tanne ran a streak of eroticism through her tales that at times bordered on the profane and the bawdy: in one tale an anecdote depicts Joseph in the shade of the great Sphinx pleading with Mary to think of him as the Holy Ghost, if only for a moment, and in another, there are coquettishly veiled references to the Greek way of love and its effect upon "the ladies" who learn that "everything Greek" is not always "le dernier cri" in "frocks and coiffures." To her mother, Tanne would remark that "Nothing in my . . . life has caused so much hatred and contempt in me as what is generally termed 'morals.' "[9]

As a result of his finickiness, the expansion of Andreas's family did not come easily and domestic turmoil had taken place before each of his eleven children was born. Reveling in the physical side of marriage, Andreas preferred to play the innocent, refusing to acknowledge his part in its consequences; he became surly and abusive, unable to forgive his secretive wife when she finally, with apologies and excuses, broke down to tell him of her pregnant condition. After each birth, he had a turn of mind, and pleased and preening, rewarded his wife with a diamond bracelet. Emma for her part reacted in a muted rebellion, leaving each of the eleven diamonds carelessly about in a manner bordering on disdain, until all but two of them were stolen by thieves. Often depressed by his moods, Emma never uttered a word of reproach against her husband. This sense of generosity toward the male prerogative did not always extend outside the Hansen home. When her sons gleefully came running home from school with a remark that the schoolmaster had made about a woman being nothing more than a "cross between a fish and a snake," their mother sent him a reprimand and received an apology in return. She made sure her children grew up respecting the suspect notion of "women's rights"; Mary's favorite sister Ellen later in life remained convinced that her devotion to feminist ideals was worth the martyrdom of spinsterhood. When John Stuart Mill's *The Subjection of Women* was translated by Georg Brandes, Mary herself came down strong on the proper side of "the woman question" and convinced her own children to do the same; her daughter Bess, Tanne's aunt, became the standard-bearer of the feminist flag.

Emma, Tanne's great-grandmother, watched over her children's education carefully, and all the schoolbooks and songs were in her native language, English; the only time this changed was when they studied God—then the elegant was invoked and they switched to French. When her daughter Mary grew up to become Mama, this immersion in English at an early age would make her own children view her as having a foreign aura, giving her a power of the strange and exotic. Her Dinesen grandchildren would be drawn to her, unable to penetrate her fatal allure with any word of rebellion or protest— Tanne would remark on this indefinable power surrounding Mama (and her daughter Ingeborg, Tanne's mother), making her a center point of harmony in the family circle.[10] In one photograph, Mama is seated unperturbed, staring dreamily from her fine delicate features, in the "majesty of gentleness," her own children seated around her in childish disarray. She is wearing black, the color she always favored after her husband died, in regal imitation of Queen Victoria.

The Dinesen children perceived the men and women in their family through a classic historical split: keepers of the family conscience and its spiritual life, the women were soothing, if inactive, in their stability, and as Tanne would write in *Ehrengard*, "Balanced to perfection in the manner of those little toy figures with lead at the base of them, who cannot be overturned."[11]

It was the men "who boldly strived toward zenith," to the visionary men that the great adventures of the world belonged—and the excitement of teasing the unpredictable military edges of the world.[12] Mama, however, vicariously had strayed over the line, her life defined by a military moment which took place in the spring of 1848 when she was a young girl—it was the same year Denmark would sign a democratic constitution, the monarchy giving way as Grundtvig's Folk High Schools aided the common people in their growing political participation.[13] Waking up from sleep, she heard a group of soldiers singing about a young girl who sees her brave beau off to war, and denied the possibility of joining him, is given his promise that he will return to her. This experience was so powerful that its martial lyricism took on the significance of a spiritual quickening.

Her daughter Bess, the Dinesen children's *Moster* Bess, would have as her highest ambition to experience a similar moment in life. But Bess's own life was marked by a political moment: after confiding her plan to Tanne and charging her to keep it secret from Mama, *Moster* Bess gathered her skirts and outrage about her, marching through the resounding halls which had never before heard a woman's steps, into the all-male Parliament, and grabbing the bell from the astonished presiding officer, announced, "Gentlemen, while you sit here discussing the fate of the country, know that the women of Denmark despise you"—the women of Denmark were trying to get the vote and were disgruntled with the Danish Defense Plan.[14] The officer could only repeat, parrotlike: "She has taken my bell! She has taken my bell."

Her illegal action created an uproar that spilled over into the newspapers. Tanne told her official biographer that it was this overbearing and overly religious (though the Church as concept and institution meant nothing to her)[15] spinster aunt she fled when she left for Africa—fled most likely her unhappy spinsterhood.[16] But in Tanne's letters home from Africa it becomes clear that Aunt Bess was a serious intellectual force against whom, and because of whom, she was forced to articulate more clearly her own, often different moral views; and it was *Moster* Bess who became the patron of her art.[17]

Many of Tanne's women characters emerge as young Valkyries; it may be *Moster* Bess who provided a model.

In a letter showing her to be a daughter of the Westenholz women, Tanne wrote *Moster* Bess from Africa that

> I once read an article on feminism written by a man, in which he actually criticized women for their foolish efforts to acquire the glories of life on their own initiative when they could get them so much more easily through a man who loved them. In his argument he used the fable of a flying competition held among all the birds of the world in which as far as I remember the eagle mounted to a great height by means of great effort and then the little goldcrest,—which had hidden itself in the eagle's feathers and which, when the great bird had reached the uttermost limits of its capacity and was obliged to stop, flew a very little bit higher still—won the first prize. He felt that this illustrated how a woman could gain everything in the world for herself by allowing herself to be supported by a man and his work and efforts instead of in sheer foolishness attempting to take an independent part in life's flying competition. And he was absolutely right; one need only read history to see how much more easy it was for a *charming* woman to acquire wealth, influence, excitement, than for anyone else. After all, it is not so long ago that the only way for a woman to travel was through the invitation of a man. Not only would she have been murdered if she had gone down to Nyhavn to haggle with a skipper for a passage on his smack, or on the highways and in the inns. . . . The only way to reply to all this is: but what if we want to fly ourselves!? What if we love wings and the air rushing past us?[18]

Tanne, who longed for "wings" in an early poem, would chafe at the restrictions placed upon her as a woman, and moved to free her women by decking them out in literary "wings."[19]

There is another aspect to the woman who can fly which intrigued Tanne and deviated from the godly bent of the Westenholz women. Fransine announces "I can fly" in "The Poet," looking very much "like a young witch" (an "angel" could never fly, trapped by her pedestal);[20] in fact, in early drafts of "The Deluge" Miss Nat-og-dag is referred to as a witch—women of power, even with the power of madness, are often aligned with the potency of the witch's brew.[21] Even if it meant swinging on the devil's tail, Tanne would set her sights on transcending her immediate reality by realizing feminine power imaginatively.

5.

The Captain and the Lady

1880: "Miss Ingeborg. Her or no one!"

🐦 *Regnar Westenholz early in his life had started as a grocer's boy in Hamburg, sleeping under the store counter at night. He moved up quickly through his talent for practicality and when the grain law was changed, eliminated the middle man in Hamburg, having his ships sent directly from Denmark to England, where the Danish ships loaded with grain caused a stir among the rowdy sailors on the docks. He made his fortune off of his practicality and the elimination of the grain law in less than six years—his granddaughter Tanne thought of him when she wrote of "people capable of making a fortune on their own [in] . . . an abrupt willed act of creation."[2] A "grand Merchant," he was tapped for various financial positions, briefly becoming minister of finance and an occasional member of Parliament. He claimed his roots through Jutland, the dark side of Denmark, and was a champion of the railroad there. Along with his partner, he was responsible for Jews being admitted to the stock exchange, and whenever he met Jews in the street they would ever afterwards remove their hats to him.*

He had long thick mutton chop whiskers, thinning hair on top, rather short straight hair, and looked awkward—perhaps indifferent is closer—in his clothes. Mama was twenty when she fell madly and wildly in love with him. He was thirty-seven. When his beautiful first wife died in childbirth, fulfilling a fortuneteller's prophecy, he asked for her hand in marriage and named his first daughter after his deceased wife, Ingeborg. All accounts of him describe his unselfish nature and warm spirit, but there are hints of a cold streak that revealed itself at the most unexpected times.

Mama would throughout her life begin trembling when she recalled a misunderstanding with her father during a scare over an outbreak of cholera. More testy than usual, he asked whether one of the brothers had come home. Sitting on the porch, Mama answered that she had not seen him—when it turned out he had been home all along, her father went over and angrily slapped her. She ran upstairs to her room, refusing to unlock the door even when her father, shouting, repeatedly knocked and kicked at the door. Writing to her fiancé, Regnar, she received the reply: "If you had been my daughter, I would have sent you from the house." They married, and Mama, whose taste in clothes was execrable, wore a simple wedding dress which she then burned.[3]

Married life at Matrup for Tanne's grandmother and her husband Regnar was not entirely removed from the excitement and amorous intrigue of royalty. Countess Danner, who had graced the female heads of Copenhagen with stylish hats as a milliner and who had lightly danced her way through ballets as a young woman, one day heaved through the door at Matrup, her double chins keeping time to her laughter, the smoke from her pipe circling the air while her husband, the king, stood nearby. Unpopular with her subjects, the queen, a commoner, was unable to convince Mama to be godmother to her child.

Matrup—mentioned by Tanne in her African letters home to her mother and grandmother—was a large estate with "four big farms, four churches, two mills, a wild area of woods and moors, several smaller places, and a number of houses with or without adjoining pastures."[4] There were farmhands, maids, caretakers, drivers, dairy hands, gardeners, cattlemen, and a dozen or so servants, all mingling with the brood of Mama's seven children. When her husband died from overwork and the strains of the 1864 war with Prussia, Mama could barely stand it and took her children by the hand, flying to Switzerland, London, and Italy. On one of the journeys her ten-year-old son died and her oldest daughter Ingeborg caught malaria which would plague her for years in the form of fevers; Ingeborg's daughter Tanne would in turn be broken by the repeated malarial fevers she caught while in Africa.

Back home at Matrup, afraid of losing Mama, some of her children conspired to hide her away in a closet if the Germans came—"the Germans are coming, the Germans are coming" was a national fear which preoccupied the Danes.[5] The Germans ended up occupying Matrup several times and Mama worried about the prospect of one of the children being run over by a German on horseback. Tanne's grandfather Adolph Wilhelm had been imprisoned for three days when German soldiers occupied Katholm Castle; they had finally let him go for the cantankerous man he had become. Fascinated by German military might, Tanne would have her own reputation in Africa tarnished by her friendship with the German officer von Lettow; sleek furred and red lipped she would later briefly flirt with the Third Reich before turning against it.[6]

Usually poised and self-contained in the running of Matrup, when she was betrayed in the dealings of a financial loan, Mama fell to her knees and repeatedly beat her head on the floor. Her balance was further thrown off by the charming entrance of Captain Dinesen—now irresistibly handsome, with his carefully groomed beard and penetrating eyes—who swooped in one fine summer at Matrup and gallantly kissed her hand.

"His genius," recalled Tanne's Aunt Bess, "his poetical gift, his life up to this point, so out of the way, so far from the conventional or philistine, appealed to her from the very first."[7] His courtship of Ingeborg (rather than her much more beautiful sister Bess, who favored frilly polka dot dresses) made Ingeborg Mama's favorite child.[8] This did not prevent Mama from an intrusive subversiveness into the courtship, which in her way she encouraged. The courtship took place on small bits of paper which Mama insisted on reading—the small pieces were used to make it easy to rewrite a letter Mama objected to; Ingeborg ended up hiding the long letters she sent without Mama's consent. They exchanged almost daily letters during their courtship of ten months.[9]

Wilhelm was quite taken by Ingeborg, who, in her unadorned blue and white cotton dress, her dark hair pulled back into a simple bun, presented a plain appearance made appealing by a face that radiated kindness; the looks of his fiancée and mother were remarkably similar. Wilhelm played the ardent pursuer, looking forward to the day he might address Ingeborg without using "Miss." Ingeborg, only twenty-four to the captain's thirty-five years, worried about being thought "impious" in her strict adherence to being a "free thinker."[10] Wilhelm rushed to reassure her that "I myself am rather lost religiously speaking and am perhaps many times more of a 'free thinker' than you. I have witnessed . . . such strange religious practices that all religion seems insane, absurd, idiotic, and at times abominable";[11] falling into line behind her father, Tanne later referred to herself as "a humanitarian heathen."[12] Her brother Tommy, writing about his participation in World War I, caused a minor scandal by proclaiming himself an atheist.

The differences between Tanne's parents were underscored in the courtship poems they sent each other. Wilhelm suggested the disturbing duality in his nature:

> I long away for sleet, war,
> Flash, bang, and the white clouds,
> The long marches, the wild screams
> The watch fire, the bugle, the bloody corpses,
> The barracks, the splendid towns.
>
> I long for the 'captain's seat'
> By the waterfall far in the forest,
> Where no strife is known;
> The falling water is as free
> as the land and the air above.[13]

Ingeborg wrote in trust:

> . . . I look deep within my heart;
> There your image lives. . . .
>
> And into this heart I shall live
> And here I shall find, confident and tranquil,
> The firm rock of my happiness."[14]

Their poetic gifts their children inherited; this understanding of life through its lyrical possibilities would be the most pronounced in their second-born child, Tanne.

During their courtship Wilhelm chose a Paris riding hat for his new fiancée while on a journey to France, but Mama wrote to him refusing such a scandalous gift for her daughter. Tanne would later show the letter to a friend, observing the sharp differences which existed between the two sides of her family; as with any number of such incidents, the references to a Paris riding hat found its way into one of her tales.[15]

Meeting Ingeborg, Wilhelm had imitated his father's courtship cry, charging forth in his diary: "Miss Ingeborg. Her or no one!" To Ingeborg he wrote that winter that "When I have to wait I can be vicious and mean."[16] It was a particularly bitter winter when there was much sickness in the Matrup home and the postal service was broken by the long, hard cold, and even the ice boats had trouble on the sound.

They married the following May 17, 1881. Spring was late and no buds or leaves could be seen on any of the trees. "Will you always remember," he asked his shy young bride, the bleak gray woods running behind their new home at Rungstedlund, "that it was beautiful and that we were happy?"[17] The words held a shadow of the conscious fiction Wilhelm Dinesen was seeking to maintain in believing he could settle down; his children would eventually suspect this inclination toward a false reality—his son Thomas in a family memoir accused him of writing letters to a nonexistent person, detailing the war in Turkey he had watched.[18]

6.

Daguerreotypes

"The best thing about Byron was Byron."

❦ *Through the sitting room windows draped with long lace falling like billowing veils onto the wooden floors (a sign of Danish wealth), Tanne and her sisters and small brothers could watch the ever-changing sea outside their home.[1] In the dead of winter, when the ice was frozen in pearled-gray swirling peaks, a fisherman would appear, a small figure trudging across the sound to Sweden. When Parliament was in session, their father's horse could be seen disappearing down "the shore road, . . . a shady, uncertain path along the beach . . . past the thatched houses of the fishing hamlets with net-drying grounds."[2] He would ride past damp heavy woods down to Klampenborg where the train could be caught for "Merchant's Haven"—Copenhagen—with its winding canals and fish wives selling their smelly wares among the brightly colored houses blooming flat against each other. Here among the brawling taverns and tattoo shops the bustling sailors and fishermen gathered, their small splintered boats bobbing in the canals outside.*

The crippled figure of Søren Kierkegaard had wandered in a dark sleek-fitting coat at the nearby Royal Theatre. The brooding philosopher—on whose head, observed Tanne, "the Mediterranean sun had never shone"[3]—appeared at the theatre regularly each evening, for ten minutes, long enough to hide his intellectual seriousness behind the fiction that he was an empty-headed dandy.[4]

Copenhagen was a busy harbor city in the mid-1880s when Tanne Dinesen was born. Swaying carriages brought men in tall black hats and women in long dresses and shawls to exchange news and conduct business in the chilly air while the cobbled streets resounded with the hooves of sweating horses. Bent over her writing table in later years, the shadows slipping along the wall behind her, Tanne would find herself lingering here in these streets.

Denmark was struggling with being a young democracy and politics meant more to the average Dane than ever before. Tivoli had become an exotic national institution, growing up from the political uneasiness Denmark was experiencing.[5] "Your majesty . . . when the people are kept amused, they forget politics," had reportedly been whispered in the king's ear, and so it was that Tivoli Gardens had grown up on the fortifications of the city with the understanding that in case of attack it would have to be burned down.[6] Cataclysmic social changes had shaken Europe, and Denmark had recently found its own political influence abroad considerably reduced from the days when the Vikings had muscled their way across the seas, leaving their language on England's shores.

As protection, Copenhagen had been surrounded by moats and ramparts against possible enemy attack, and to prevent smuggling, searches were made of all carriages and carts clattering across the bridge into the growing town of "Merchant's Haven."[7] Wilhelm Dinesen was preoccupied with Denmark's military defense, even during his defeat for his first bid to Parliament, writing articles for the newspapers calling for arms for every Danish man and for "more shooting, more history of war, and more teaching of war in the schools" as part of a plan to defend Danish land against covetous intruders, "the spiked Helmet" of Germany in particular.[8] He considered himself politically independent (unlike his father, who had written many pamphlets supporting "king, church, and class"), but was associated with the group of men arrayed against Prime Minister Estrup, and therefore labeled a leftist, a political label, rather than with the extremist connotations it has come to have today.[9] Like his own father before him, Tanne's father was a respected member of Parliament, often taking the long journey to the city for political meetings.[10]

Georg Brandes, the great Danish intellectual, wrote that at a time when "aristocratic radicalism" was about to break into the national spirit, Wilhelm Dinesen coolly appeared on the horizon, "not touched by considerations of convenience or mercy."[11] It was the aristocrat as unrelenting—revealed, for example, in Tanne's disdain for compassion, and the comfort of the bourgeois feather comforter—in living out a code of symbol and ritual which his dark-haired daughter always upheld.[12] Even as a young girl she would test her limits, casually throwing out her lunch on the train ride to Copenhagen. Learning that the free-thinking Brandes (whom she had never met) was ill, the young girl Tanne sent him a bouquet of flowers, remaining unrepentant when the sweet smelling blossoms caused a scandalized furor among her relatives.

Wilhelm Dinesen would return from Parliament through the gaslit streets, the lamps on passing coaches twinkling, to the boarding house where he stayed a few nights a week. The tensions of the city, its echoing alleys and winding streets, invigorated Wilhelm, providing a respite from his almost too perfect domestic life, the galloping horses sparking the ground around him. The driven restlessness of his youth still possessed him. Twenty years after being a soldier he missed the dramatic confrontations war provided, writing of his "longing after the white clouds of smoke and the thunder of the fight."[13] War he loved even more than the women he seduced.

He had been back to America with some officer friends, revisited Paris, and was now trying to convince his wife to travel with him around the world.[14] His books *Paris Under the Commune* and *Letters from the Hunt* were doing well—Georg Brandes would hail him as the greatest writer of nature to appear in Scandinavian literature; but there was an internal disturbance which would not leave him.[15]

Darwin had stunned the world with his theories of natural selection, and the eye of the ape was looking disconcertingly human as the naturalist's ideas were discussed over clinking wine glasses in the murky light of parlor rooms. Those in privileged positions were confirmed by Darwin in that privilege: "The nobility of Denmark," Tanne would note, "was stirred and intrigued by his doctrine—shocked by the assumption that one's ancestors were no better than oneself, attracted by the statement that a high rank in the universe was in itself the proof of genuine fitness for that rank."[16] The adventurers of a whole upcoming generation would be defined by such a self-preening.[17]

There was rumor of the Copenhagen railroad going past the Dinesen home to Elsinore, increasing the value of the land. It was one of the reasons Tanne's father had bought Rungstedlund when he had returned from the midwestern wilds of America, and why he chose to raise his family here along the shore road. Talk around the table in the evening was of the inventions of Edison, Daguerre, and Alexander Bell—Tanne's father had laughed at the scratchy voice coming from the new telephone box and no one thought much of the invention. Her aunt, *Moster* Bess, however, was taken by the idea of capturing some semblance of reality beyond the moment, and had become one of Denmark's first photographers.[18]

A black and white photograph passed down through the family shows Tanne and her sisters, Ea and Ellen, as little girls posed in the somber Victorian manner. Not so long ago a metal rod had been placed down the backs of those sitting for portraits, to make sure no unexpected movements took place. Now *Moster* Bess stood a long time beneath the black draping of her camera before being ready to take the picture of the three sisters, insisting that they ignore all itches and not blink to make sure a rare, miraculous likeness of them could be made, prettily grouped in a semicircle. Their dark eyes soft and dreaming, their hair cropped straight, they might be mistaken for boys, except for the identical pleated dresses with light trim which they are wearing. Tired of always having to dress exactly the same as her sisters, in the same straight, simple dresses and sensible shoes, the same fur capes and pompon hats, one time Tanne decided to pin a ribbon to her dress. Grumbles from her astonished family threw the house into an uproar all day: "Oh, Tanne, why do you always have to be different?"[19]

Claiming to have no particular interest in photography herself, Tanne found the daguerreotype of interest as a cultural representation of historical ideas, the "small yellow surface" of the daguerreotype "a symbol of the structure and ideology of an epoch, . . . the fine, true essence of a departed culture."[20] There was, she said, "a mystical inner connection between the principles, ideals, ambitions, prejudices, and dreams of an age—and its sofas, bouquets, and women's hats":

> Because Estrup as minister of state was prepared to carry out the defense of Copenhagen, cost what it might; because the czar of Russia as a happy and attentive son-in-law was paying a summer-holiday's visit at Fredensborg Palace; because *A Doll's House* had just been performed at the Royal Theater and had occasioned violent discussion in the newspaper and within families; because on other evenings, on the same stage, Emil Poulsen as Ambrosius had caused young ladies to dissolve in tears; and because Edison had just astonished the world by inventing the phonograph—because of all this, my mother's old friend, the wife of Admiral Bardenfleth, had—at an early stage of her life as a young seaman's bride—to be photographed with a shy little smile, beneath a complex of braids and curls, and in a dress with tucks, flounces, pleats, and a train, before a background of agitated waves in which could be seen pieces of a wrecked ship and—as a symbol of hope—an anchor.[21]

The moving in of the Industrial Revolution had created a split in the human psyche. Throbbing new machines attested to the power of mechanical restraint and sterility as humans were removed from the nature of their beings with the dizziness of the whistling train. Darwin had further confused the Victorian self, bringing back from his tour of the Galapagos Islands notes—just when progress meant a forward metallic streak—that linked human beings to the animal ladder. Marx added his machinelike voice, inveighing against the devouring power of the machine, eerily visionary in his warning that, like a magician's uncontrolled fantasies, the creations of society were about to overwhelm it.[22] And Freud, the last great Puritan, was about to observe demons seething in a dark medieval abyss of the unconscious, suggesting paradoxically that as human beings became more civilized and more removed from their original nature, more and more unhappiness could be expected.

Byron had sought to transcend human limitations by sacrilegiously wresting from God divine powers, the possibility of creating the self, and had fashioned himself as the tempestuous Byron, tortured by a deep secret. Tanne as a young girl played the role of Byron when she and a friend, Ellen Wanscher, invented a continuing saga starring Lord Byron and Lady Arabella. Many years later she still signed her letters to her friend with the poet's name.[23] "The best thing about Byron," Tanne would say, "was Byron."[24] The romantic imagination saw beauty in the order that was to be found before the Fall, before the individual had lost an idyllic place in the hierarchy of things through grave error, and the creation of the self ensured an understandable order made possible through artistic design, a return to a closer form of perfection.

Kierkegaard extended the Byronic character into the mid-1800s, with his own melancholy dandyism and cursed secret. He straddled the century's rational and imaginative conflicts when in *Either/Or*—in the section "Diary of the Seducer"—his seducer argued for the poetic removal of the individual from itself in objective reflection upon that self.

By the end of the century Wilde had taken this elegant, objective pose with an aesthetic vengeance (along with others such as Aubrey Beardsley), the self abstracted into something other than itself, which the machine had forced. The individual needed to be rearranged, stripped of unwieldy passions, into an elegant work of art, the *pose* made possible by artifice in tribute to "art as the supreme reality and life as a mere mode of fiction" argued Wilde.[25] A world made painfully alien by the ascendancy of the scientific and industrial mind—where Bartleby would be afflicted by a psychic stutter—could be reassuringly dismissed as mere fiction. Others joined Wilde, both Melville and Mark Twain concluding that reality was, soothingly, nothing but a "dream of the eye."[26]

This confused split in the nature of the self erupted in literature in such works as *Dr. Jekyll and Mr. Hyde,* Poe's "William Wilson," *The Picture of Dorian Gray,* Dostoevsky's *The Double,* and Melville's *The Confidence Man.* Tanne in "The Monkey" would pick up Kafka in this theme, part of a new century's anxiety over the struggle with passions and forces greater than oneself made particularly unpalatable in a world newly revealed as godless and efficient, where a benevolent ordering force could not be counted on to restore a world unpredictably thrown into disorder. Kafka found no solace in a world uninhabited by the gods, but Tanne found consolation in the whole thing being a jape of the pagan gods. The secular prioress daintily chews cloves, forsaking her perfumed lace handkerchief and manners long enough to run up the walls of Closter Seven in transformation into "The Monkey" (Darwin's monkey), mockingly landing on the bust of Kant in a mockery of all careful systems affirming rational thought, as we are warned the gods are capable of great laughter at our expense.

The best revenge, Tanne decided, was to fashion oneself in great style, in a vast articulation of will and protest that would give way to a graceful alliance with the creative powers of the divine, an alliance capable of reciprocal laughter. Her choice of Isak as the first name of her pseudonym—"he who laughs"—was a deep throaty chuckle, a belly roll, back at the gods. "The comic," concluded Tanne, "is the true art of the gods," and the aristocrat: "the very same fatality, which in striking the burgher or peasant, will become a tragedy, with the aristocrat is exalted to the comic."[27]

7.

The Dinesen Children

"shall I, shall other people see a stork?"

🐛 *Tanne's earliest memory was of her father helping her climb up Ewald's Hill,[1] to come upon a dreamer's view, the blue sea beyond edged in white, the dirt road below running out past their house along "a stretch of windblown land covered with willow trees and [purple] heather."[2] At the top of the highest hill, the little chubby girl of three sat with her hand to her mouth, her father's dog Osceola lying at their feet. Her father had been called Osceola by the Indians, and he told his daughter about his life among them, stopping to imitate the sounds of the cuckoo's song for his wide-eyed daughter. From him she learned the power of nature to console, the sharp cool smell of the sea hitting their faces as they walked back home down the hill to the Strandvej.*

"We were," Tanne remembered of her childhood, "not observers, as children today seem to be from birth, of their own accord; and not utilizers, as they are brought up to be: we were creators":[3]

Children of my day, even in great houses, had very little in the way of toys. Toy shops were almost unknown; modern mechanical playthings,

which furnish their own activity, had hardly come into existence. . . .
Our knotty stick, . . . came nearer to Pegasus himself, than any mag-
nificently decorated horse from a smart store.[4]

Living in a self-contained poetic world, the Dinesen children "owed
their existence to a romance."[5] Riding Pegasus on their gnarled
wooden sticks through the high-ceilinged rooms that looked out over
the sea, the "gold dust of romance" dreamily sifted over them from the
intrigues of both the barroom and royal courtroom that had been
acted out within its walls when the Rungsted Inn stood there.[6]

As a child, Tanne ducked in and out among the ghosts of men in
plumed hats stopping along the King's Highway at the inn. Shaking
the dust from their long, full capes, they downed a warming brandy
and ale, their horses waiting at the worn hitching post outside. Then
they would be on their way to the castle at Elsinore where Hamlet
haunted the rat-infested dungeons no prisoner had survived beyond
six months, or they returned to the shrieks of red-scarved fish wives
rending the air of "Merchant's Haven."

As an old woman, Tanne would recall in her famous radio talks the
history of the inn,[7] using the formal old-style Danish which made the
Danes shake their heads a bit and chuckle.[8]

She chose to ignore the meaning of *Rungsti*, pigs, which had given
the inn its name, for the 300 or so pigs that squealed out back when the
Dinesen children were small. Instead, her low voice crackled from the
radio that here Kirstine Munk, suspected by her husband Christian IV
of carrying an illegitimate child, was said to have whispered with a
Swedish gentleman of her husband's plots against Sweden. A young
Charles XII was rumored to have stayed here during his attack on
Denmark, his military dreams for a triumphant Sweden ending in
imprisonment. Shunned by the woman he loved, Johannes Ewald had
joined in the Seven Years' War; after his return, ravaged by alcohol and
disease, he sought refuge from a cruel stepfather by taking up lodging
at the inn.[9] Hearing the stories the fishermen and seamen told each
other over their thick, foaming ale, their nets thrown on the floor
nearby, Ewald used them in his poems, leading the way for Danish
romanticism.[10]

The inn had a long tradition of storytelling while the presence of
Ewald's poetic spirit served as a point of pride and inspiration for the
Dinesen family. Here at the Rungsted Inn, wrote Ewald, "the song-
stress builds, and chirping reveals her nest."[11]

But there was another storyteller, Hans Christian Andersen, who had traveled with her grandfather, and to whom she turned as a child. In the evenings, Tanne recalled, when she was "a little girl and had been put to bed . . . , my old Nurse used to read one of . . . [his] tales to me":

> Then when . . . [she] had said good night and was gone, and there was only the small night-lamp to light up the room, I used to call out in my thoughts: "Uncle Andersen, come and play with me."
>
> "Why, not at all," he answered me. 'I have had a long life, and have told my tales to many children. I have made them laugh and cry. Now I want to be left in peace in my nice, quiet grave here in the Copenhagen churchyard, and not to be worried by spoilt little girls." . . .
>
> He had that talent that he could make big things small and small things big. I lived in the country, and there were horses there that I loved to ride on, but they were so big that without assistance I could not get onto them or off them. He now made them quite small, like my kittens, and me, myself, much smaller than I was, and I had some lovely gallops round and round the bedroom with my slippers as hurdles, and, as I was alone, I always won the race. But my little dog, when we were walking together in the woods, he made as big as an elephant, so that I was very proud of leading him, and all the time he remained quite soft and curly, a lovely new kind of elephant. I also had two dolls, who were named Southcarolina and Goodfrida; those he made big, like grown-up ladies in long frocks with trains and tight, stiff stays, so that the three of us could have tea together looking exactly like Aunties and talking about how difficult it is to make little girls sit nicely at a tea-table.
>
> Uncle Andersen could make all things speak, . . . The old black stove in my bedroom and the bedroom door quarreled so terrible that in the end the door banged itself with an ear-rending boom. "I shall never speak to you again!" it squealed. "You are terribly rude," sighed the stove, "but although I am made of iron I have got a soft heart, and I forgive you." . . .
>
> "Not at all," I said, "if you are with me. For you can make big things small and small things big and everything talk, and I am much braver since I have known you than I was before. Just wait till I grow up, and you will see that because I have known you, I am not even afraid of lions."[12]

In her little-known introduction to *Thumbelina,* about the diminutive heroine who acquires gauzy wings, Tanne tapped the disingenuousness of the *naif,* and wisdom.

Water lilies like those used by Thumbelina to ride through the air spread over the pond near the footbridge at the back of the Dinesen home next to the sloping woods. As the Dinesen girls sang to the frogs hiding in the pond, Andersen's fairy tales ran through their heads. An elf tumbles through an early collection of Tanne's stories, Andersen-like, running into trolls and mischief, his hat snatched away by a muskrat. The elf meets a young girl, Henrietta, who is less than delighted to send her porridge to any elves, despite a servant's warning of the pitfalls lurking in the New Year if she ignores them. "To tell the truth," Tanne wrote about her heroine, "Henrietta believed in elves, although she denied it shamelessly."[13] What is already apparent in the early stories and plays is the youthful draw to contrast and the unexpected, which Tanne, a characteristic wry twist to her smile, was to develop into the high irony that would distinguish her writing as reality slipped into an elusive guise under the ironic grin.

The dramas the Dinesen children performed were great family fare and often called for the girls to exchange with the boys' roles and the boys to dress as girls, causing a bit of balking and giggling, especially during the love scenes. Once a family member was asked to act out the part of a blue mist, while another time the characters decided on stage to omit the next scene, agreeing it was too "tedious."[14]

Tanne's first dramas appear to trace back to the age of ten or eleven, around the time when family tragedy struck. The characters included Columbine, Harlequin, and Pierrot—with Tanne insisting on playing Pierrot.[15] Her interest in Pierrot was less for his foolishness than for his tragic sadness, his unrequited yearning; and his popularity.[16]

The pantomime tradition had found a permanent stage at Tivoli in 1844, winning out in popularity over all other entertainment: the huge yellow balloon carrying as many as sixteen people into the air, the acrobats leaping through hoops of fire, and the spear-carrying Bedouins riding in the caravans of elephants and camels. The tragic long-curled Elvira Madigan had been watched by the royal family in her breathless high-wire act before her romance with Baron Sixten Sparre ended in a suicide pact. The first bicycle race took place here, with riders wearing visored caps and tight britches as the huge front wheels of their cycles spun dangerously around steep curves. But the crowds pressed around the peacock stage where Pierrot, Harlequin, and Columbine bumbled in a love triangle.

White costumed, white faced and black eyed, Pierrot wore a large red heart on his back for the elusive Columbine, or nursed a crying babe with his white pompon. The victim of his foolishness, he was buffeted around the stage by a masked Harlequin; the children in the audience, who would have included Tanne and her brothers and sisters, delighted in his confusion, at the same time identifying with his unhappiness. When the actor who played Pierrot died during Tanne's childhood, the entire city of Copenhagen followed in his funeral procession.[17]

As a child Hans Christian Andersen had wandered in the Deer Park near Rungstedlund—where the Dinesen children raised dust with their horses—watching the pantomime troupes perform while servants flirted with each other on their afternoon off. After seeing a patched harlequin, he announced that he, too, wanted to become a harlequin; he ended up making and dressing his own puppets instead.[18] The melancholy Kierkegaard scribbled clowns into his writing,[19] and the great choreographer Bournonville used Pierrot in his ballets;[20] the young Tanne sat expectantly in the audience after making the long journey to Copenhagen to view his dances.[21] She appropriated the fanciful and the playful from the *commedia dell'arte* which appeared in Danish life; the image of the marionette became an important one in her tales.

In the Deer Park next to Rungstedlund, North Rungsted, stood the castle and royal hunting grounds of Christian VII, now empty after the scandals of his rule.[22] The Dinesen children were protected from the details of his reign, but as they grew older his entire history seeped into their consciousness, and Tanne's piqued disavowal that she was "a Danish writer"[23] was further contradicted as she capitalized on Danish history in such tales as "The Poet" and "Converse at Night in Copenhagen."

The events surrounding Christian VII's reign had crystallized the fine powdering of theatricality and drama that permeated much of Danish history.[24] In a fit of madness, said Tanne, Christian VII had pronounced that he would " 'rage' for a year" as he ascended his newly acquired throne in 1766.[25] In his lucid moments the king intended to improve the lot of the peasants, beginning with the abolition of serfdom in Copenhagen. But those moments of clarity were far too few. There was speculation on the reasons for this weakness of the brain: it was the cause of beatings his chamberlain, Count Reventlow, had given him as a youth, it was the result of being innoculated against smallpox with "matter" taken from Count Reventlow's feebleminded daughter. Only the immediate court seemed to know of his mental failures, but later generations would be entertained by the king's wild and bawdy behavior,[26] and as Tanne noted, "within the long row of kings of Denmark, of Christians and Fredericks," he was recognized first in their gossip.[27]

In the late afternoons after the girls' lessons were done, Mama would sit recounting stories of Danish history to them, *Moster* Bess, the "Old Victorian," rushing in to interrupt her. As the fire crackled in the fireplace, the wind outside blowing in the dark winter days as the three sisters sat bending their heads over their embroidery hoops, Mama warned them about the perils of a girl giving her heart away unwisely and too easily as she recalled the tragedy of Christian VII's young wife, Caroline Mathilda. Court memoirs refer to the English Caroline Mathilda's plight as that of "royal slave," who at sixteen was sacrificed in marriage for political reasons.[28] Neglected by the king (who attended the masked balls at the palace with his mistress, a former young harlot), Caroline Mathilda fell in love with the court physician, Johan Struensee. She abandoned her long jeweled dresses to ride dressed as a man with her German lover through the country-side, "attire which," sniffed Tanne, "one cannot imagine, from her por-traits, to have been very becoming"[29]

Isak Dinesen would always be drawn to the exotic, and the atmo-sphere of Denmark as a faeryland, with its royalty (and royal intrigue), castles, waterways, and the small pantomime theatre at Tivoli found its way into her tales; the gaiety of Tivoli appeared in her work, partic-ularly in *Ehrengard*. She ended up perpetuating the side of Denmark given to the brooding romanticism of a Kierkegaard and the shadowy faeryland of a Hans Christian Andersen.

Every Sunday morning Mama would greet them as the Dinesen children arrived at Folehave (Mama had moved to Folehave after Inge-borg's marriage to Wilhelm) to sing hymns while their mother played the piano and Elle the violin. Ea's voice was particularly pretty, though her dream of being a singer would be cut short because her voice was too small to fill a hall with Schumann. A dancing tree became the center of festivities on their parents' anniversary, and chocolate and white strawberries were served.[30]

During the week, the three sisters (the boys were sent away to school) were tutored at Folehave by Mama and her daughters, *Moster* Bess, and Ingeborg, as well as a medley of demanding governesses (once their father threatened to advertise for a governess who would share a bottle of red wine with him, since none of the Westenholz women, including his wife, would).[31] Mama carefully supervised their education and it was rigorous and romantic.

As an intellectual catalyst, Mama was responsible for a brilliance of education in the Dinesen children largely unknown today. She was strongly versed in the Bible and Latin, and ignored the abstractions of science and mathematics, which would later make her famous granddaughter bemoan her own gaps in knowledge, even though governesses were brought in to teach those subjects.[32] She deviated from the strictly religious and orthodox thinking of the time, believing that Jesus Christ was only a man, and convinced her grandchildren that the idea of one man taking someone else's crimes on his head was immoral, that the crucifixion was brutal and barbaric as a belief.[33] At the same time she believed unswervingly that there was a supreme God guiding the world, something her granddaughter Tanne wished for, but which the weight of her tales show she suspected was a fiction.

By twelve the Dinesen girls knew Latin, had read Molière in French, written an essay on Racine and Corneille, and translated Sir Walter Scott's *The Lady of the Lake* into Danish verse, which they quoted for years after. There was much enthusiasm about discussions over the books they read; Shakespeare was a favorite, and reading him for the first time "was," rhapsodized Tanne, "one of the really great events of my life." They had numerous essays to write—Tanne's topics anticipated her later interests: "It's the Will that Counts," "Women in the French Revolution," and "Matter and Spirit."[34] The school exercises became a way of testing her mettle and a child's battlefield. As a governess ordered "Essayez!" in red letters across her blue exercise book, Tanne, her dark eyes flashing, proudly wrote back "Still I am unconquered," and conscious of her military family, her father's claim to have no fear of anything, even death, "Often in difficulties, never afraid."[35]

Their mother, Ingeborg, their lessons done, gave Tanne and her sisters and brothers great freedom in the household but made rules against any childish sounds of discord, any hitting or screams taking place in the long corridors of the house, but granted them absolute authority in their own playroom, where, she said, a slight hidden smile in her edict to them, "everything is permitted which does not draw blood or inflict injury. No one, however, may cry for help from the grownups for what goes on in the playroom."[36] This for a time protected her children from the larger world and gave them an instinctive reassurance that outside of their own circle of childish turmoil an amiable spirit ruled, harmoniously—but in the tussles that took place at their own level, all chaos could unexpectedly break loose if a brother or sister was thwarted. In this way they were given, paradoxically, absolute control in their own unpredictable world. Ingeborg added that "All spiritual conflict is permitted, but no anger. Whoever is angry must absent himself from the public spaces, and from the stairs and corridors, so long as the anger lasts."[37]

In the evenings they played chess and cards, and tried to best each other at word games. One of their favorites was a game which required two words to be given, then a poem to be made over them; Tanne and her uncle invariably won.[38]

But one game particularly impressed itself on Tanne, a story told while lines were drawn on a sheet of paper in a "kind of moving picture," by the teller. The story began "In a little round house with a round window and a little triangular garden in front there lived a man . . . ," who took many different roads in search of the cause of a loud noise.[39] Searching for the noise, always in the wrong direction, he fell over stones and into ditches repeatedly before finally discovering that the noise came from a broken dam where water and fish rushed through. Repairing the damage, he went to sleep. Waking in the morning, the man "looked out of his little round window," and "what," the young Tanne was asked, "did he see?—A stork!"[40] She picked up the theme of this childish game in "Sorrow-acre" by interpreting the landscape in geometric shapes, leading to her conclusion that all of life's "mazy" tragic and comic shapes contribute to the design of the harmonious whole; it was this—the "stork"—she wrote from Africa, that she believed in and pretty much nothing else.[41]

8.

"the black sheep"

circa 1900: "One can do anything
when it is necessary."[1]

🐦 *Above the heads of the Dinesen children a secret was being whispered by their
mother and grandmother, their aunts and uncles, they cannot be sure what, exactly,
has happened. The family nurse Malla is heard to say that she thinks she has heard
their father walking the floor late at night, muttering to himself over and over again,
"I'll have to do it, I'll have to do it."*

The painful events from her tenth year became blurred with time,
and Tanne never knew whether the increasing intensity of her
father's talks with her were real or imagined. To the young Danish girl
on the verge of adolescence, the memory would linger of her desire
and inability to comfort her father in some way.

When Tanne's father hanged himself in the boarding house in
which he stayed while in Copenhagen during sessions of Parliament,
he created a scandal. The ignominy of an officer choosing to die by
hanging rather than by shooting himself impressed itself on everyone.
The Danish newspapers were filled with Wilhelm Dinesen's suicide,

an outspoken member of Parliament and famous author of a long line of decorated military soldiers choosing to hang shocked everyone, and tainted the purging by a deathly penance suggested in his self-inflicted punishment.[2]

There are different versions of how Tanne first learned her father was dead, but it seems most likely that a servant burst in with the news.

"Look, Tanne is trembling so" was heard while the family sat in a hushed circle. The Dinesen children could not comprehend the news right away—the sense of conspiracy and whispers increased as the family members closed in great matriarchal protectiveness to keep from the children the manner of their father's death. Although there were rumors that he was financially on the brink of ruin, that Danish politics had depressed him, even perhaps that he could not forget his love for his dead cousin (whose fragile beauty made her "*une princess de conte de fees*"), family tradition evolved to say Wilhelm had killed himself because he did not want to be crippled by the syphilis he had contracted and for which no cure existed.[3] Four years earlier in his *Letters* he had admitted his envy of all youth, noting, "But thank goodness, we still have plenty of time ahead of us, I hope"; he had also suggested that possibilities existed for a gentleman to keep a mistress in town, as well as waiting on the large estates to greet the gentleman hunter, who in the evening put aside his rifle to appear for dinner carefully dressed in coat and tails.[4] Love, which he intertwined with hunting and the battlefield, was incompatible with peace—"They hate each other," he wrote, "and persecute each other and destroy each other like fire and water."[5]

All church bells were silent at the news of Wilhelm's death. The family receded into great gloom and sadness, and Tanne, screwing up her thin face into a scowl beneath her heavy crown of twisted braids, withdrew into herself.

Thomas, a plump sunny-eyed boy of two still in his petticoats when his father died, became, in some sense, the man of the house as he was presented with his first rifle and expected to carry on the military tradition of the Dinesen men; his petticoats catching at his heels, he went stamping through the woods with his rifle, hunting. Their mother could not bring herself to say much about her husband's death, and a grief-stricken look descended on her face as she stepped into the widow's black she would wear all her life. Ingeborg's mother, Mama, had suspected that Wilhelm Dinesen would make her daughter unhappy, questioning what such a cosmopolitan man could see in her provincial daughter, and had feared the results of the union.[6] But she had been drawn to the dashing Captain Dinesen, even slightly infatuated with him, and had swayed her daughter in his direction when at first Ingeborg showed no special leaning toward him. Now, she was stunned at the news, and feeling responsible for her own daughter living through the pain she had seen her mother live through in a different way caused her to lapse into moments of paralysis, a condition which went on for several years.[7]

A letter written by Ingeborg to her son Thomas when he was a young man explains her own reaction to that time and suggests how her daughter Tanne was touched by it:

> It is not at all incomprehensible to me that Tanne can write of death so calmly. I know that I have talked so little to you all about Father's death,—perhaps I really should have been more outspoken to you, but it has seemed like holy ground to me, that no one must walk on without being able to understand what had happened. To Father the thought of having to live as a sick and stricken man was intolerable, and when I felt,—especially during the initial painful period,—as if he had failed me, it immediately grew clear to me that it would have been impossible for him to live like that,—and so he chose the only solution available to his nature. Many times have I thought that it would have been harder to see him growing old and feeble; speed and movement were essential factors of life to him, he had to be experiencing something, whether it were joy or sorrow, anything but stagnation, "respectability." How he could ever have come to choose me, and during all the years we lived together show me,—and feel, as I know that he did,—the greatest love and understanding, has always been a riddle to me,—it must have been something in him that needed another side to life, perhaps during a period when he needed more peace and quiet after a stormy spell. I have no doubt that he was happy here in his home,—happier than Tanne has ever been."[8]

Ingeborg's letter, more than any other direct testimony we have about her, makes clear, contrary to the commonly held belief that she was a bit of a bore, that rather she was a woman of unusual intelligence, sympathy, and selflessness.

Tanne did not reconcile herself to her father's death in the way her mother eventually did, calling it "my greatest misfortune."[9] In recalling her father's death, Tanne would accusingly say that he knew she would not be able to take care of herself without him; she shifted the truth slightly by claiming her father had said "the rest can take care of themselves—it is Tanne I worry about."[10] The one note left from Wilhelm to his daughter is an attempt to pacify her childish anger over some small incident: "from Papushka to Babushka in her belligerant mood."[11] But traces of the rebellious anger at being abandoned by him so dramatically never disappeared.

"It was," said Tanne of her father's death, "as if part of oneself had also died . . . the desolate feeling that there was no one to remember the talks on Ewald's Hill."[12] Suddenly one was pushed out into the foremost row of life, bereft of the joy and irresponsibility of childhood." Coming to feel that her father had failed her in some major way, the somber-eyed daughter who was most like him would seek just retribution from her family, coercing them into doing what she wanted by calling up his memory.[13]

When the family seemed to finally be coming back to itself, three years after the father's death, the farmhouse burned down, killing a farmer. The silence of the children's home without all of the farm animals accentuated the feelings of sadness and change which had descended on the household.[14] Thomas, reticent about discussing his own father's death, allowed himself to say in his memoirs that he and his brother were most troubled by the loss of an Icelandic hound: "For years Anders and I talked to Mother and the girls about why things like that happened and what death was like: 'He must have been killed outright, don't you think so, too, Tanne?' "[15]

Thomas Dinesen tells us that in a gift book written by friends and relatives "for Mama's amusement," his sister Tanne contributed a condensed version of the events of her life from 1885 to 1908.[16] Not surprisingly, her father's death is not mentioned, but the farmhouse fire is. Tanne lists having various teachers, and her authorship and "performances of several great dramas." The rest of her notations record her lessons in painting and drawing, her interest in ice hockey, sailing and bicycling, travels to Norway, Scotland, and Holland (where she saw Rembrandts). She "sacrificed" herself "to high society," was given "a lovely police dog named Natty Bumpo," and held "Soren's cap." Perhaps because of the nature of the gift book for Mama, there is a curious mixture in the presentation of events, the burning down of the farm appearing as significant as holding her cousin's cap—the balance of the account is slightly askew.

In her own imaginative life, Tanne, after her father's death, would always be seeking to find the stable point in a world thrown dangerously near the abyss; her tales often attempt to reconcile the disastrous and the calm in what turns into a search for the eye of the storm. In this there was an instinctive impulse to reconcile the experience of the world presented to her by her mother, the pure, clean "white Lamb" Tanne fondly called her, and her father, the restless "black sheep," who like Jeremias in "The de Cats Family," an early story, becomes the focus of turmoil in the family. In another early story, "The Ploughman," Tanne reversed her family experience by describing the "wild witchblood" of the mother and the "staid bourgeois heritage" of the father—she hinted at the emotional confusion this parental duality set up in her own life when she depicted a male character paralyzed by this familial conflict, making it impossible for him to succeed at anything.[17]

Tanne reacted to the family tragedy by sharpening her sense of self through an adoption of style, through an "arrangement" of the self which implied a triumph of the will in a reality which had become for her, with her father's death, confused and unclear. She confided to a friend that in the evenings, as she combed her sister's hair, she would insist on telling stories, until Elle, tired, would beg her to stop. One of the first tales she ever told, recalled Tanne, at the age of fifteen, was called "John Vorbech's Eterfølger." Two men chase each other, switching positions with each other throughout the pursuit until they are discovered, dropped over from exhaustion; they have become so alike it is impossible to tell who is who.[18] Reality had dissolved, losing all clarity. As a mature writer, Tanne would elaborate on this idea in "Deluge at Norderney," a tale of self-creation and recreation in a spinning back that negates the creative and noncreative self and all its understood lines of reality.[19] In "Deluge," the mask becomes a nihilistic disguise against fate—or an attempt to enter into a cabal with destiny—as life is engaged within the lineaments of an artistic pose in the attempt to keep death, the fear of nothingness, at a distance.

Reacting against her father's death and the blurring of her world, she moved into a life that depended upon memory for its definition, the memory "of her beloved father"; living in a world made vague and indefinite by its adherence to the past, she was rebuked by her mother for being "a sleepwalker" as she became forgetful about even such favorite chores as arranging the flowers in the drawing room. Shaken, she looked to Katholm for comfort.

All of Wilhelm's children felt his spirit at Katholm, and sought to bring him back by walking the same steps he took: the two brothers Anders and Thomas were delighted to have their father's rifle and go hunting as he had done along the wilds stretching out near Katholm. Claiming Katholm as her home—it being, Tanne told her mother, her "father's house"[20]—became a way of adolescent rebellion against the Westenholz women surrounding her.[21] It brought a pained look to her mother's face, while putting her into a heady and symbolic alliance with her father. She remained perceptibly and imperceptibly, her father's daughter; when she finally left for Africa the family nurse Malla remarked wistfully: "There goes the last of the Captain."[22]

At the great castle of Katholm, their great large hats circling above the soft, slim folds of their dresses, Tanne and her close friend, Daisy Frijs, shared their secret flirtations, carried on while dancing through the late night balls; the mild friendships Tanne formed with the young men were kept from her mother for fear of disapproval.[23] The social whirl brought her into frequent contact with Katholm where the bathhouse on the long sandy beach still ran up a flag when her aunts were in the area changing for a swim into long, full dresses and floppy hats.[24] Times had changed little since Tanne was a child gossiping with her sisters about their uncle being forced to propose to Aunt Lidda after catching a glimpse of white from under her uplifted dress.[25]

While she enjoyed the attentions of suitors vying for her hand at Katholm, the Danish papers were filled with a pressing fashion debate: "the corsetless women's gowns" question. No one cared much for the proposed "reform gown," but no gown design that made the figure feminine without the obligatory restraining wires and stays was thought possible. Tanne would pick up this quandary over fashion to test an argument against marriage: in the same way as "resistance" to corsetless gowns, argued Tanne from Africa, a proposal for the abolition of marriage would have an initial outcry.[26] The marriage relationship was not to be trusted.

Not having the money of the aristocrats surrounding her at Katholm, Tanne grew despondent.[27] After a time the life of endless parties and flirtations came to have a meaningless ring to it; her intelligence demanded more.

9.

Paris, 1910

1910: "Dear God, this old worn childish . . . life which you have given us to play with and which might have been good enough for the people who you created 20 centuries ago, we have grown out of it. . . . "

❦ *The Paris of 1910 was the mysterious Paris of a smoky Atget photograph, darkly handsome men with slicked down hair and twirled moustaches staring secretly from the grills of wrought iron doorways, engraved men in metal armor hovering overhead. Parisians in swirling dark capes and long foxtail furs moved through the gaslit streets past elegant tea salons and sultry cafés, hats tilted coquettishly above their eyes. It was the Paris of style and engaging charm.*

"Amaze me," intoned Serge Diaghilev as he swept into Paris with his corpulent bulk, flowing cape, high hat, and penciled moustache, bringing with him the diaphonous red and purple lushness of the Ballets Russes in his *Scheherazade;* shop windows beckoned to passersby with fashions inspired by the thinly veiled storyteller and Nijinsky's writhing slave as Parisians rushed to imitate the exoticism of the Arabian tales.[1] Diaghilev and his circle demanded the extravagant gesture and replied in kind—at one opening night the front row of fifty-two seats was filled with the most beautiful actresses of the time, their seats carefully arranged so that the blonde and brunette heads alternated. The artistic design was not lost upon the audience who burst into applause at the sight.[2]

Tanne later confided to friends that she had seen Diaghilev, and despite a dispute among her biographers over whether she actually did, given her repeated trips to Europe when the Ballets Russes reigned, it is not unlikely that she was in one of the audiences.[3] Certainly she was aware of Diaghilev's influence, and drew a subtle line between herself and a Diaghilev favorite, *Scheherazade*. In an early story, "Carnival," she borrowed from Diaghilev's plot, using the same Pierrot and Harlequin figures he used in his own ballet *Carnaval*. A record given to her by a lover in Africa was the music from the Diaghilevian ballet, *Petrushka*, about a Pierrot, a helpless puppet and the all-powerful master—a recurrent theme in her tales.

Overcome by a terrible melancholy, Tanne left for Paris with her sister Ea in March 1910, writing in the beginning of her Paris diary:

> I thought to myself: Dear God, this old worn childish enormously embarrassing life which you have given us to play with and which might have been good enough for the people who you created 20 centuries ago, we have grown out of it.[4]

Aerlig, aerlig,—honest, honest—she had marked her diary, in a reminder to herself that she would be adhering to the truth more than she ordinarily liked to. She was relieved to be traveling with her sister Ea who was not demanding and would "not let herself be bothered in ways others do."[5] The ferry ride to the train on the Continent had been a lonely one, punctuated by the racy talk of some Swedes; once on the Paris train they passed up into Germany, a country which, huffed Tanne, they saw "through a fog of railway idiocy."[6] Even though it was Good Friday, from the train window they could see men working along the rails, while the lights and smoke from the nearby chimneys gave out the sparkle of spectacular fireworks. Their arrival at the French border was signaled by the two sisters having to carefully watch their skirts as they stood on the seats while the customs officers checked below for smuggled goods.

Tanne had turned into a stunning beauty who wore her hair fashionably swept up into dark curls, a style of the muses, who from behind a pert smile suggested a veiled flirtatious manner that was accented by a preference for gauzelike chiffon, cut daringly low, clinging to shoulders and arms in colors of pink or pale blue. In the first stirrings of youthful love, she had become infatuated with a Swedish cousin of hers, the Baron Hans von Blixen-Finecke, whose bold exploits intrigued her. The baron rode the newly invented shining plane and madly raced horses—once he won a flying contest, then landed in time to place first in a horse race—and fluttered the hearts of the young Swedish women around him; being of an aristocratic line he could change someone into a baroness and with his striking Nordic looks was thought to be a prize catch. He showed little interest in his petite Danish cousin.

Pencil in hand, Tanne dreamily drew a mermaid over and over again throughout her early notebooks, finding an echo of her own personal pain at her first unrequited love (even perhaps at her father's abandonment) in Hans Christian Andersen's fairy tale "The Mermaid."[7] Andersen's tale is a classic depiction of romantic love, its bitter ironies and its overwhelming irrationalities. In an attempt to win the love of the prince she has saved from drowning, a mermaid exchanges her lovely voice for the shape of a human woman. Every step she takes brings the literal pain of her love in silence while the prince remains oblivious. He ends by marrying a woman he believes has saved him from drowning, mistaking her for the ideal he has been seeking. The story struck deep, playing out Tanne's own fatal attraction to elusive men which would wrap her in an emotional straitjacket whose grip was tightened by the prevalent romantic attitude.

Depressed and tired, Tanne had confided to Ea that she hoped the trip to Paris "might give a little bit of charm to life and at least make it worth living for me."[8] They had arrived in time to attend Easter Sunday Mass at Notre Dame, the pungent clouds of incense drifting as organ music filled the great church. Her mood began to lift when they went to the tower after the service, and in the din of the midday bells saw Paris spread before them. It did not last and Tanne complained about "how idiotic and meaningless the whole trip was."

The two sisters decided to stay in separate lodgings, and Tanne moved in on the Rue Boccado where she confused the taps and was forced to take a cold bath. She bought two birds and a cage, some fresh flowers, writing supplies, ink and inkstand, brushes, charcoal, and had tea and cakes up in her room with Ea—but still, "how trivial everything seems."[9] It was best, she decided, to go to art school while her sister studied music, "so that at least I'll have a feeling that I'm doing something useful—though God knows nothing useful goes on in a school for artists." Bringing over one of her artworks she was accepted at the school of painting at Simon de Menard—she had studied at the girls' school for artists back in Copenhagen.[10] Every morning anew the problem of whether to attend class or take a round of the city presented itself; the decision was invariably based on trivial considerations—getting up one morning she decided to attend class that afternoon to get away from Düring, one of her more fickle suitors. The school made scarce impression on her, except for the bearded student who asked her to leave because she was painting the "nice young girl" from his place. Most of the students were English, the only one interesting her being a French artist.

Walking through the cold Paris rain wearing fashionable black hats and silk stockings, the two sisters were on the lookout for a husband, and Tanne was pleased to receive some good advice on men and marriage from the matron at Rue Boccado. They had many friends in Paris, among them Count Wedell and the Comte and Comtess d'Elbée, and were pursued by scores of men—one, a Hoskier, brought a "terribly ugly bouquet of flowers and kissed Ea in the vestibule" wrote Tanne with mixed feelings, "now the servants treat us with much more respect"—and they were drawn into a whirl of French theatre, roulette, the racetrack, and art museums.[11] Art museums were not a favorite with Tanne, who was nevertheless rather taken by the French Impressionists, more than the modern artists who distressed her by reflecting her view of a dispirited and meaningless world; the Louvre, decided Tanne, was embalmed, like a tomb, and should hold a dead king in its recesses.

French and German officers and a divorced French woman who had considered suicide within the month crowded around Tanne at one luncheon; a Rumanian officer gave her a medal and she heard military music in the Tuilleries Gardens. A Madame Gallembert offended her by refusing to believe that "father had been a French officer" and she was glad to be rescued from her anger by the Duchess Bourbon.[12] Anyone who irritated her made their way into her Paris diary as an "idiot."

At night, in a pink gown, Tanne and her friends prowled through the expensive cafés, the Café de Paris and Kafé de la Paix, where they watched dancers and ate fresh fruit while sipping champagne. She alarmed her mother when she went out with an American, a redhead with dandruff in his hair, whom she found "nice" but singularly unappetizing. With one favorite escort from the consulate, Eduard Reventlow, she went down during intermission at the opera to smoke, and played cards and drank whiskey, not coming home with him until 5:00 one morning, when not a single soul could be seen walking in the early light along the Champs Elysées. She noted flirting with Eduard Reventlow and with others, but added in her diary: "I don't really have any feeling at all—that they are real people."

The only quarrel she had with Ea took place at a tea salon, her sister scolding her and putting her into a bad temper by accusing her of disturbing the relationship between Reventlow and Else Bardenfleth, a woman he planned to marry. Reventlow eventually married Else and stayed with her the rest of his life; it did not prevent him from sending Tanne a letter fifty years later:

> Above all your letter has made me think so much of being together with you half a century ago. It was a moving time of my life for me. I never forgot the sorrow of your leaving, or of missing you when you were away. I have never been very communicative when it concerned something very close to me, but you could not have been completely without knowledge of my feelings.[13]

With him at the cafés she discussed the kind of hat the husband she chose should wear and "exclusivity" between the sexes. Perhaps Reventlow was too easy a conquest or offered the possibility of too predictable a life; at any rate, despite her fondness for him, he did not strike a deep enough chord in her.

Her search for meaning had a religious cast to it which had been obscured by her stay among the Parisians—Paris had done its job and captivated her—but which had not disappeared. In the Kafé de la Paix with Reventlow she discussed the "meaning of life" as they drank tea, and he stared at her intently across the table; it was a question which would not leave her, her tales becoming an artistic—and often romantic—quest to solve the existential dilemma which would characterize the twentieth century, the question of the ultimate significance of internal and external reality; it was a question to which a new age would offer little belief as answer.

Picasso was beginning to think of cubing the world; small gatherings of artists sparked with new excitement as perceptions of the world broke unforeseen ground. Diaghilev was infusing Paris with a curious mixture of the romance of a past era, extending the self-conscious dandyism of the Oscar Wilde epoch, heralding at the same time the dawning of the twentieth century with Picasso's sets and Stravinsky's music as backdrops to his ballets. His art tapped into the primitive and the modern as the world pulled into a new century where the individual was proving inferior to its own metal creation, the machine, where the rational and objective was meant to rule, where science (and soon, the Great War) was making God into a question mark, bringing on an unfulfilled yearning for a reminder of one's essential being. Mark Twain had argued in a prescient comment on the century that God could not exist in a world which had run amuck; better to think romantically and reassuringly of everything as a dream of the imagination and nothing else. D. H. Lawrence was busy recording the complexity of the emotional life as it became clamped under by the worship of industrial forces, while Faulkner was about to create out of America's Southern consciousness the quintessential twentieth-century individual in Quentin, facing the self in existential *angst*.

But Paris would eventually give out its own answer to the young Tanne. Once in Africa Tanne remembered the "harmony" to be found there: "that indeed I think is the greatest charm of Paris and of France as a whole—and the great gift of the south, where everything is in harmony; they can assimilate all the various elements of life into one beauty. Everything that in less perfect natures exists in a state of contradiction: body and spirit, nature and ideal, theory and practice, art and life, life and death,—there becomes the most delightful harmony"; the feeling would be tentative.[14]

Trying to decide whether to leave Paris, there was one last walk around Paris with Reventlow, and Tanne could remember standing on the bridge over the Seine counting the automobiles and finding violets on a green beach, or the talk of symbolists and the anointed right of kings. Mario Krohn, who had published one or two of her stories back in Denmark, had shown up recently and sent her roses when she couldn't meet him because her sister was ill. She decided to leave for home the next morning with her sister Ea, shortly before Diaghilev's successful flirtation with Parisian society.

II

THE ADVENTURER

10.

The Baron, Bror von Blixen-Finecke

"a strange stinging of the blood"

🐝 *The Baron Bror von Blixen-Finecke had the kind of looks and manner Hollywood would build its empire on: a sturdy physique, dark hair and a penetrating blue gaze that was edged by a suggestion of the wild, a gaze that promised great mischief and humor, and a gift for storytelling. He had never taken to books, preferring to be out on the estates hunting, invigorated by what he called "a strange stinging of the blood": "I cannot," Bror reminisced, "say how old I was when I had a gun in my hands for the first time, but that my fingers itched to hold a weapon rather than a book is beyond question."* [1] *When Tanne later pointed to the differences between herself and Bror, she referred to his ignorance of the Crusades, whether they came before or after the French Revolution.* [2] *One of his women friends recalled that even after many years of friendship a telegram from Bror stirred excitement, and admiringly described his courage and disarming modesty and—here affectionately—his "never being significantly silent."* [3] *A loneliness of the spirit, she added, showed itself late in the night when he was left without company, having drunk everyone else under the table.*

The baron's interest was sparked by his older Danish cousin, who in her precocious wit and intelligence ran counter to the prevailing vogue of the shy, retiring Victorian lady; he was charmed by her flair for elegant grace and a style sharpened by Paris, framed by beguiling *fee*-like looks and a caressing voice.[4] Better still, her family had money. He decided to woo her interest away from his twin brother, Hans.

Flattered by his persuasive attentions, Tanne felt drawn to him and after he gave repeated proposals of marriage, agreed to marry him. He offered the lure of adventure, and the possibility of going to a foreign country in search of fortune; he was not in line for a great inheritance back in Sweden, his future being set up to be the manager of a farm in Skåne and to remain in dim competition with his more flamboyant brother—so he agreed with alacrity to going abroad. It has been suggested that it was the possibility of life in an exotic country and an aristocratic connection which finally convinced Tanne of the marriage; her mother, eager for news from her, would regret opening a letter Tanne had written to her brother, in which she admitted "that I got married and put all my efforts into emigrating in order to get away" from the cocoonlike atmosphere of her Victorian home.[5] But in her story "The Pearls," she hinted at other feelings surrounding her decision to marry Bror:

> The gossips of Copenhagen would have it that the bridegroom had married for money, and the bride for a name, but they were all wrong. The match was a love affair, and the honeymoon, technically, an idyll. Jensine would never have married a man whom she did not love; she held the god of love in great respect, and had already for some years sent a little daily prayer to him: "Why doest thou tarry?"[6]

Tanne was of a rather advanced age to not yet be married, twenty-six, when she decided to become engaged to her younger cousin.[7] He was not her first choice.

Bror's family was against the marriage—she was not of the right aristocratic breeding, her father had had the bad taste, in a failure of gentility, to kill himself, further tainting the blood of the family.[8] Her own family was suspicious of the baron, his high-spirited sense of adventure and dashing good looks reminding them a little too much of Wilhelm—even though he was not an officer, for which he suffered slights.[9] And Bror's mother was the sister of Agnes Krag-Juel-Vind-Frijs, the cousin around whom Dinesen family legend hovered, insisting that Wilhelm's tragic love for her had made him unhappy all his life—an appealing connection for Tanne, if not her family.[10] Despite the reticence of both families (her mother "was taken by storm"[11] reported one relative, while Aunt Bess prophesied that the "only good she could see in it was that . . . [Bror] was a poor man"),[12] the two second cousins went ahead with plans for the wedding.[13] Bror himself would remember fondly their decision to leave for Africa, where the marriage would take place:

> The human imagination is a curious thing. If it is properly fertilized it can shoot up like a fakir's tree in the twinkling of an eye. Tanne knew the trick, and between us we built up in our imagination a future in which everything but the impossible had a place. The promised land which hovered before our eyes was called Africa, and our golden dreams included a large farm, teeming with fine fat cattle.
>
> Nor was it just a castle in the air. Behind our imaginings lay a reality, named Aage Westenholz, an uncle of Tanne's. This excellent man was, among other things, the owner of a rubber plantation in Malaya.
>
> "What would you say to exchanging Stjärneholm for my rubber plantation in Malay?" he asked me one fine day.[14]

But another uncle, Mogens Frijs, just back from hunting in Africa reported that a million could be made from owning an East African farm; the sight of profits and gleaming gold carried to the bank was an invigorating one, and the family was eager to buy shares in the scheme to grow rows of coffee plants instead of rubber trees.[15] After the exchange of many letters, a farm of seven hundred acres was bought.

11.

Mombasa Wedding

1914: a world that as if "by some
magic, had been turned . . . upside down"

❦ *Wooden dhows laden with rugs and spices of the Orient sailed into the harbor
town of Mombasa on the winds of the monsoon, and their powdery mounds of spices
rivaling the fire reds and oranges of the sun were weighed out in the marketplace. For
thousands of years the coast of East Africa had been the run for trade in ivory, gold and
jewels, swords and silks. It had provided a ready market for the rugs made by small
children who by the age of eight or nine became deformed from the minute sewing of the
oriental rugs. "The Dreamers" was set nearby, at Lamu, Tanne setting asail one dhow
that hid opium, a "secret load, which was about to stir and raise great forces, and of
which the slumbering countries which she passed did not dream" as it "carried full
sails before the monsoon" with its additional "freight of ivory and rhino-horn."[1]*

There was good reason for interest in east coast trade. The loads of
the dhows marked a lavish life for the privileged: "A single dhow of
eighty tons could take on sufficient elephant tusks to furnish every
room in a maharajah's palace with ivory chairs and tables, enough
rhino horns to keep a dozen sultans in aphrodisiacs for a year. Slaves

and concubines were easily obtained on the coast."[2] An ornate style emerged from all of this importing:

> Splendid mansions mushroomed. Built of wood, cut stone of coral and lime, these houses had pillared verandas and arched porticos, and they girdled spacious courtyards that glowed in smotherings of oleander, jasmine and roses. Indoor furnishings bragged tastefully. Alongside the polished crystal glassware on any well-set table lay silver cutlery and emerald-encrusted gold fingerbowls. Retiring for the night, one mounted a silver stepladder to reach an elevated bedstead of ivory-inlaid rosewood. Gold-embroidered silk robes were everyday garb. Thumb-sized rubies set off the silver hilts of the curved, razor-sharp jembias worn at every waist. Some towns had their own mints, which struck coinages of silver and copper. The historian Basil Davidson has likened such places as . . . Mombasa to " 'city empires' in the same sense as medieval Venice or Genoa."[3]

Mombasa had been crucial to Great Britain's launching—blundering is perhaps more accurate—into East Africa.[4] This reaching into Africa was brought about for any number of reasons not the least of which was the inalienable belief in the divine right of Christians and in the superior civilization guaranteed by the white skins of English gentlemen, boredom at the Victorian-lacquered society at home, excitement at new ports of trade offering renewed chances of corralling the golden *El Dorado*, and a peevish dislike of Germany's upstart forays into Africa. All of this was informed by a moral righteousness interpreted by the Victorians as humane intention. The empire became synonymous with the *organizing principle*, a triumph of the rational as embodied in the idea of progress, set against a spiritual belief in the duty of Christians to remove all lingering vestiges of original sin.

The *Arabian Nights* spilled out onto the crowded streets as teeming crowds sent a melodic Arabic into the air at the Mombasa harbor as the boat docked, their brilliant oriental costumes a shock to Tanne after the blue monotony of the sea.[5] It was a land where all fantasy was possible. A fifteenth-century writer, Abu al-Mahasin, had written about the mysterious rule of apes in Mombasa: "the monkeys have become rulers," he said. "When they enter a house and find a woman, they hold congress with her."[6] The story would be echoed in "The Monkey."

Stupored by the heat, when she finally caught sight of Bror, Tanne felt "it was wonderful to be with someone one feels one belongs with again."[7] She left von Lettow in a "narrow, fiery street in Mombasa . . . overlooking the blue Indian Ocean."[8] He was going on to nearby Zanzibar, the island known for the pungent smell of cloves where the notorious slave trader referred to in "The Dreamers," Tippu Tib, had conducted a thriving business at the crowded auction block, parading and selling slaves. That was when caravans with hundreds of slaves slowly wound their way through Africa, vultures marking the route as they waited for the dead flesh that would fall their way.[9]

They went over to the old part of the Arab town, to the Mombasa Club overlooking the small boats dipping in among the palms along the sea. Next to it was the massive Fort Jesus, the coral- and charcoal-blasted fort that had been the site of the bloody battles of the Portuguese, when the town had filled with the stench of corpses and even the birds were reportedly shot out of the skies.[10] Battles between the Arabs, Africans, and Portuguese were common and on one rare occasion when Mombasa failed to be triumphant, the failure was blamed on the superior witchcraft evoked by the brass pot and gong hidden in the ground at Lamu.[11] Only a few years before Tanne and Bror arrived in Africa the hollow echoes of slave children dragging long poles from their metal-bound necks had been heard, as they slowly walked to the water's edge to dip their bare feet; slavery had not been outlawed until 1907.[12] There was in the heavy heat a dreamy timelessness to the place, as the mosquito netting fell into folds on the bare floors around wooden beds, the Arab women wearing black *bui buis* silently gliding through the old narrow streets outside glassless, white-barred windows. There was, Tanne remembered later, a sense of a world that as if "by some magic, had been turned . . . upside down."[13]

The wedding took place near the sea, in a room where a leopard's eyes gazed down at them from the stark whitewashed walls. It was a civil ceremony overseen by a seated, sickly looking man, who prepared to record the marriage with his rusty pen onto the oily papers placed before him. The governor's deputy: "And now I ask you . . . oh yes . . . what's the name, it was so strange?? . . . oh yes, if you will take this. . . . " He dates the document carefully, January 14, 1914. The baron, notes his friend Prince Wilhelm of Sweden, one of the witnesses, wears "white clothes, which . . . [have] not been pressed in a long time."[14] The blue eyes shine from a face bronzed by the African sun, his broad shoulders and solid bearing exuding the confidence of a hunter and conqueror. Searching for the pedigree in the young woman about to be titled baroness, the prince finds it, describing the bride:

> She is slim, shapely, with deep-set and intelligent eyes and regular features under up-swirled chestnut hair. The simple but well-cut morning dress betrays the handiwork of a first-class fashion house. Not used to this heat which is like a baking oven, she wipes some shining pearls of sweat from her forehead with a handkerchief. A lovely and courageous young girl now far away from all that. She has come alone to join her destiny to the man at her side. No family, nor any friends besides those gathered on the way out. Really, to do this self-assurance and love is required.[15]

The prince further records a jarring detail:

> The ceremony is over. At the same time as the deputy closes his book with a thud, an animal which lives behind the leopard skull on the wall comes out and catches a fly. Quick as lightning soon a frayed wing hangs out of one side of its mouth, while the rest of the insect is chewed to mush in the broad mouth.[16]

After the wedding, the salty sea spray lingering in the air, they drift away in a rickshaw through the blazing heat which makes everyone feel languorous, to a seashore villa for lunch "with Hobley,"[17] the man with malaria and whiskey in his blood who has married them.[18] Hobley has been here for years, first coming out to search for precious metals in a geological exploration.[19] It is not unlikely that he entertains his visitors with stories of his visit to the site of the "man-eaters of Tsavo," where the Indians halted all work on the railroad for three weeks in a protest—they have, they say, come out to build the railroad, not to provide food for two hungry lions.[20] Hobley: "I was besieged by my men begging the loan of my guns to protect themselves, and they clustered round my tent all night. Guns went off at intervals in the various coolie camps around us, and altogether I had a very disturbed night."[21] A friend of Hobley's will later note that the African land is ready for a Kipling to emerge and record its stunning beauty and wild brutality.[22]

Then the newly married baron and baroness catch the train for Nairobi. Prince Wilhelm has reserved the train for their special use; advertisements for the Uganda train refer to the new African playground, "a Winter Home for Aristocrats has become a fashion."[23] Around the wedding supper that night (prepared by the corpulent millionaire Macmillan's special chef), as they sip champagne and toast to the future in time to the clicking rhythm of the train, everyone sits in their pajamas cooling off while the hyenas cackle in the distance. As the Baroness Blixen-Finecke raises her glass in a toast, she is slightly uneasy. The choice of her handsome Swedish cousin for a husband has set the paradoxical rhythms of her life; she has recently been in love with the baron's daredevil twin brother Hans, and now, looking at her husband, she finds herself bound to a mirror image.[24] A fatal decision, as her father's destiny is prepared to be repeated in her own.

Den fürgterlige Begivenhed i Rigsbagen.

»Hun har ta'et min Klokke«

Gikuyu men dressed for a tribal ceremony. From
The Life and Destiny of Isak Dinesen

12.

Arrival in Nairobi

1914: "Everyone called me Baroness every other word. . . . "

❦ *Tanne's distant voice was next heard from the heart of Africa, as she wrote back home to her mother:*

My own little Mother.—

I ought to have written long ago, but you have no idea how time has flown, and I wanted so much to write something sensible and worth-while. But now I am sending this by runner, so you must take it as it is and despite the muddled style try to get an idea of this great new life and everything that has happened out here. I am in bed, not on account of illness but of night hunting, in a little log cabin, two rooms with wooden floors, with a fireplace in one of them, and all around on every side the most magnificent and wonderful scenery you can imagine, huge distant blue mountains and the vast grassy plains before them covered with zebra and gazelle, and at night I can hear lions roaring like the thunder of guns in the darkness.[1]

"But now," continued Tanne, "to begin at the beginning."[2]

Leaving Mombasa behind, the "landscape had completely changed," marveled Tanne, "and then it was the real Africa," with the "vast grass plains and the mountains in the distance and then an incredible wealth of game, huge flocks of zebra and gnu and antelope right beside the train."[3] She and Bror had arrived in Nairobi in the morning exhausted from the train ride, and despite the blanket and sheets the baron had brought, they were streaked with red dust from the countryside, only their eyes showing circles of white.

The train ride in from the coast could be trying.[4] The train might be besieged by a marauding lion, a human leg dangling from its mouth as it made off with a bunkmate. If the train ran out of fuel, the passengers obligingly climbed out and chopped some firewood; if an official took a fancy to hunting, the train patiently waited while he stalked his game. Later, the locusts, like huge gusts of smoke, would stop the train, oblivious to the passengers frenziedly waving sticks at them in all directions. As the first sign of the industrial age lumbered into Africa in the form of the chugging train, it was accepted by the tribes on the basis of personal ornament, and the train engineers had much trouble to keep cable lines from disappearing, only to reappear handsomely adorning someone's bare arm.

"The lunatic line" had grudgingly been built to forward England's interests under the ostensible excuse of obliterating slavery—and because it was just plain fun moving powerful machinery around. Mogo wa Kebiro, medicine man for the Gikuyu, had warned in a prophecy of the dangers to be carried by strangers from a far land who would "bring an iron snake," the train:

> In a low and sad voice he said the strangers would come to Gikuyuland from out of the big water, the colour of their body would resemble that of a small light-coloured frog (*kiengere*) which lives in water, their dress would resemble the wings of butterflies; that these strangers would carry magical sticks which would produce fire. That these sticks would be very much worse in killing than the poisoned arrows. The strangers, he said, would later bring an iron snake with as many legs as *monyongoro* (centipede), that this iron snake train would spit fires and would stretch from the big water in the east to another big water in the west of the Gikuyu[5] country.[6]

One of the fixed markings of the train station at Nairobi was the figure of the Ali Khan, parading along the platform with his black riding whip, his makeshift fleet of carriages ready to whisk newly arrived settlers to the Norfolk Hotel for rest and refreshment.[7] In the worst rains canvas was handed out to the rickshaw runners of the Norfolk working Sixth Avenue among the dozens of other rickshaws ducking between galloping horses, buggies, stubborn mules, and a rare car wheel.[8] Nairobi stood by after the rains, dusty red and tingrazed, with its teeming Indian bazaar, while over on Government Road—where banana trees had been planted in the potholes as a protest by angry settlers[9]—complained one settler, the daring khaki could seldom be seen, replaced instead by pretty, gayly colored frocks, as real Bond Street as any English lady could desire.[10] Scattered swamps hid fevers and disease, as killing as the loneliness which could grip a settler out in the vast, deserted, windswept spaces surrounding Nairobi.

The arrival of the newlyweds in Nairobi was a heady one for Tanne as she and Bror attended a reception given by the governor. "Everyone," recalled Tanne in a pleased tone, "called me Baroness every other word; to start with I didn't realize they were addressing me."[11] As they drove up to their farm, the road reminded Tanne of the woods back of her home in Denmark where the pantomimists had roamed and the doomed young queen had ridden with her lover: "It is the most enchanting road you can imagine, like our own Deer Park, and the long blue range of the Ngong Hills stretching out beyond it. There are so many flowering trees and shrubs, and a scent rather like bog myrtle, or pine trees, pervades everything."[12]

Once at the MBgathi farm, vast crowds of brown faces—made up of at least a thousand Africans, estimated Tanne—shouted a welcome to them. The few white men on the farm, looking somewhat questionable in appearance, had made a tea and arranged for wedding presents. She was touched by the pains taken by the homeless men who had tried to make her a wedding welcome. The whole thing made Tanne feel she had arrived in Africa during its Golden Age.

After a walk with her husband along a thin path covered with green through a deep forest which led to a coffee field, the baroness settled in on the farm, convinced that it was the only one in all of B.E.A. which had a lavatory. Rather delighted with her new life she advised her sister Ellen back in Denmark that "If you ever get married, which you really must, *then allow yourself plenty of time* to learn housekeeping properly first"; she had found that she lacked the domestic knowledge to easily train her servants—the small boys, *totos,* she had ordered whipped for drunken reveling and stealing.[13] She was not, she wrote home, afraid of the African boys even when one ran into her room with a bloodied club, no more than one was of "savage dogs." To her brother Thomas, continuing a conversation she had had with him before coming out, her keen eye on the golden *El Dorado*, she wrote: "As far as writing books out here is concerned, that will not amount to much. I am more of a tradesman. With a capital of 3,000 rupees I make between 400 and 500 rupees a month on my sheep."[14]

13.

The White Hunters

"There's an old adage . . . translated from the ancient Coptic, that contains all the wisdom of the ages—'Life is life and fun is fun, but it's all so quiet when the goldfish die.' "

🐝 *Inside, in the darkened rooms the walls of the house are wooden, covered with canvas part of the way up. The dining room and corridor are green. In the bedroom there is a pale gray with pink rugs and cretonne, flowered. Soon her furred slippers will stand neatly by the bed, which could be draped by white mosquito netting. The sitting room is brownish-gray, with her husband's inlaid cupboard standing there. The house needs a new veranda, the rooms are hot, there is difficulty in breathing, no breeze reaching the inside rooms. The air outside is limpid and free, making for a feeling light and giddy, like a bird's wings veering off in flight. The present veranda is little good since it is where the men gather, those who have left their homes in sometimes rather desperate situations, and serves as a kind of smoking room and office, filled with men eager to talk to Bror—"Blickie" or "Blix" as they like to call him. His wife has fallen ill with malaria and is rarely seen.*

The talk is about the "Cole Case"—Galbraith Cole has been deported for shooting to kill a native African guilty of stock theft. The men, as they light their pipes, their khaki shirts carelessly unbuttoned, sympathize with Cole, agreeing among themselves that the government is not doing very much to help the settlers. Cole has been acquitted by a jury of Europeans, but pressure back in England has forced him to be deported. The men, their voices—often in Swedish accents—rising through the smoke, agree that such treatment cannot be tolerated; they want more political autonomy. Cole is no agitator and has, it is clear, been driven in an arthritic fit to his wit's end.[1] Not like his quick-tempered brother-in-law, Delamere, who fires his manager for dismissing some Masai for stealing cattle while he is away. Though even "D" one time tracks down a Masai chief to ask who has stolen his cattle from Equator Ranch. And who has known of the theft? Everyone, replies the chief, his teeth showing, except those still in their mother's wombs.

The Masai believe that at creation they were given the sole right to all cattle. Too convenient a belief, grumble the settlers, who are trying to convince the different tribes that they will benefit by being subordinate and working for them; Bror is himself impatient with the reluctance of the different tribes to fall into line with the colonial vision being shaped. A hut tax has been passed to make money a necessity for the tribes and so help convert them into laborers. But the proud Masai won't have any of it. For their part, the more obliging Gikuyu will tell a story about the invasion of their land by the Europeans, comparing the invasion to an elephant taking up too much room in a native hut.[2]

There is mild admiration among the B.E.A. settlers for the South African Nationalists who quote Darwin in support of rigid restrictions upon the native tribes, seeking, as they arrive, to ensure their entrenchment in South Africa. There is a disdain for the humanitarians among them who find racial superiority meaningless, something the newly arrived Baroness Blixen unpopularly believes—"twaddle about humanity," says one settler, cannot be considered—but it is not felt very practical by those who look to imitate the Boers.[3]

Confronted with each other the two races, the Europeans and Africans—the Indians are somewhere in between—react from one emotion, that of "astonishment and derision." This attitude is not much different from that encountered by the Englishman who completed a study of Kiswhaili, instrumental in furthering England's empire and pressing forward the moving in of Europeans.[4] England's emissaries were at a disadvantage before acquiring a knowledge of the native language, making it possible for interpreters to subvert the officials by pointing out, baldly, in the company of Crown representa-

tives, to slave traders potential places of sabotage, or presenting officials with papers to sign which turn out to be secret bills of sale for
slaves.[5]

This Kiswhaili gentleman reported that the tribes recoiled from, or
made fun of, his person: "Especially . . . my shoes, which they took
for iron, my hair, which seemed to them like the hair of an ape, and my
spectacles, objects of astonishment and derision."[6] The Victorians
were no less taken aback by the complete disregard for clothing (and
occasional preference for animal skins) of the tribes under the burning
sun. Other points of failure in comprehension will grow up between
them: the Africans cannot understand a legal system which depends
on someone's innocence until proven guilty even when everyone
knows that person guilty, the Europeans cannot understand the Africans who want compensation for crime that is no one's fault.[7] There is
an uneasy tolerance as each race eyes the other.

The men here in Bror's study are in their element in Africa; it is a
bachelor's paradise, as they are given free reign to test their mettle
with their rifles out against the beasts of prey and have at their service
hundreds of tribesmen—with some persuasion.

The "great beasts of prey give color to the country. . . . Beasts
and birds of prey are really," says Bror's wife, echoing her father, "the
most magnificent fruits of the earth, and to have one's life truly
affected by them, have one's stock devoured by them, see them at lib-
erty [is] . . . an extremely strange experience for a cultivated person. . . ."[8] The natural brutality makes the blood surge.

Roosevelt is an inspiration to these hunting men, who are
expanding European domination. Coming out for safari (at a time
when no one knew what the word meant), he had 600 porters to carry
supplies, each load weighing 60 pounds, echoing Stanley and Living-
stone's explorations.[9] The hunters are already adding to the raucous-
ness of that "gold-digger's camp," Nairobi; Europe's princes and
counts pay high prices to join the white hunters in shooting at the big
game roaming through Masai lands. After a safari they troop over to
the Norfolk where it is "nothing," recalls one visitor, "to have an
Italian baron or an Austrian count thrown through the window on to
your bed in the middle of the night."[10] East Africa, he adds, is "beginning to earn its reputation for unconventionality and the pica-
resque."[11] In July and at Christmas the local settlers arrive to stand
with the hunters, cheering their favorites at the breathtaking horse
races.

Bror, quite taken by the life, will become the best of the white hunters, opening up the Tsavo country[12] to European settlement and taking on safari Hemingway and Vanderbilt, providing Hemingway with a model for the hunter Wilson in "The Short Happy Life of Francis Macomber"; caught in a tight situation, Bror impresses Hemingway by quoting: "There's an old adage . . . translated from the Coptic, that contains all the wisdom of the ages—'Life is life and fun is fun, but it's all so quiet when the goldfish die' "[13]—then asking for some gin.[14] His broad smile, boisterous good humor, and generosity make him a leader among the men. He infuriates his wife by moving the dining furniture into the hills,[15] giving all the men a good laugh— "Oh, that Blix," shaking their heads.[16] He has a quality of the anarchist, appealing to his wife—and to his women.

He will be called "the toughest, most durable White Hunter ever to snicker at the fanfare of safari as to shoot a charging buffalo between the eyes while debating whether his sundown drink will be gin or whiskey."[17] He swears in Swedish when he finds himself nose to long nose with an elephant, and when the meeting looks to be going from bad to worse (the elephant about to pulverize Bror and the tree he has fallen against), switches into English and Swahili. After such an occasion—"Blix never knew when he was dead"[18]—Blix leans back with his drink and delicately pitches away an insect, calling up a Dr. Turvy who has, he claims, recommended the fine benefits to be gotten from gin and wine. Everyone comes to believe in this Dr. Turvy even though he was never seen by anyone in what, says Blix, flashing a grin, "was bedside manner carried to its final degree of perfection."[19]

His safari hunts cost him, and he "went about for years in Africa with enough malaria in his system to cause the undoing of ten ordinary men."[20] Once stranded out in a particularly treacherous area of Africa, surrounded by floodwaters, he is rescued by a free-lance pilot, Beryl Markham. In order to make it possible for Beryl to land in a wall of thick brush and trees, he works into the early morning while everyone sleeps, clearing out at least 1,000 scraggly trees with a panga.

Long after his wife had returned to Denmark for good, Bror traveled with Beryl to London in her Leopard Moth plane. On the trip she is awakened by Bror's knock at her door in Shepheard's Hotel: "Beryl, I hated to do it, but I had to wake you. The head rolled eight feet from the body."[21] Beryl, thinking Bror out of his mind with drink, wondered how best to soothe him. But Bror had done what he said, gingerly cradling the head before bringing it back to where it belonged, to the shoulders of the man killed in the murky late night streets of Cairo.

14.

The Great War

"it may be said that hunting is ever a love-affair. . . . It is a fine and fascinating art, in the spirit of that masterpiece of my countryman Søren Kierkegaard, *The Seducer's Diary*, and it may, in the same way, provide the hunter with moments of great drama with opportunity for skill and cunning, and for self-gratulations."

🐦 *By spring Tanne had fallen ill with malarial fevers, made more difficult to endure by Bror's frequent absence. As summer drew on she recovered her strength enough to walk out to see how changed everything was, where the deep, green forest had stood were neat rows of coffee plants.[1] She could reflect that "the god of love . . . had perhaps granted her prayer with vengeance, and that her books had given her but little information as to the real nature of love";[2] she had found she was not Bror's main point of attention, as he was hers—the wildness of the country was claiming him to the hunt, making her fear for his safety. He was oblivious to danger.*

One day as Tanne and Bror prepared to leave for safari—the doctor had recommended a change of air—Bror, his smile "caught, like a strip of sunlight, on a familiar patch of leather," appeared in the doorway dressed in khaki pants and shirt with empty pockets, worn moccasins, and a helmet.[3] He was impatient with watches, able to tell the time by the sun—or without the sun—and did not wear the obligatory dangling binoculars or revolver, relying only on a rifle and ammunition.[4] He played the handmaiden to his wife, taking care of all the packing and gathering of supplies for the safari: the cooking pots, water jugs, knives, plenty of bullets and rifles, gin, and tents. Any of the blue-shirted safari porters might be asked to carry anything from champagne to collapsible tubs.[5]

Bror had taught his wife to shoot (he himself had gone out after one week of practice) and out among the scrub brush, out in the Mara, an apocalypse blast of thorn tree desert lands where the Masai wandered with their cattle, the flies came crawling and buzzing into their eyes, until all that could be done was to leave them be.[6] The game was abundant, and they shot at least twenty different kinds of game on this particular safari—impala, gnus, cheetah, marabou, eland, lions, and leopard—bringing through the mails a moral reprimand from her mother. But Tanne was exhilarated:

> I experienced a real night of game in the *boma*,—the most wonderful thing you can imagine. There was bright moonlight, and as you are sitting in a boma with your kill not 8 feet away, you can watch the big animals as if you were actually sitting among them. The first to come are the shy, shadowy hyenas, they retreat a couple of times before finally daring to start eating; more and more of them come gliding out of the darkness, you can hear every sound from their teeth in the meat. Then the eager little jackals come, they resemble foxes and are tremendously lively and attractive; I saw mothers playing with their young ones many times in the mornings and it was really delightful. You can see everything quite clearly in the moonlight and could almost touch them with your hand while you sit there as quiet as a mouse with your cocked rifle resting on a branch ready to shoot.[7]

The shooting of the male lion impressed her the most, "the life ebbing from its eyes." Out along the wide blue and yellow ribbons of sky and land which offered no resistance to the eye, the heat and sun bringing about a stupor, a hypnotic trance, they met one man who told about stalking lions, and then being circled and attacked by all fifteen lions in the light of the moon. Care had to be taken; tracking an animal might backfire when the rhino or elephant turned out to be tracking the hunter instead.[8] Years later Tanne would remember hunting as having the aura of a love affair, offering ground for conversion to an artistic vignette of high drama and manipulation:

> . . . . it may be said that hunting is ever a love-affair. . . . It is a fine and fascinating art, in the spirit of that masterpiece of my countryman Sören Kierkegaard, *The Seducer's Diary*, and it may, in the same way, pro-

vide the hunter with moments of great drama with opportunity for skill and cunning, and for self-gratulations.[9]

Hunting became a carefully delineated—and veiled—erotic exercise, as the emotions stirred; the moment, heightened by danger and brutality, depended upon an object yielding up its being; the excitement of seduction gave way to a sense of power and control, and became cause for self-preening.

Exhausted, but excited by the hunt, the baron and baroness returned home, Tanne bewailing "how drearily civilization lays its pall over life!"[10] Before long, Europe was embroiled in playing out its own deadly conflict. Rumors were rampant. The young protectorate would be plunged into war, a ragamuffin version of the one being waged in Europe.

The August 8, 1914, issue of one of the local rags, The Leader, reported that everyone who had come to Nairobi on business had ended up gathered around its doors to hear the latest news about reports of war filtering through from Europe. The freak assassination of the Austrian archduke had caused Germany to rear up on its hind legs. Large, floppy pages bearing the news—"We are officially informed that war has been declared between Great Britain and Austria and Hungary"[11]—were passed around while everyone stirred, agitated, muttering disbelievingly "Germany's mad."[12] The same paper briefly noted that a woman had stabbed Rasputin in his home village,[13] then went on to devote nearly an entire page to the best methods for preparing coffee.[14] In Europe there was speculation about a changing of the map as the war geared up: André Gide confided in his diary that "One forsees the beginning of a new era: the United States of Europe bound by a treaty limiting their armaments; Germany subjugated or dissolved; Trieste given back to the Italians, Schleswig to Denmark; and especially Alsace to France. Everyone talks of this remaking of the map as of the forthcoming issue of a serial."[15]

As the colony began readying for war, a reader wrote in to The Leader, arguing that for forty years the German mind had been fed on Nietzsche, which explained the origin of Germany's present brutality as it moved against the other European nations. Nietzsche, continued the reader

posits the production of the superman, a being who shall be as greatly superior to the man of the present as he is to the ape. The features of life which are to find their fullest development in the superman are essentially appropriation, injury, conquest of the weak, suppression, severity. The supreme thing in life is the will to power. Where Darwin placed the struggle for existence, Nietzsche placed the struggle for power.[16]

The war played itself out against the panorama of daily life as the chants for the fast month of Ramadan cut the early morning air and prayer rugs spread out facing towards Mecca. Tanne railed against the English, having little liking for their tastes and conversation.[17] The settlers' treatment of their farm laborers disturbed her, and she hid one boy who was threatened with three years imprisonment and a beating by one of the settler women; one tribesman had been given three months hard labor for stealing a bottle of whiskey.

No one knew when the war would end, in six months or three years, but expectations were that England would emerge triumphant.[18] Reports came through of thousands of Germans and Austrians being arrested in Great Britain, and the protectorate followed suit, arresting the Germans in its midst.[19] The Swedes had made Bror their gathering point and because they were more fearful of Germany than Russia, sympathized with the wrong side, making Tanne nervous. Bror's plans for settling large tracts of land had aroused suspicion, and he complained to the local paper of "certain rumours started, accusing me of introducing German money into the country and hinting at me being a Hun." The baroness would soon fall under a cloud of suspicion for being part of the Scandinavian crowd and for her friendship with von Lettow, the leader of the German forces in East Africa, and her agreement—now treasonous—to send horses for his cavalry. Feeling ran high: when she ate at the New Stanley, all the tables near her cleared out.[20]

From Paris claims were being made that in Munich French prisoners were being put on display behind bars for the public to view at 2d.[21] Readers of *The Leader* were admonished not to forget "the little ladies" who were learning how to bandage; the war was largely a masculine affair. Sandwiched in between the news was an occasional report of a lone woman traveling with only a small entourage through Africa, and news about vaudeville and moving pictures playing in town. The modern woman was cautioned to be careful of public life or she would become wrinkled like the men and kill off all feelings of chivalry in her sons; settler life called for an Amazon woman, but what was wrong with the old-style timid woman, *The Leader* had asked plaintively, who had, after all, produced able men to fight the Crimean War and Indian Mutiny.

British East Africa, struggling to eke out a vision of European progress, was not prepared to fight a war within its borders. The only military available to protect the vulnerable railway, all 500 miles, was the King's African Rifles.[22] The immediate problem was to get what troops there were out to protect the railway in a vast, dry, hot country that was thick with small thorn trees and "scrub" bush, where tropical disease ran rampant.[23] Before long the worry became keeping von Lettow out of Nairobi.[24]

The settler men, wanting to join, found there was really nothing to join. Those who turned out came with stubble on their chins, their eyes shaded by helmets, their waists hung with knives and water flasks above the mules they urged into Nairobi, the more dapper wearing an ostrich feather gallantly stuck from a felt hat and a bright kerchief round a sunburnt neck. Others came in a steady stream of horse, buggy, pony, cycle, waggon, by train and on foot, with Stetsons and boots, tennis shoes and terai hats. These all ended by forming the East African Mounted Rifles. One of the squadrons was eventually ambitiously armed with lances of bamboo poles flying colorful pennants which startled the mules.[25] Fear of flying machines gave rise to the ditty:

> I thought I saw an aeroplane
> Upon the Athi plain:
> I looked again and saw it was
> A kavirondo crane.[26]

The officers were jumpy and could just as easily attack a thunderstorm, mistaking it for an enemy troop. The men couldn't protect themselves against charging rhino and lion for fear the Germans might hear them, so resorted to stones against the lions. There were problems with the sweltering heat, dysentery, malaria, blackwater, septic wounds and gangrene, and rotting bodies in the heat. (In addition to daily mishaps; Bror, in an absent minded fit drank some Lysol, burning his mouth, and another time chiggers burrowed under his toenails.) The Germans had their own troubles; using British maps which were largely mistaken they attacked the rail line at the wrong point. Reports from recruits came of pianos and settees making their way to the front.[27]

Government officials were aware of the delicate problem of arming black and brown men to fight a white man's war after priding themselves on stopping tribal warfare (where before a few men were lost in tribal conflict, thousands would be lost in the "great war for civilization"). But when 800 Somali volunteers showed up Berkeley Cole (brother to Galbraith) organized them into a troop.[28] And the Masai, the ones who knew the country best, were organized by Delamere to watch along the 200 miles of vulnerable border.[29] Taking along chocolate and cooking utensils, he set up a communication center and put Bror in charge of being the liaison between himself and an official heading intelligence in Nairobi, Captain Woosenam.[30] Still infatuated by his wife, Bror ended by tracking Tanne for eighty-six miles on foot, charming her by suddenly appearing unexpectedly, arriving so stiff and cramped that only with help could he be bent in half to sit down.[31] Runners were sent looking for the elephant skull hung outside the game office, and carrier pigeons used, who had much trouble keeping from being plucked quite clean by the hawks.[32]

Tanne wrote home that,

> It is dreadful to be away for such a long time. But when we telegraphed home it was already then impossible to get back, Suez is still blocked. They think there will be disturbances on the frontier here, and Bror has joined the volunteers with the other Swedes; that is, not as a soldier, but among themselves, they have organized a kind of telegraph service with motorcycles and cars and cycles from the frontier to Kijabe. There is nothing to do here on the farm; we have dismissed our boys and stopped the transport of wood, because no one knows when money will get through again and whether Swedo* will ever get any.—And the repair work on the house is at a standstill.[33]

News came through from back home that Mama had fallen ill and did not know of the war; her close friend Daisy had died, someone who, said Tanne, had made of life "poetry."[34]

Tanne felt the terror of the war, but as her brother Tommy carried on the family military tradition by joining in the fighting in Europe, she felt great dramatic forces were let loose from which she was excluded.[35] The dramatic change brought by the "great adventure" of war was not, she felt, entirely unnatural: "When I think of how von

*Swedo-African Coffee Co.—the coffee farm bought by Bror.

Lettow and I would sit and gossip on the deck of the 'Admiral,' and how he was traveling straight into such a fearful great adventure, I can hardly comprehend that it is the same existence,—but it is hard to see which is the most natural form for human beings."[36]

While she was disturbed by the loss of so many men in the fighting, Africans in particular, she was entertained by the hunting game being played between the British and von Lettow, vicariously basking in the respect accorded to the old slippery lion—after attacking with the force of a raging, ruthless storm, his uncanny disappearance behind trees and into swamps upset all British stratagems, turning him into a legend. British East Africa had not responded to him quickly enough and von Lettow had managed to grow from a force of 2,750 to 15,000, still a small force against the 92,000 men mustered against him.[37] Daily talk had it that von Lettow wanted to stay undefeated until the end of the war so that at the surrender the Germans could be in a better bargaining position about German East Africa.[38] Near the end of the war when he had only a few men left, and little supplies, his men had had to turn to using tree bark for bandages. One story told about him was of someone who had gone out in the line of battle to bandage the wounded. Afterwards, an officer angrily reprimanded the man for doing the bandaging in a sloppy manner. Von Lettow, overhearing the exchange, finally said after a pause: "Well, I can understand, Colonel, . . . that you are annoyed because this man has put on the bandages so hastily, but what I cannot understand is, why you didn't yourself crawl out to the wounded and put them on better."[39]

When Klapprott, the man running transport was arrested for a German, Tanne took over; tired of only the men being heroes, she made herself into a heroine.

What occurred on this trip is marred by some confusion. Tanne went out with eighteen boys and her trusted Farah who had insisted that as a talisman she carry von Lettow's signed photograph in case they were so unlucky as to run into German troops. She had had to walk from Kijabe to Narok with the forty-one oxen and waggons since the road was too difficult for horses to traverse, Narok being layered with a yellowish powder like ancient Egyptian papyrus, no green leaves showing through the dust. Somewhere along the route, stopped by a stone Tanne was holding a lantern to, the oxen were attacked and clawed. Here there is agreement.

At this point the story diverges.

To her mother, Tanne recounted the incident, telling how she had had to sight the lion on the back of the oxen and shoot him off their back. It was fortunate, she added, that someone along the road had given her a rifle and ammunition which could be used by Farah. Her trusted cook sat up with her during the night, and with his kitchen knife was never far from her side. To her husband she reported that lions had attacked the oxen and that, the rifles packed away, she was left with no alternative but to whip two lions off with no help from the others, who had all disappeared: "If I'd had a gun I'd have used it, of course; but the stock-whip isn't to be despised."[40] Since Tanne had unhesitatingly reported home on Africa's dangers—recommending *The Man-Eaters of Tsavo* to understand what her new life was like—the lion whose paws could be seen under the door, and the siafu which had devoured a kitten litter in her kitchen leaving nothing but bone and scraps of skin, it is not likely that she here chose to lie to protect her family from worry. Rather, it is more likely that she lied to Bror. Why?

If we turn to the story "The Pearls" (a story giving yet another version of the necklace theme made popular by Guy de Maupassant), which it is possible to read as a thinly disguised version of her early relationship to Bror, we can surmise her motives. In "The Pearls," Jensine, like Tanne, comes from a family capable of making a great fortune by "its wit" and whose wealth has saved her new husband Alexander, a gambler and nobleman. They take their honeymoon in the high mountains of Norway, where the air is reminiscent in its lightness and sweetness of Africa's air. Here Jensine makes a discovery about her husband. She realizes that he does not understand limitations or boundaries, knows no fear, which causes her to feel dizzy, her balance thrown off, the anchor she expected of her husband not there:

> He was, on the contrary, the cause of the turbulence in her, and he was also, in her eyes, pre-eminently exposed to the dangers of the outward world. For very soon after her marriage Jensine realized—as she had perhaps dimly known from their first meeting—that he was a human being entirely devoid, and incapable of fear.
>
> . . . all the phenomena of life, love itself included, were his play-mates within it. . . . Now she felt, with horror, that here she was, within a world of undreamt of heights and depths, delivered into the hands of a person totally ignorant of the law of gravitation. Under the circumstances her feelings for him intensified into both a deep moral indignation, as if he had deliberately betrayed her, and into an extreme

tenderness, such as she would have felt towards an exposed, helpless child. These two passions were the strongest of which her nature was capable; they took speed with her, and developed into a possession. . . . it seemed to her that for her own sake and his, in self-defense as well as in order to protect and save him, she must teach her husband to fear.[41]

Using her parasol for balance, Jensine prettily leans along a deep chasm, looking for a protective reaction. But the result is unexpected:

her daring did her no good. Her husband was surprised and enchanted at the change of the demure maiden into a Valkyrie. He put it down to the influence of married life, and felt not a little proud. She herself, in the end, wondered whether she was not driven on in her exploits by his pride and praise as much as by her resolution to conquer him.[42]

Originally told to Bror in a way to pique his interest (so we can speculate)—and his "fear"—when in *Out of Africa* she recalls the incident, it is kept in a variation of the version given to her husband, that of the image of the lions being whipped away, and becomes part of a self-mythology: the myth of Gefion is popular in Denmark, Gefion turning her sons into oxen and whipping them until Sealand was carved out of Sweden. It is this mythical image that Tanne very likely had in mind. This movement toward a myth of the self which runs through *Out of Africa* becomes a way of compensating for a reality less than splendid, less than satisfactory, that could be trying and boring and lonely, and became a way of defying fate through the grand gesture, of lifting herself onto the universal plane.

In *Out of Africa,* Tanne ever the artist, would adapt the facts of her life to the purpose of self-creation. *Out of Africa* has the clarity of the artist, who observing the faults and imperfections of reality, consciously seeks to perfect it according to the unrestrained play and demands of artistic creation. Life had to be experienced as dramatic perfections which became like completed self-contained scenes of artifice on a vast stage. This insistence upon staging reality, so obvious in *Out of Africa,* resulted in a series of personal imaginative rituals. Tanne as Isak Dinesen became increasingly drawn to the dramatic gesture as the way to declare her existence; this bold declaration broke through the dreaminess that enveloped everyday reality for her, pulling her back from the overwhelming abyss of feeling, and reassured her that she indeed existed within the sharp outlines of reality. By extension, *Out of Africa* became autobiography written as dramatic ceremony, as

Isak Dinesen coalesced this imaginative ritualizing into a literary self-mythology that defined her in an extraordinary way.

Soon, with the war going into full play, and her husband often absent (though charmingly attentive when he was home), Tanne fell ill again.

15.

The Faustian Pact

"But what is it to be a writer? Writing is a sweet, wonderful reward, but its price? During the night the answer was transparently clear to me: it is the reward for service to the devil. This descent to the dark powers, this unbinding of spirits by nature bound, dubious embraces and whatever else may go on below, of which one no longer knows anything above ground, when in the sunlight one writes stories."[1]

🐝 *Sitting in a ruffled light shirt, looking worn and pale, her hair pulled partly back, some curls escaping, she looks out hesitatingly, shyly from the hospital bed. It was this stay in the hospital that Tanne always referred to later as shaping her artistic life. Thinking herself alone in the room, she felt a presence, a pressure which made her look round. In that moment—dramatically—"I met the devil."[2] In that instant her pact with the devil was sealed. But "the Devil," she discovered, has his price: he "is expensive to talk to, a sparkling glimpse of his fiery tail of stars costs more than most people can pay."[3]*

Tanne had been diagnosed as having syphilis from her husband, within one year of her marriage.[4]

The illness caused a crisis in the marriage, and forced her into a conspiracy of secrecy against her family. Making her way back to Europe during the war was difficult, but she returned there, staying first in Paris—where she was told that the disease would most likely not be cured—and then returning to Denmark for over a year, visiting the National Hospital for tests and diagnoses which took three months in all; she had told her mother that she was being treated for a severe tropical disease. Treatment in those days was prepenicillin, when the medicines prescribed were the nerve-destroying mercury and arsenic.[5] The best that could be hoped for was that the disease would be arrested, which it was, in the second stage, before it reached the brain. Her ability to have a "little Wilhelm," which she desired, was now called into question. Her sense of irony sharpened as the same fate which had descended upon her father now descended upon her, making her feel that she was the carrier of the family curse. Despair settled down around her.

While Tanne always insisted later in life that the disease was not as bad as all that, and scandalized Denmark by claiming that the disease was worth the title of baroness, those kind of statements were a form of bravado which smoothed over what was a devastating disease that completely dislocated her life.[6] While life in B.E.A. was in many ways unconventional, the settlers had brought with them European mores which made the stigma of such a disease as taboo as in a Denmark still lingering in Victorian times.[7] That it marked her life irretrievably was confirmed by friends who remembered that as an old woman she said to them, do you know what it is like as a young woman to experience such a disease, to feel through no fault of one's own a sapping strength which is dissipate and means that the love relationship would no longer, could no longer, be experienced as normal.[8]

More than forty years later, the emotional power of the experience was recalled in "The Cardinal's Third Tale" (which has resonances of D. H. Lawrence's *The Man Who Died*) where Tanne tells the story of Lady Flora, who has "vowed never through a marriage or a love affair to repeat her mother's misery" of a husband too easily seduced by young women.[9] Lady Flora recoils against her own physical nature and shuns all human touch. When, in a movement to break her isolation, she enters a church and kisses the foot of St. Peter in the same spot left moist by a young man's kiss, she finds, after four weeks, a lip sore. A visit to the doctor confirms that she has contracted a venereal disease.

The nature of the disease belies the nonchalance of Lady Flora's revelation—"I was not ignorant, I knew the name"—a revelation intensified in its power by the ironic bite of the ending, a reference to an earlier conversation with a priest who urged her more into life.[10] Lady Flora ends the story by asking: "To what, I thought, does this [venereal sore] bear a likeness? To a rose? Or to a seal?"[11]

The disease forced Tanne into a pact with the nether powers through a deeper understanding of life in all of its different possibilities—a knowledge bought at a Faustian price—that she later insisted gave her the ability to write, to tell a story. It contributed to a circularity of thinking which manifested itself in such tales as "The Monkey" (where the tension is often between sheer physicality and tight restraint), where the prioress quotes in Latin that from "disease comes health"; as early as 1905 she had written that "light comes from darkness, daybreak from night."[12]

It was in the symbolic form of the disease, as "devil," that Tanne was finally able to make her peace with the illness—perhaps peace is too strong a word for the corruption of self suggested by "devil," her own feelings of the disease as a tainting coming in the myth she eventually created around it. Better is an integration made possible by the imagination, a transformation through the artistic impulse, a belief that "surely, then, the transformed will have power to transform"[13]— which does not preclude a steely nihilistic gleam showing itself through the question "The Cardinal's Third Tale" ends with: whether it is God or the devil who is served, "a risk which the artists and the priests of the world have to run."[14]

Lucifer's existence as religious paradox—he is both angel and devil—provoked Tanne's imagination, his appeal to her became apparent early on, as she wrote her brother: "Lucifer is the angel whose wings should be hovering over me. And we know that the only solution for Lucifer was rebellion, and then the fall to his own Kingdom!"[15] What at times gives Isak Dinesen's writing the peculiar force of paganism and religiosity intermingled is that the points at which good dominates and evil is submerged are not always apparent, indeed are not always of interest to her.[16]

But before all of this, at her farm, having learned of the disease, Tanne felt a despair at her very real condition, and in a semiconscious gesture of carelessness about her life took too many sleeping pills because, she said, of her restlessness at not being able to sleep. Bror had, with effort, to bring her round from the coma.

Her husband was gaining in reputation as a womanizer, and, in a modern-day version of the Dinesen men's battle cry—"Her or no one!"—would become infamous for the remark he was heard to make in Nairobi while watching the daughter of a client out for safari: "She's mine for the night." Bror's hunting instincts had not stopped with the wilds. There have been suggestions that Bror reveled with tribal women, picking up syphilis from a Masai *manyatta*.[17] This is not very likely, since social relations between the Europeans and the peoples of Africa were then strictly prohibited by strong social taboos on both sides; such reports may have more to do with wanting to flesh out his portrait as a rogue.[18] This is not to say that the type of relations that could be found in American slavery—the seizing of the slave woman by the master—did not eventually find its way into colonized B.E.A. But entering a tribal enclave of Masai warriors and proceeding to make merry would not have been such a simple matter.[19] Ironically, Tanne's father has been accused of the same behavior in America, resulting in the same serious consequences. But his illness showed up way past the time of his American visit, physically affected no one in the family, and it is not unreasonable to assume that he was an observer of social taboos, if not intellectually, then emotionally.[20]

In leaving Africa, Tanne was seeking the best medical attention available, but there was an element of flight and anger at her husband. Farah accompanied her part of the way to Paris, where Tanne had decided to go in the interests of secrecy, but she finally decided to send Farah back and to go on home to Denmark where she saw a Dr. Rasch,[21] whose Salvarsan injections (a precursor of antibiotics) arrested the disease.[22] Bror arrived in Denmark over a year later, probably to convince her to go back to Africa with him. Apparently the long separation between them brought about a reconciliation of sorts. Tanne could not get away from feeling quite fond of Bror, and, romantically, that she had married a truly great man. She excused Bror to her mother on another occasion by saying *"If he steals twopence from a blind beggar and buys poison for his mother with it, you will say it was only his high spirits."*[23] In a less generous, but still humorous mood, she eventually confided to her secretary: "There are two things you can do in such a situation: shoot the man, or accept it."[24]

A macabre mood and humor prevailed in *Shadows on the Grass* when she referred to taking an overdose of arsenic (for the venereal disease) by mistake, and, panicked, she prepared to die. Then she remembered reading of King Charles IX who had saved himself from the poison which had clung to his finger as he touched his tongue while turning the pages of a hunting book. Sending for Alexandre Dumas's *La Reine Margot* to discover the remedy, and preparing to take the king's antidote of milk and egg white, she recalled that someone had told her from an overdose of poison one turned green.[25] And what was the use of staying alive if one were to be green, she wondered. She called for a mirror and prepared to watch the greenish shades overtake her, no longer caring about life. But she recovered, no worse, she said, a mischievous gleam in her eye, for the experience.

In a different context, she sought reassurance of sorts by concluding: "For whether there be no venomous snakes in the world, or whether you shall have arrived, by injecting ever-stronger doses of venom in your blood, at a stage of perfect immunity to it, in the end it must come to the same thing."[26]

16.

The African Farm

"Such a glance did Adam give the
Lord when He formed him out of
the dust, and breathed into his
nostrils the breath of life, and man
became a living soul. I had created
him and shown him himself. . . ."

🐝 *Traveling back to Nairobi, Bror was attentive to Tanne, while she turned to her
paintbrushes. The baron and baroness stopped in Zanzibar (the air there pungent with
the cloves fancied by the prioress of Closter Seven) and had seen the old slave auction,
markets, and ruins of old fortresses. The sultan had been paid a handsome sum by the
British to give up slave trading; Arabs had done much of the slave running.*

The marriage between the baron and baroness was renewed in an
escalated financial cast, as they managed to obtain a loan of 1,000,000
kroner from a Danish bank; named after Tanne, the Karen Coffee Co.
Ltd. was formed and shares bought by her relatives.[1] Their farm of
seven hundred acres was sold and a much larger farm bought at the
foot of the Ngong Hills, the one made famous in *Out of Africa*, "from
Mr. Sjögren the Swedo-African Coffee Co., owning 4,500 acres near
Nairobi, and about the same area near Eldoret." It had been decided
that a fortune could be made from coffee in a world market craving the
drink favored by the Arabs. The dark liquid was advertised in London

as early as 1657 as "a very wholesome and physical drink," trumpeted
The Leader,

> having many excellent vertues, closes the orifice of the stomach, forti-
> fies the heat within, helpeth the digestion, quickeneth the spirits,
> maketh the heart lightsom, is good against eye sores, coughs or colds,
> rhumes, consumptions, headaches, dropsie gout, scruvie, king's evil,
> and many others.[2]

Tanne liked the new coffee plantation and named it Frydenlund,
after the cabin her father had stayed in while in Wisconsin, and rode
out horseback into the Masai Reserve daily, in culottes and with her
hair pulled back, chatting to the people as the red dust floated up in a
dreamy haze around the fires burning outside the huts. Tanne's
admiration of the tall, proud Masai as warriors, her description of
them as noble and chivalric, was part of "the warrior caste of Europe
recognizing its equivalent in another continent";[3] in her African letters she admitted that "Africa is Robinson Crusoe,"[4] appropriating to
herself Defoe's fictional exhortation to expand British empire.[5]

The feudal implications of her African existence were not lost on
her, and in notes Tanne wrote in Africa she named the different people
on her farm, listing them as slaves, herself as owner.[6] When she later
caused a stir by an interview with *Life* magazine when she claimed she
wouldn't mind owning slaves, the wish was fanciful; she was thinking
of the slavery in the *Arabian Nights,* a glamorous and exotic phenomenon—she had little interest in the real problems presented by political
systems, all too dreary for her.[7] Instead she embraced the old style of
things, the coherence of the aristocratic code underlying feudalism.

She was criticized by the settlers for not working to improve the lot
of the Africans, in, for example, not working to start hospitals for the
women (who often became seriously infected from circumcision) or
improving their social status.[8] When she tried to help out during a
famine, her efforts came to nothing, though she eventually started a
school to make it easier to get workers on her farm. She herself
wanted her brother Tommy to become part of the League of Nations
in order to help the Africans. Her own role was not, she felt,
"preaching," but best confined to setting an example for the other
settlers by being a gracious hostess—"even my glasses and my big
cupboard must work in my mission for 'my black brothers.' "[9]

But while she respected and felt strong feelings for her servants
and the workers on the farm, it did not prevent her from being inter-

ested in them as showpieces. She dressed up African boys to carry cigarettes in slim gold boxes in to her guests, causing titters among the settlers when the cigarettes spilled onto the Oriental rug during an invariable stumble. [10] On one trip to England she dressed up a servant, Abdullah, and had him walk behind her through the London streets wearing his colorful turban; [11] at night he ended up sleeping in the bathtub because of a lack of space. (When she brought him to Denmark, it was a bust, her family reacted against her actions.) [12] Respecting and admiring the African people, she nevertheless felt free to transform them (as she did the Europeans) into backdrop, into the feudal tapestry she described in *Out of Africa*.

Her admiration and sense of kinship with the different tribes was always the kind that kept her at the head. In one of her most sympathetic descriptions, she described the suffering of a young African boy, Kamande:

> I came upon him for the first time one day when I was riding across the plain of the farm, and he was herding his people's goats there. He was the most pitiful object that you could set eyes on. His head was big and his body terribly small and thin, the elbows and knees stood out like knots on a stick and both his legs were covered with deep running sores from the thigh to the heel. Here on the plain he looked extraordinarily small, so that it struck you as a strange thing that so much suffering could be condensed into a single point. When I stopped and spoke to him, he did not answer, and hardly appeared to see me. In his flat, angular, harassed, and infinitely patient face, the eyes were without glance, dim like the eyes of a dead person. He looked as if he could not have more than a few weeks to live, and you expected to see the vultures, which are never far away from death on the plain, high up in the pale burning air over his head. I told him to come round to my house the next morning, so that I could try to cure him. [13]

But Kamande—whose suffering was set at a distance, objectified into a geometric shape in the landscape—given some sugar, then treated by Tanne (who served as a doctor on the farm, as did many settlers on their own land), was only cured when she took him to the Mission hospital. Grateful that she had saved his life, he eventually became her cook and a Christian, and came to adore her as his mother. Yet he has made clear that all *social* conversation (as equals) between the Europeans and Africans did not exist, was not possible. [14]

Tanne wrote home with an understanding absent from many of the settlers when she reported that life on her African farm could have the intensity of unfiltered tragedy: Esa, her cook of five years, had been poisoned, apparently by his wife; a group of totos had gathered in a hut, and one of them, using a shotgun left on the veranda, had injured many of the young boys, killing one and taking off the jaw of another; a young girl had died after falling off a passing cart and her body left unattended, it going against tribal custom to touch the dead. There had been a murder on the farm, and Tanne was convinced that she had come face to face with the murderer.[15]

Nevertheless, Tanne came in for a virulent attack by the Africans in later years after her death when strong anticolonial feeling turned against her memory, fueled by her depiction of Kitosch in *Out of Africa*. Kitosch, wrote Tanne, was brutally beaten by a settler because he had been disobedient. She left out, nihilistically, any moral judgment of the jury's decision to acquit the settler on the grounds that Kitosch had willed himself to death. She ascribed to Kitosch the aesthetic pose of transcendence, ignoring the political and human consequences of the beating.[16]

Much has been said about Isak Dinesen's relationship to the Africans on her farm, and more will be written. Like the contradictions she was so often drawn to, she has been called on the one hand a racist, and on the other a radical liberal.[17]

In *Out of Africa* Isak Dinesen writes from the privileged position of the generous ruler at the head of feudal lands. While she is both sympathetic and compassionate in her portrayal of the native African, she never has the moment of recognition in which the African as *other* ceases to be seen in that otherness and fuses together with the European whites in a commonly experienced humanity. It is ultimately as *emblem* that the native African's greatest appeal is felt by her. They are felt to be in connection with and extensions of a nature no longer available to the European, a connection made impossible to the European through the accumulation of thought. If the native African shuts out the European through innocent participations in Africa's natural rhythms, recalling Adam and Eve before the Fall, then we are reminded by implication that the Fall gave to Adam and Eve greater knowledge and brought them into a different and momentary closeness to the divinity of God. Isak Dinesen ascribes to the black Africans the characteristics of different animals in their different natural postures, poised in the freedom of obliviousness. The white European, on the other hand, is described as separate from and in some way finer for being in a refined state of nature, imaginatively embroidered and ornate, as an actor or a possible wanderer from an Elizabethan court.

The presence of Isak Dinesen in *Out of Africa* is that of "white female divinity" giving to the male native African his being—and to the animals—as he is imagined by her for himself and herself. She says, for instance, about Jogona Kanyagga, a native African: "Such a glance did Adam give the Lord when He formed him out of the dust, and breathed into his nostrils the breath of life, and man became a living soul. I had created him and shown him himself: Jogona Kanyagga of life everlasting."[18] This happens once or twice with white Europeans who gain their significance in their eyes (and ours) for their role on stage, Isak Dinesen's theatre of life. About Emmanuelson, a self-described vagabond, Isak Dinesen says:

> I sat in the car and watched him, and I think that as he went he was pleased to have a spectator. I believe that the dramatic instinct within him was so strong that he was at this moment vividly aware of being leaving the stage, of disappearing, as if he had, with the eyes of his audience, seen himself go.[19]

The aristocratic Europeans, on the other hand, tend to be displaced in their relationship to the stage, becoming viewers with her. And they all are elevated by having "the tragic mind."[20]

Isak Dinesen is always the creator and *Out of Africa* reminds us throughout that nature's creative force is echoed by her relationship to the land and its people; it is when she is most specifically evident as an imaginative being that *Out of Africa* transcends its "tragic note." We are given Africa through the poetry of its land and its people. We are given Africa through the force of Isak Dinesen's transforming presence which gives us the sense of life lived on a vast stage of shifting dimensions where the layers of reality shift, undulate, waver but are never quite what we expect of them, where nothing is ever completely explained, where the strangeness of the land and its people becomes cause not only for adventure but for imaginative celebration.[21] This method of staging her experiences in Africa creates a romantic distance between her and the people she writes about. At the same time a type of grandeur is conveyed, as ordinary experience is lifted into the extraordinary, as universal experience appears to be unique.

17.

The "charming" English Gentleman

"He did cut a figure in his own age, but it did not quite fit in anywhere."

🦎 *Everyone felt that things were beginning to fall apart. Coffee was banned as an import to Great Britain; prices had gone chaotic and were sometimes very good, other times bad. The war made farming difficult, since the government had started conscripting African men; the Germans had been using tribesmen who knew the country, while B.E.A. had delayed.[1] Drought would rear its head and famine further affect the tribes.*

Shortly before the end of the war a slaughter took place in the reserve through the government's incompetence. Early on the Masai warriors, *moran*, had been anxious to fight, but had lost their enthusiasm for the enterprise as the war progressed.[2] Askaris were sent to the village of Ol-Ahunga where the warriors refusing military service were rumored to be hiding among the huts. Without orders from the officers, the askaris opened fire on the village, killing two women and wounding several others. The incident caused unrest in the Masai nation, and fears of a massive uprising arose as the Masai attacked in retaliation, killing fourteen people, and burning dozens of stores out-side of Nairobi.[3] Lord Delamere's aid was enlisted and he managed to work out an agreement with the Masai to end the angry roaming bands.

Soon word came through that an armistice had been reached. Celebrations were held in Nairobi's streets with a parade of 5,000 Africans carrying torchlights to the beat of music. *The Leader* announced on its back pages that "Those who have the privilege of knowing Baron-ess Blixen, will learn with pleasure that her brother Private Thomas Dinesen, Quebec Rifles, has earned a VC," for distinguished service in the war, putting an end to the rumors of her being pro-German.[4] In a desire to be part of his military victory, Tanne wrote her brother that she and Farah had visited an Arab sheik, giving him 1,000 rupees and followed his instructions to bury passages of the Koran on three suc-cessive Fridays. The sheik had predicted that twelve of the enemy would be slain, the number that Tommy had killed to earn his award; Africa was bringing the idea of witchcraft more to the forefront of Tanne's imagination—witchcraft, she insisted, was essential in writing.[5]

Soon after Tanne met General Polowtzoff, the former governor of Petrograd, who had been forced to flee during the Russian Revolution. Back in 1911 the general had met Tanne's Aunt Fritze—who had sat during the meeting with her trouser legs hidden by a parasol—when she visited Africa with Uncle Mogens.[6] He invited the baroness to ac-company him and his wife to Paris to meet the aristocratic Russians who, deposed during a side note to the Great War, had been forced to sell their jewels and flee to Paris. She was tempted, but declined the invitation.[7]

Still more interested in her easel and paints than in paper and pen, Tanne was thinking of going back to art school when she was back in Denmark; the best thing, she said, was to "assimilate one's personality in some kind of art," then transform oneself through that art.[8] Her husband had announced he was intending to write a book on Africa. He agreed with her that they should think about returning to Den-mark, to settle there.

Those plans soon changed.

The Muthaiga Club was a favorite meeting place of the settlers in B.E.A. Here hunters, government officials, and military personnel gathered. There was a comfortable fireplace, with the Swahili words "Na Kup Hati M'zuri"—"I bring you good fortune"—engraved in the stone, and a bar and dining room where Wedgwood china and fine linen took over.[9] The conversation swirled among the hunters as quickly as the drinks at the bar as the dangers of the hunt were called up:

> "I stood here . . . my gun-bearer there . . . Tusks?—just under two hundred . . ."
>
> "Black-maned devil—big as they come—my heavy rifle in camp . . ."
>
> "Ah!" says the red-jawed Russian, "lion? Listen, my friend, I have fought Siberian wolves."[10]

Tanne wrote home about "Denis," a really "intelligent" and charming English gentleman she had met at a dinner party at Muthaiga. Before long Tanne confided to her mother that when he became ill with fever he had stayed with her until he was better. If she had a son, she would, she decided, send him to Eton. Soon Tanne had lost her head and heart to "Denis" Finch Hatton, convinced she had met her ideal man.

Denys Finch Hatton, born to the Earl of Winchilsea and Nottingham, was a classicist, remembered for wearing a red silk dressing gown at Eton.[11] Once, to distract a tutor who was about to give him extra work, he pointed out the dizzying path an imaginary mouse had taken, putting his tutor into such a state that he fell down into a crawl, jabbing about with a poker.[12] At Oxford, he was remembered for wearing an emerald waistcoat and gold watch and chain, and for playing cricket, throwing the boomerang, and winning second place in a singing competition. His name was a variation on the Greek god, Dionysius, who had reveled with intoxicating grapes, women, and song—he himself, all six foot three of him, was called a Greek god.[13] As a child he had played with his brother Toby in the Monastery Garden—the monks had once used his home as their monastery; his mother's favorite, like the Baroness Blixen he had rebelled at the uniformity of childhood dress. Now as he lounged into a room, everyone's attention turned to him; there was a softness to his presence that was described as catlike, "dove-like," some of which came from his sinking into "fits of vagueness" and depression, a dreamy quality which made him memorize long passages of *A Midsummer Night's Dream*.[14] It was a manner belied by a sarcasm which earned him the name Makanyaga— "To Tread Upon"—among the Africans.[15]

Out of an apparent ambivalence at the blurring of lines which informed his life, he reacted to a lack of preciseness: out on a hunt away from any towns in Africa, he received a message from London which had taken many days and which to reach him was picked up by runners using sticks to relay the message: "Do you know George Robinson's address?" The reply sent back through many runners: "Yes."[16]

A story is told that while at Oxford, Denys was inspired by *A Midsummer Night's Dream* to perpetrate a smashing hoax.[17] Invitations were sent out to everyone whose name contained some form of the word Bottom, inviting them to attend a gathering at a London hotel. An announcer was hired to read out the names as each guest arrived: "Winterbottom, Sidebottom, Bottomley."[18] He himself gave to Tanne the nickname of Tania, a variation on the queen's name of Titania in *A Midsummer Night's Dream*, a name she often used throughout her life. It was a joke on himself, for Titania, queen of the fairies, was blinded by a secret potion and fell in love with an ass.

He was the quintessential charming English gentleman who had gone astray, finding that the world had not been gotten quite right, giving him the license to participate in it only on his terms; the war had held little interest for him and he had thrown puddings across the enemy lines at Christmas.[19] Lord Cranworth spoke for many who knew him: "with his vast talents he might doubtless have made a success in public life, but it just bored him. I remonstrated with him in later years for his apparent lack of ambition and the more than partial burial of his great talents but he was quite unrepentant and pointed out that one had but one life and that he reckoned that few people had had more out of it than he."[20]

At Oxford Denys had been part of a group called "The New Elizabethans." It was a label which stuck, friends describing him as unfit for the twentieth century, being instead "like one of his Hatton ancestors of Elizabethan days—a man of action and poetry."

Tanne added:

> Denys should be set in an earlier English landscape, in the days of Queen Elizabeth. He could have walked arm in arm, there with Sir

Philip, or Francis Drake. And the people of Elizabeth's time might have held him dear because to them he would have suggested that Antiquity, the Athens, of which they dreamed and wrote. Denys could indeed have been placed harmoniously in any period of our civilization, *tout comme chez soi,* all up till the opening of the nineteenth century. He would have cut a figure in any age, for he was an athlete, a musician, a lover of art and a fine sportsman. He did cut a figure in his own age, but it did not quite fit in anywhere. His friends in England always wanted him to come back, they wrote out plans and schemes for a career for him there, but Africa was keeping him.[21]

Denys had come to Africa to hunt and trade.

He bought a stucco home with dark, heavy Arab doors of wood with scroll, up along the coast near Mombasa, in what was called white man's grave.[22] There was old coral in the ground which made it difficult to grow vegetation. Set up on a cliff, the arched veranda windows looked out on a brilliant sea, and as the white foam swirled, the sea and sun was revealed like so many facets of glittering jewels. Nearby were the hushed and secret recesses of moss overhanging the ruins of a mosque. Tanne came here, though rarely, with Denys, the place considered too hot for white people. But she remembered it as a place of romance. At night, "You slept," said Tanne, "with the doors open to the silver Sea; the playing warm breeze in a low whisper swept in a little loose sand, on the stone floor. One night a row of Arab dhows came along, close to the coast, running noiselessly before the monsoon, a file of brown shadow-sails under the moon."[23]

Had Tanne's marriage to Bror not been such a difficult one and had she not been so lonely while he was away on long safaris, it is likely that Tanne would not have allowed her interest in Denys Finch Hatton to take hold more strongly; he became reason for an emotional reaction against Bror's philandering.

Erik von Otter was another man she had met in Africa and gone on safari with, a man whom she described as being like Wilhelm, her father, living only for war—though with an unpleasant moral streak. He read Mohammed, stirring her own interest in Mohammed and the Moslem acceptance of life and individual superiority, and had shown interest in her and wanted to marry, trying to convince her to divorce Bror.[24] Tanne explained her reaction to him by comparing his temperament to that of her Aunt Bess, who would never have been able, she said, to refrain from trying to persuade Shakespeare to abandon his bawdiness and Michelangelo to forget his nudes.[25] After his early death from blackwater,[26] she reflected on her relationship to him: "I think I made him very unhappy, but it would have been impossible for me to have made him happy, and the worst thing that could have happened to him would have been my marrying him, for I, like the majority of human beings, am incapable of 'living for' one person and still less of letting another person 'live for me,' and could not possibly have done it for him."[27]

But von Otter was himself married and how available he was, really, is not entirely clear. Nevertheless, the appearance of Denys crushed any hopes Erik von Otter may have entertained. The way was made clear for what Tanne herself referred to as a serious problem, that she was only attracted to unattainable men, fatally.[28]

18.

Divorce

"To be forced to silence, as I am
here, when one has great difficulties, as I have now, feels as if one
is buried alive, and you must
imagine me as if you saw me lying
in darkness with the weight of the
earth on my breast, and forgive
me for this screaming."

🦋 *The Danish baroness was thinking of going down the Nile with her
Englishman—who had received "orders to get demobilized in Egypt"—and her husband was encouraging her to go.[1] But the plan fell through. Before long the repeated
illness which killed many settlers hit her, this time in the form of the Spanish flu which
would kill twenty million people worldwide. When the baroness fell from a mule that
had been startled by a jackal, the resulting wound refused to heal in the hot sun, even
five months after, complicating things further; mischievously, the baron expressed
hope that not too many people would see the long scar left by the wound along her thigh.
She ended up having to travel to Denmark for treatment, and when she and her
husband stopped in London, they visited the Honorable Denys Finch Hatton.*

When the baron and baroness finally arrived at Rungstedlund, it
was clear that life had changed. During the war, the announcement of
Mama's death had been sent in a black bordered envelope to the coffee
farm at Ngong.[2] Both of the Dinesen sisters left in Denmark had married, and Ea had had a child, a reminder to the family of the second

daughter's barrenness. The arrest of Ea while on a singing tour of private homes in north Schlewswig had once again brought Germany's spectre to the family door. Dressed in her evening gown, Ea had been taken to the German border under guard, part of the way by foot.[3] Their brother Anders, with a stutter and guileless social manner seemed not particularly interested in marriage; when Katholm passed to him, he had sold it.

Tanne stayed in Denmark several months; impatient, Bror returned to Africa alone. With Tanne's help, her brother Tommy had tried to obtain acreage through a plan parceling out land to former soldiers of the Great War. The factory he would build, its dusky stream of coffee beans spilling down through whirling machinery, would provide a pleasant respite for his sister before a fire destroyed it. Now Tommy packed his books about Einstein and the New Testament (the same books on which his discussions could drive his older sister to distraction) as he prepared to visit Africa without knowing exactly how long he would stay.

Before taking the train to Nairobi, they stopped along the sea at the Mombasa Club, the heat taking on an almost palpable form as the palms appeared to be swaying the sun. Rumbles reached them throughout their journey of troubles at Ngong; with all the plantation's debts, Bror did not expect a hoped for loan from his wife's family to come through, and had depressed her with dismal communications. The arrival at the farm was not an easy one. Many people moving in and out of the house had made it a shambles. Bills of sale had been taken out on the furniture, and the china and fine glass lay in fragments after the baron used them for target practice.[4] Perhaps because Tommy was a witness to his brother-in-law's actions, his sister for the first time let her usual restraint fall and angrily reported back home on Bror's bad behavior.

Bror was not up to the task of director of the farm; a gambler and drinker, he would carouse and flare into tempers, creating havoc as he rode around the farm in a rickshaw.[5] In hunting matters he was not much better; if he liked a client he would give him all the safari fees back in the form of a party on the last night of the hunt.[6] This nonchalance in money matters and an inattention to detail put him in a bad way. A manager had quit, complaining that no books were being kept, the oxen had been sold so the fields could not be plowed, and that after being prohibited by the bank from signing any checks, Bror had gone back on his word in a financial matter.[7] The local papers were filled with a controversial land scheme of his which came to nothing; things came to such a bad head with him and his financial affairs that he ended up hiding out shoeless in the Masai Reserve from the police who threatened arrest in an attempt to collect on his debts.

As a way out of their financial troubles, the baron and baroness would consider buying a farm near Ingrid Lindstrom, a kindly Swedish woman who became best friends with them. Bror's plan was to convince his wife that trees should be planted in between the coffee plants, to be sold for charcoal in Nairobi. The coffee would gradually be eliminated. Their own farm was, admitted Tanne, a bit too high up to always bring the coffee plants to full flower "like a cloud of chalk, in the mist and the drizzling rain"; the distant railway further affected the crop price. "But Tanne liked coffee," recalled Ingrid, and resisted the idea.[8]

Tanne was proud of her ability to plow the land while her dogs ran nearby and liked, now, to wear daringly the khaki trousers, blouse to the knee, leaving her legs bare. But the land was not always strong enough to hold her, and there were many months on her farm when she became bored, longing for the European landscape and Italian and French paintings. She entertained herself with the tragic (and, at times, comic and pathetic) characters who walked into her life on the farm near the Ngong Hills. Old Knudsen, a drunken and blind Dane, wandered into her life, and reminded her of the Danish language, which she had not spoken in nearly a year. He was filled with schemes for making gold, but they came to nothing—much like his speech, which was marked by anticlimax: "It was in 1880," he would begin, "—no, wait a minute, that's not true, it must have been in 1888 or 1887,—now, let me see, it was—," all this to tell about a brick being dropped by a major.[9]

Another Scandinavian, a Swede, Casparsson, an actor whose major role had been Armand in "The Lady of the Camellias," had shared with Tanne her faith in the imagination; during their talks together, he proclaimed that "with the exception of God, I believe in absolutely nothing whatever."[10] He set himself the task of walking to Tanganyika, and Tanne, with trepidation, gave him some shillings and a bottle of beer to help him on his journey. In *Out of Africa,* she gave him a rare bottle of chambertin and painted her own backdrop for his departure: "Exit Emmanuelson. Should not the hills, the thorn-trees and the dusty road take pity and for a second put on the aspect of cardboard?"—for Isak Dinesen, life was not to be distinguished from the ceremony of the stage, and was lived intensely only when it was arranged artistically.[11]

News came back that Casparsson had last been seen riding atop a lorry.

In 1921, Uncle Aage Westenholz arrived at Ngong—impressed by the elegantly furnished house set up against the green hills and woods—and was greeted by his niece standing charmingly under the Danish flag. Eventually he would feel that his interest in Karen Coffee Company put his reputation as a businessman in question (among other investments, he owned cement shares in Bangkok); but partly because of his feelings for her mother, and because he felt that of the family, Tanne was the most clever, he could not but feel that risk and sacrifice must be taken "so that," as he put it, "Tanne can obtain what she considers her life's goal."[12] Uncle Aage had come out to help make arrangements for Tanne to buy the African farm.

Afraid of the bankruptcy so many settlers fell into, Uncle Aage preached thrift to his niece, finally convincing her to build a modest cottage of three rooms with a thatched roof and cement floor, and to let out the "lovely" farmhouse.[13] She had resisted, then agreed, entering the game by calling the cottage a "mudhouse."[14]

Before long, he and his nephew Thomas aligned against Bror, whom the uncle had found pleasant enough at first, but maddening in the financial embarrassments he continually put Tanne and her family in—in what was shaping up to be a scandal of some proportion, Bror had taken out a mortgage on the furniture, which would have to be sold off if the loan, obtained on an astonishingly high return of interest, could not be paid.

As he prepared to leave for home on June 20—(the loans had fallen through and Tanne was left as manager of the farm)—, Uncle Aage recorded in his diary that his niece and nephew, sitting awkwardly on top of piles of luggage, had driven into town with him. Bror had not been able to come with them for fear of being caught and arrested for debts. The uncle noted that "I bought second-class fare to set a good example of thriftiness ('Be thrifty' was one of my last words), and at 1:45 we parted, thank God as the best of friends . . . I hope she doesn't have too many plans I don't know about."[15] Clearly, she did.

After he left Tanne would write home about the impossibility of finding tenants to pay the high rent on the farm and never moved into the "thatched cottage," despite a letter from Uncle Aage urging her to demonstrate sincerity to the "skeptical board," and that she was worth her salary: "may you quickly be able to show proof of your determination to *work* and *be thrifty;* reports and financial accounts will be helpful in the former case, the thatched cottage in the latter."[16]

Letters were exchanged between Tanne's brother and her uncle. Thomas was furious at Bror for all of his lies, which had made his stay in B.E.A. a difficult one—at one point he even insisted that Bror be given money on the condition that he never be seen in B.E.A. again; but he was particularly upset at the precarious financial position Bror repeatedly put his sister in.[17] Uncle Aage confided to Thomas that he believed in Tanne's desire to make the farm succeed, but concluded that she was "weak as a woman" before Bror, and that the family needed to provide support against him, even if that support looked to be "a prison wall."[18] They knew she was shrewd enough to run them round in loops when it suited her.

A rupture nearly ensued with her family over Bror, as Tanne threatened to cut off all communications back home. When the family sided with Tommy over one of the quarrels with his brother-in-law, Tanne defended Bror, reminding her mother of her own marriage to Wilhelm Dinesen. Calling up her father's image, Tanne blamed his abandonment for her troubles, at the same time that she looked to his memory for consolation.[19] Her uncle, meantime, was obviously peeved, writing to Thomas that "while we here at home are gradually losing our shirts for the sake of KC she has maintained her elegant house, kept her costly furniture, her expensive houseboys, her riding horse, and, above all, her risky husband."[20]

Convinced of her family's unreasonableness in now pressing for a divorce because of Bror's incompetence—and humiliating behavior—in financial matters (though there is reason to think that by now her mother, at least, knew of the syphilis), Tanne regretted ever having bound herself financially to the Karen Coffee Company and her family.[21] As for a divorce, she did not want one. To her mother she wrote:

> During these six months I have come to realize that I am very, very reluctant to separate from Bror. There is so much here that binds us

together, and it is impossible for me to stop believing in the good in him, and to think that his various inexplicable and heartless outbursts are other than a kind of frenzy, that should surely subside. Perhaps it is simply that I care too much for him; I feel that I cannot abandon him now, when things are so difficult [financially] for him.[22]

At a management meeting, Aunt Bess compared her to a fine horse which could use the discipline of whipping. Her niece replied swiftly and caustically: "I find it altogether degrading to be compared to a horse, especially one that needs whip and spurs, because that is a worthless horse."[23] Irritated by the hold her family had on her, Tanne found herself defending her actions in Africa by arguing against *Moster* Bess's fondness for the calling up of fictional characters to test her niece's morality. This importance of literature as a moral model for the Westenholz women contributed to their adventurer Dinesen daughter increasingly blurring the boundaries separating art and fiction, even as she would proclaim that the line between life and death was an illusion.[24] In her form-fitting riding jacket and darkly shining boots, her hair pulled back into a short tail, looking stylishly ready for the hunt, she could see the wisps of smoke slowly winding up through drifting red dust surrounding the tribespeople and their huts; in the distance, the heat-laden horizon took the sharp lines away from sun-bleached thorn trees and stubbles of brush, confirming the world as impressionistic reverie.[25] Sifted through such great distance, her reflections on life back in Denmark, of the continuous flow of Danish generations, took on the dimensions of a work of art.

The baroness kept to herself that she had discovered her husband's relationship with a vivacious woman, Cockie Birkbeck.[26] Married, the beautiful Cockie suited the irreverence and mischief making of Bror. When the Prince of Wales came home for breakfast, Cockie would yell down that she was getting up for no one, not even the prince, to make breakfast. Come on, shouted the prince in reply, you must have some eggs that can be scrambled.[27] Another time, while on ship, she was reported to have appeared on deck with both legs mistakenly wearing only one single pajama leg, a bit of blood on her forehead from a parrot that had bitten her.[28] Cockie and Bror had a brief "walk-out" while Tanne was away in Denmark; when Bror's wife returned, Cockie sent a letter asking to quit the affair, keeping it as their "little secret."[29]

Tanne had been willing to tolerate Bror's affairs as long as he was discreet—and as long as she knew nothing about them. But now the letter fell into Tanne's hands and Bror soon found himself thrown out from the farm, Tanne's anger having been festering with too long a list of wrongs.[30] Not long after, Tanne reported back to Denmark that Bror had found an "English lady" to help him with finances (he had been completely cut off from management of the farm by his wife's family) and wanted a divorce;[31] Thomas wrote home that Bror had harangued his sister endlessly for one.[32] Eventually Cockie pressed a string of cultured pearls into a grocer's hands to keep the creditors away.[33]

Back in Sweden, Bror's family—and his friends in Nairobi—complained that, the uncle reported to Thomas, "Tanne sits as a millionaire while her husband goes around begging. It is exaggerated, but it is essentially true of course as long as there hasn't been a divorce."[34]

The African letters record how difficult it was for Bror's wife to break such an intimate relationship as marriage, thereby disrupting the basic emotional continuity in her life. She wrote very much like a woman in love with her husband, although other reasons also contributed to her reluctance to divorce.

In Nairobi, a social awkwardness would result from Bror's desire to remarry: there would now be two Baroness Blixens, and strictly speaking, Tanne's title could no longer be retained.[35] This aristocratic accouterment of the marriage has been blamed for Tanne's distress over the breakup of the marriage. But the social stigma which caused her to divorce and what she saw as a personal failure concerned her more.[36] She herself was unable, she confided, to think of returning home to face her family for several years after the divorce *shauries*.[37] But the worst was the "terror" she felt overwhelming her, as she was once again plunged into feelings that her life lacked any real and vital meaning (her own brother always felt that the first year of her marriage was the happiest, and that the "substance" of the first year would never return).[38] Out of this frightening perception of a deepening void, her enthusiasm for Denys Finch Hatton took hold more strongly, as she moved to exchange one painful relationship for another.

The Danish baroness was soon having her own problems with her Englishman. His unexpected step in the doorway would make her feel that the snows of winter were nothing, that death was nothing, she wrote in a euphoria to her brother. Other times he would be away for months, appearing and disappearing at will, often without notice; when he was away she would drift into a deep depression.[39]

Denys, a modernist, leaned to art which took its impetus from the war, breaking icons in a machinelike staccato, while she lingered in the known order inherent in old and traditional forms; he would not have minded new paintings and prints on the walls, but she could not bring herself to hang any. Though she preferred Tchaikovsky, Stravinsky's *Petrushka*—about an abandoned puppet—had been given to her by Denys and played scratchily on her Victrola.[40]

A tame bushbuck had entered the household, and Tanne, taking a rest from bringing the flowering coffee to harvest and market (she was seen in Nairobi every Friday afternoon wearing her red shawl) would write, the bushbuck Lulu at her feet.[41] Denys was never far from her mind. During her brother's stay, Tanne had become convinced that she was pregnant by Denys and when she discovered her mistake, took her brother by the arm, pacing late into the night. Later, a second false alarm would bring a telegram from Denys (who was in England) urging her in a terse message to "cancel Daniel's visit," to consider her mother and that he could not enter into a "partnership" with her.[42] When she wrote nothing to him for months after—aside from an apologetic "Thanks cable I never meant to ask assistance consent only Tania"[43]—he sent a poetic letter to her, showing how distance drew him in, just as any approach toward him pushed him away:

> I shall be glad to see Ngong and your charming self again. Those sunsets at Ngong have an atmosphere of rest and content about them which I never realized anywhere else. I believe I could die happily enough at sunset at Ngong looking up at the hills, with all their lovely colors fading out above the darkening belt of the near forest. Soon they will be velvet black against the silver fading sky—black as the buffaloes which come pushing softly out of the bush high up under the breasts of the hills to feed with sweet breath unafraid upon the open grass of the night. I am very much looking forward to seeing you again, Tania. You might have given me something of your news—nothing—no word even of Daniel.[44]

Throughout Tanne's *shauries*, the one man consistently by her side was Farah, her Somali servant. He is given a permanent place in *Shadows on the Grass*—as servant, and his private complaints of being "a miserable coloured man" are missing as their relationship is elevated onto a mythic plane.[45]

In the evening as his memsahib sat at her desk smoking a cigarette and writing in her notebook (filling one side with scattered financial figures from the farm, then turning it upside down to begin a sketch or story),[46] Farah might emerge from the shadows to refer to a household problem with fleas: "only cats and dog, these two people bring them in."[47] One day while Farah watched his memsahib painting in the dark browns and streaks of blue she favored, the realistic portrait was thrown to the floor as she angrily ordered him to burn it. Then later, heard from Farah: "Try one more day, then think that God shall help you and it shall be very good."[48] He served as a continual reminder of a higher law, as he reassured his memsahib that God's presence would help with the problems of daily life, with the dogs and motorcar, and everything else.

As she rode along a red dusty road with Farah, the wild flowers stirring to the side looked as despairing as she felt. The impending divorce weighed heavily on Tanne's mind, making her burdens harder to bear. Finding nine Indian carts caught along the road, the memsahib and her servant helped move them by loading and unloading their wares, until Tanne discovered that her own motorcar was stuck, and tired, fell to weeping, much to Farah's distress.[49] Back at the farm, the final insult had been a brass rooster which fell on her head.

Shortly before their divorce came through in 1925, Bror came down with a high fever and experienced a kind of paralysis of the limbs; he was out in Uganda, broke and stranded. He received an invitation to stay with his estranged wife, who offered to care for him. The divorce was too difficult to bear (Tanne asked that it be kept secret back home), and she decided to go to Denmark that year, for her third visit. Once she was at Rungstedlund, her brother convinced her to return to the farm when she wavered, seriously thinking of never seeing Africa again.

A vignette in "The Dreamers" is emblematic of what takes place in *Seven Gothic Tales* thematically, and can be read as a reflection of her feelings at the time. The tale of an old sultan is told, and of how he sends for a young bride who has never laid eyes on a man. He is defeated when she catches sight of a young water boy, and mistakes him for a god or an angel (Tanne herself took pride in showing pictures of Hermes and then bringing out pictures of Denys as a comparison). And the tale continues:

> So the Sultan became very sad, and he had the virgin and the young man buried alive together, in a marble chest broad enough to make a

marriage bed, under a palm tree of his garden, and seating himself below the same tree he wondered at many things, and at how he was never to have his heart's desire, and he had a young boy to play the flute to him.[50]

The possibility of love and ecstasy bring the silence of burial, of death. The tale itself is suffused in longing and a turbulence and violence of feelings and experience that is masked over by the moment of repose, of the soothing flute, of art, which makes everything appear in order. Even when it is not.

Tanne complained to her brother after the divorce and her return from Denmark that her troubles (quarrels with Denys, as well as the financial disarray of the farm) made her feel a suffocation, and she wrote of burial in different form:

> To be forced to silence, as I am here, when one has great difficulties, as I have now, feels as if one is buried alive, and you must imagine me as if you saw me lying in darkness with the weight of the earth on my breast, and forgive me for this screaming.[51]

This feeling of forced muteness during emotional upheaval was transfigured in *Seven Gothic Tales*, which, she said, was born from "a scream, a lion's roar" after her African life had ended.[52]

Because her travel between Denmark and Africa undermined her fragile sense of stability as she fell into a "completely meaningless seesawing" about life (now set into motion by the disappearance of Denys from the threshold), she resolved not to undertake any such journey for a long time.[53] As she swung in wide arcs of mood and thoughts—a lifelong problem she recognized—, in a hopeful clarification of self she asserted anew the conscious development of her person as personality, and her surroundings to support it, despite her sister Elle's chiding: "I myself feel that a certain kind of shape and color in my surroundings, a certain amount of 'showing off,' . . . is the expression of my personality. . . . Without these things I am . . . but an actor without a stage . . . I am not myself"; her adult fairy tale *Ehrengard* is the fullest working out of this idea as her seducer Cazotte creates a rococo setting of pink tones within which to best showcase (and contemplate) himself while planning a seduction.[54] This impulse of hers to "show off" she felt was divinely informed as she noted that Judgment Day would undoubtedly bring as sharp a rebuke for having mismatched colors as for lying about a neighbor.

Her writing would become the most sustained effort at achieving a glimpse of the symbolic stork of her childhood play, a reassurance that the possibility of feeling centered existed, even as the writing moved back upon her to suspiciously question whether such a possibility really existed. When she unexpectedly caught sight of a long-legged stork walking on her farm, she was delighted.

19.

Happy Valley

"I don't think the Devil himself
could have had a greater effect."

🌰 *It was Beryl Markham—who was "absolutely ravishing," really, said Tanne
about her after one dinner—who gave the Danish baroness trouble on two fronts, in
her personal life and in putting the lie to her imaginative world.[1]*

Beryl had come out to Africa with her father as a child; her father,
Charles Clutterbuck, had left a divorced wife and son (and prizes in
Latin and Greek) in England to come to Africa to train horses and live
in straw-thatched huts with his four-year-old daughter.[2] Ignoring her
math and grammar lessons, the barefoot Beryl had slipped out among
the bamboo trees and leopards to go hunting with the Nandi Murani.[3]
By eighteen she was training at Nakuru (a place the Baroness Blixen
praised as lovely and "free,"[4] where thousands of flamingoes turned
the lake pink) against long odds, her first prize-winning horse, Wise
Child, who broke the racing record in the Kenya St. Leger,[5] giving rise
to the rumor that Beryl fed her horses a magic potion known only to
herself and the Nandi.[6] She was undaunted by danger: by the time she

was a young woman, a lion had clawed her and a sword cut her in a feud with a young African boy she had bested in wrestling.

She became one of the first pilots to scout out elephant for safari, sending down messages attached to silk ribbons of yellow and blue, her racing colors.[7] She flew out in the dark African night through uncharted land with no radio, runways, or night lights, only swamp waters and the sharp mountains below; rags soaked in oil and burning in tins lit the way as she came to the rescue of stranded dreamers hunting their fortune, their dreams ending in blackwater and death.[8] Morphine was pressed upon her, to be kept with her compass and log book, should a wind shear near Mt. Kenya or Kilimanjaro be unexpectedly swift, bringing her down into the deep forests; or somewhere else. Carrying a branch of heather she was the first to cross the Atlantic from England to North America, egged on by Lord Carberry: "Think of all that black water! . . . Think how cold it is!"[9] In her white skullcap of a pilot's hat, goggles, red bow lips, delicately arched brows, and finely limned nose she gave the "ravishing" picture which Greta Garbo's profile echoed.

She left the Nandi to become part of a circle of men, the white hunters and adventurers of Africa, bewitching them. She was that most fatal of coquettes, offering with a slow side look the mesmerizing draw of beauty and danger. Her rumored affair with the Duke of Gloucester (who was said to have sent bouquets of white flowers on a Shetland pony over to where the married Beryl was staying in Piccadilly) was talked about long after by the settlers, despite her protests.[10] The affair, and her pregnancy by the duke, was said to be hushed up by the Royal Palace and a large sum settled on her.[11] She ended up running through three marriages, keeping the name of her third husband, Mansfield Markham.

The Oxford-educated aristocrat Denys Finch Hatton and the Swedish Baron von Blixen-Finecke both found Beryl Markham irresistable. She in turn commented that the Baroness Blixen—whom she called unpredictable, "You had the feeling that she might suddenly shoot someone,"[12] and indeed the baroness had threatened a fidgety Gikuyu with a pistol when he refused to sit still for his portrait[13]— could not have loved two more difficult men.

Delamere's wife, "Lady D," acted as Beryl's adopted mother, and most likely brought her over to the Baroness Blixen's farm; part of her chores as a young girl had been to walk the dogs on the baroness's farm.[14] Now, the finely educated Englishman's attention strayed from the baroness. While the baroness painted quietly to the side, Denys would insolently drawl in British tones: "Beryl, come and roll my back up and down."[15] His flirtation with Beryl provoked quarrels and caused his relationship with the baroness to be brought to a head.[16] People thought that Beryl had had a "walk-out" with Denys, though her discreet comment on Denys was:

> The thing is, he did like lovely food and good things, and . . . [Tanne] was very good at looking after everything, and, of course, he was very well-bred, but I don't think it really happened. I think that's what buggered up everybody.[17]

When four "flying machines" arrived in Nairobi in a racing competition, Lady Maia Carberry's small plane was among them. Along with at least 1,000 other cars Tanne had driven with her totos in high excitement—she was fond of the totos and had playfully hidden potatoes fashioned into dolls on her farm for them to find—to see the shining machines lined up in Nairobi.[18]

Lord and Lady Carberry were part of what came to be known as "Happy Valley." The Danish baroness moved on the periphery of this "Happy Valley" crowd which had come into being soon after the War and had its playground in the white highlands. A wealthy, titled group who spent their time reveling in scandal, their notoriety reached its apex with the murder of the womanizing Lord Errol in the early 1940s.[19]

One day the houseboy Juma reported to his memsahib that someone carrying milk on a bicycle to Nairobi had sighted a plane crash; when Denys and Tanne went out the next day to investigate they found mangled wood and iron in a pile where Lady Carberry's plane had crashed. Her daughter claimed it was a suicide because of the cruel treatment her mother had suffered from her husband.[20]

Another time, when a cruise ship put in at Mombasa, Lady Macmillan brought two elderly American women over to the farm at Ngong. While the visiting Americans gossiped about the sinful goings on of the Comtesse de Janzé and the "Happy Valley" crowd for which the Kenya Colony was becoming known, the baroness listened quietly. The Comtesse de Janzé, a sultry-looking woman, had been seen in Nice walking her white-collared black panther; in a more demure mood, she was photographed wearing a large-brimmed hat and the loose chemise dress popular in the twenties, a lion cub on her lap. The comtesse had been arrested in Paris for the attempted murder of her lover.[21]

When a car was heard pulling up and the Baroness Blixen's expected guests, Lord Errol and the notorious Comtesse de Janzé entered the room, the baroness was so pleased at the expression on the faces of the Americans—"I don't think the Devil himself could have had a greater effect," she recalled, delighted—that she invited the comtesse to stay with her if she had occasion to go to Nairobi as she prepared to follow orders forcing her to leave the country.[22]

At small intimate dinners where the men dressed up in pajamas and robes and the women in off-the-shoulder gowns, Tanne would also meet with settlers who did not belong to the "Happy Valley" crowd. Occasionally, Denys would be there. While the lights darted into shadows along the walls and the leopards silently stalked the house, the settlers would click their glasses and toast the empire. The newly appointed governor, Lord Grigg, and his wife, "Gladie," who knew George Bernard Shaw and who was raising money for hospitals for the tribal women, might be there.[23] And so might the dandy Berkeley Cole, who had given Tanne two ships' lanterns to hang on her veranda in the night, and such others as Lord Delamere, "Lady D," Mr. Bulpett, Gustav Mohr. There were Lord and Lady Islington—Lord Islington had captivated the Danish baroness by referring to her as his "greatest experience" in Africa, making her slyly declare that men were not truly charming until they were seventy.[24] Only a small, trusted group knew of the clandestine relationship between the English gentleman and the Danish baroness.[25]

At the dinners on the farms or at Government House (on special occasions), or the race days held twice a year at Muthaiga, there was a sparkle to the conversation which the emerging Danish author had been bred to, to be precocious in. "At one party," recalled the baroness, "the subject came up how many of the Ten Commandments it would be necessary for the perfect gentleman, . . . to observe. . . . The commandment which the perfect gentleman had to observe was the Eighth."[26] A conversation with one friend ended with a caution to the baroness that a woman should avoid wearing wings because it would make life too impractical for her.[27]

That brilliance of conversation found its way into her writing, and it was in the unexpected provocativeness and upsetting of the conventional where the delight often lay: "The proof of the pudding is in the eating" was not to the baroness's liking, for example, for if dead rats could make a tasty meal, then, she argued, they would have to be included in all cookbooks describing elegant dining.[28]

One of the closest friends to Denys and Tanne (now often called Tania by her friends, after Denys's pet name for her) was Rose Cartwright, a shy, serious Englishwoman who had grown up in Victorian England, where as a young girl she was not allowed to board a train without a maid (her family had fifteen servants).[29] Her brothers had gone to Eton and Cambridge, while the girls had gotten a lesser education from governesses. During World War I she had driven an ambulance in northern France. Everyone had lost people in the war, and when she returned to England and its social life, the dances after World War I, it was more than she could bear. She had left for Africa to escape the memories of the carnage of the war—in one day she remembered that 30,000 men were killed and 150,000 wounded, all arriving on the trains. Her own cousin, Cara Buxton, at twenty-six had sent out a house to British East Africa, then had walked through the Congo to Kenya with ten porters and a compass; it took her six months. So Rose Cartwright had decided to come out to Africa with her brother. Rose in particular believed in the integrity of Denys and would remain loyal to him.

They could all three be seen talking together, Denys quite comfortable in a bow tie and disheveled clothes and hat, a style of casual reassurance that would be repeated in the black and white image of the lone big city knuckle-cracking man. He was sensitive about his receding hair, always wearing a felt hat, which he absentmindedly pushed back on his forehead during a conversation.[30] One time, when crossing a narrow bridge, his motor car flipped over, falling to the churning waters below, trapping his servant Billea Isa. Denys was strong enough to raise the motor, freeing himself and his servant. Having lost his hat, he quickly borrowed a lady's hat from one of the nearby houses until he could get a more proper one.[31]

He sought repeatedly the isolation of Africa's wide plains; it suited his elusiveness. In an attempt to accommodate herself to Denys's demands—or lack of demands—the baroness claimed no real interest in marriage, veering toward a "free relationship." When Tommy returned to Denmark after a two-year stay in Africa, the baroness had sent him an extensive essay on marriage. It reflected her ambivalence toward marriage, as she on the one hand appeared to support it and on the other condemned it; in the old days when the bride had stepped forward to join her groom, she was no different than innoculated cattle which had been branded, she concluded bitterly.[32]

Denys's movement, often bordering on flight, did not allow for attachments; the Denys Finch Hatton crest insisting on the credo, "conscious of no guilt," released him from any moral culpability.[33] He said a lot about his attitude toward women when in a letter to his friend Kitty in London (a woman with a gypsylike aura he had been attracted to), he pretended exasperation with her for expecting to hear from him without leaving a forwarding address. She was, he chided, displaying "a hereditary weakness of her sex—namely of expecting a little more than it is possible to give."[34] His refusal to form any permanent marital attachments led to talk after his death that he was sexually ambiguous.[35]

Tanne herself revealed the pain in her relationship to Denys in a story she started writing in Africa in the 1920s, "Carnival." One woman says to her sister, costumed as Pierrot:

> "Is it bad to be in love?" she asked. "I thought," said Pierrot sadly, "that you might have seen that for yourself."
>
> "Would you change with me tonight?"
>
> "Yes," said Pierrot with great energy, "with you and anyone else who is not in love."[36]

The identification with Pierrot's unrequited yearning had taken hold imaginatively:

> ". . . you see, it is like this: we are all dressed up, but I think that you ought to have *been* a Pierrot." "Yes, I think so myself," said Pierrot.[37]

One of the sisters voices the idea that if the man she loves knows of her need for him, she will lose him—it is an ironic reversal of the plight of Andersen's mermaid. The implication is clear: love imposes its own silence. This silence—the silent pain of unfulfilled desire—Tanne was able to translate into her own tales, in particular in "The Poet."

Tanne, who has been criticized for becoming increasingly possessive of Denys as their relationship developed, was really giving into a pervasive anxiety, giving into a fierce possessiveness fired by lack of any real possession.[38] She admonished her brother Tommy never to reveal her true feelings for Denys, if he were by chance to meet him.[39] At heart, she felt defeat, and that "never had a little ruined and lost Pierrot looked more tragic."[40]

Depressed by her life in Africa, Tanne had sent a letter to her brother saying that she wanted to achieve something, even if that—in a dramatic sweep—was her own death by suicide.[41] But suicide, she realized, was an ironic solution, because she fled from feelings of negation and nonbeing. She turned to writing for solace. She started writing "stories, fairy-tales and romance that would take . . . [her] mind a long way off, to other countries and times," away from the long, lonely evenings and the ticking of the clock.[42] What she looked for in writing was the inspiration that was revealed by the New Testament, the inspiration of truth revealed at a glance, made manifest by experience concentrated and unified in the fictional—or mythical— moment. When destiny touched that moment, redemption was possible, in a sanctification by God and a relationship of grace to the universe.

An offer had been made asking her for some marionette plays. One appeal for her in the marionette plays was in the importance of the marionette master, who, when gone, left the puppets collapsed, a metaphor for her own emotional dependence on Denys.[43] Her brother Thomas had written a book on the war that because of its atheistic posture was a minor scandal in Denmark, and her sister Elle was also writing, under a pseudonym. In emulating the family tradition set by her father, she looked to achieve independence by writing, as a way of coping with Denys's skittishness. She wrote out of a psychic crisis that had developed in childhood from being equipoised—until she felt negated and pressed off-balance—between the two sides of her family, the Westenholzes and Dinesens (the travel between Denmark and Africa recreated that split); a sense of crisis that had intensified with her father's abandonment and later reemerged in each of her failed relationships, informed by a muted anger resulting in an inner paralysis.[44]

20.

The Gypsy Moth Plane

1931: "We were afraid she would lose her mind."

🌿 *Ellen had sent out to her sister a porcelain figure of harlequin as a gift which had joined Columbine on Mama's old bureau; but it was the missing Pierrot, the yearning, dark-eyed Pierrot that her sister preferred. A Pierrot costume had been carefully packed and brought to Africa, the same one Tanne had worn to a masquerade ball as an art student in Copenhagen. For one dinner she had dressed up in the white silken costume and when she was unexpectedly called to the school on her coffee plantation, appeared wearing the Pierrot costume, the students taking it all as quite natural, thinking she was in the proper attire for exams.*[1]

During Christmas the figurines had been placed out on the mantle along with some candles, a reminder of Tivoli and the spirit and charm of old Copenhagen.[2] Mischievously, she convinced one wide-eyed visitor that the vast African plains had their own Tivoli with ferris wheel and whirling lights.[3] Now on the eve of the new year, Tanne and Denys decided that to see the harlequin become animated and turn in a pretty circle would be a curious pleasure, "that the unexpected would happen, even if it were in miniature."[4] There was, Tanne was convinced, a yearning for the magical and the fantastic in the present age, 1928.[5]

On New Year's Day, 1928, Tanne and Denys packed supplies for a safari that had gone ahead and drove out past grazing herds, taking a new road to Narok, where everything was layered with dust like old parchment. In the clear morning air they came across a lion guarding the carcass of a giraffe. Stopping, they fired and left the lion dead and covered with thorn branches to skin later. When they were forced to stop by the abrupt ending of the road, they turned back; a magnificent black-maned lion stood near the one they had shot earlier. Looking at each other, they quietly discussed whether to shoot the lion or leave it; feeling an urgency for possession, they took aim, killing it. Then, with the dead lions nearby, the carcasses stiffening, they sipped fine red wine, toasting the New Year over a breakfast of bread and cheese, raisins and almonds.[6]

Tanne missed her family this holiday, particularly her mother who had recently left Africa, after her second visit to her daughter. The visit had at first presented a problem because Denys was secretly living with the baroness. The totos had run around them during their talks as Tanne confided the truth of her relationship to her mother, who calmly accepted the news; as her mother prepared to comb her long hair by untwisting it, letting it cascade to her waist, the totos watched in fascination.[7] Her mother had sat for hours in the shade sewing crib sheets for the baby soon to be born to Thomas and his new wife, Jonna Lindhardt; to her mother, Tanne made clear that the African farm took the same place in her feelings as a child.[8]

By spring, Denys had left the farm and then reappeared for only a day, leaving again in the night. Unable to let him go so soon, Tanne had put a coat over her thin gown, going with him as far as a nearby dam, then walked back home without him through darkness lit up by the stars.[9] Tanne would sink into such despair when he left that Denys had started worrying about her when he was away on business or safari and eventually arranged with Ingrid Lindstrom—the pretty Swedish woman who had not known what her husband meant when he wrote her from Africa about going on safari, but who nevertheless had come out to join him after the war and had taken to farming in B.E.A. with zeal—to come out and stay with her after he left.[10] The first time it was quite clear and open that Denys had asked Ingrid to come out; the second time he just picked Ingrid up at the train and told Tanne he had met her in Nairobi.[11] Denys was taking precautions because Tanne had threatened suicide—Tanne, commented Ingrid about this time, "liked to use suicide."[12] But after Denys left, as Tanne rode out on horseback with Ingrid in the morning it was as if Denys had left her mind and her entire concern was the farm and its people. "She was double," commented Ingrid. "It was hard to get inside someone like that."[13]

The fall of 1928 brought an unexpected bitterness to the year. Friends believe that Tanne seriously turned to writing for consolation when the Prince of Wales came out to B.E.A. for his second visit.[14] By then Bror was married to Cockie Birkbeck, creating an awkward situation: now there was another Baroness von Blixen-Finecke, and Tanne could no longer legitimately claim the title. The Danish divorcée, to her shame, was excluded from the major festivities at Government House for the prince.[15] There was great fanfare surrounding the prince's visit, and over in Mombasa the prince had given a picture of himself to the chiefs, from one "chief" to another, with hundreds of Arabs, Africans, and Europeans milling in the ravine garden at Garden House among the frangipani and oleanders.[16] Her social status challenged, the former Baroness Blixen reacted by arranging an *ngoma,* an elaborate series of ceremonial dances performed hypnotically by the Africans to beating drums, annoying Lady Grigg for taking the prince from his schedule.[17]

For his part, the Prince of Wales created his own embarrassment. Without telling anyone, he had entered the races. Afterward, he went into the room of Lady Grigg's young son. As he sat on the edge of the bed, her son asked him what the matter was. The prince replied that he had ridden in the races.

"Did you come in first?" asked the son.

No answer.

"Last?" asked the son.

Dolefully: "Yes."[18]

As an English aristocrat known from his articles on conservation in *The Times,* Denys was chosen to be the safari leader for the prince. Much to Tanne's displeasure, he ended up calling in her ex-husband for the safari, reportedly because he himself had been unable to find lions for the prince.[19] This period in Africa was one of the most trying for Tanne, and she looked pasty and gaunt beneath her Somali shawl, no longer the full round beauty that had charmingly held a huge bouquet of lilies when her brother was there; she would never recover her vitality.[20]

Out on safari hunts it could be almost impossible to find the different animals demanded by a wealthy client. The development of flying stirred an interest in scouting from a plane, something Beryl Markham was among the first to do successfully. There was danger hunting from a plane, since no cleared landing places were easily available. Denys decided to take out his Gypsy Moth to see if elephant could be sighted from a plane, and asked Beryl to go up with him; from that time, reported Beryl, she knew Denys "liked" her.[21] But her flying teacher, Tom Black, on a premonition, asked her not to go; one child burst into tears, also preventing another woman from accepting his invitation.[22] Denys settled on his Gikuyu servant for company and flew to the Mombasa coast, not far from his home there. While landing, his propellor cracked, and he sent for another one. The next day he took off again, the new propellor in place.[23]

Then the accident happened.

Others learned of the accident before Tanne did. It was Lady Macmillan who finally, quietly, told her after lunch that the plane carrying Denys had circled the runway, then crashed. No one was sure why.[24]

Afterwards she learned that people had run to the plane with branches and earth, to cover the fire, but they had been stopped by the heat. A few charred oranges had rolled from the wreckage.[25] Both Denys and Kamau, the boy with him, had been killed.

The burial was arranged for up in the hills, where they had driven out one day after Denys had said to Tanne: "Let us drive as far as our graves"; once there he had settled down into the grass to peel an orange.[26]

The day of the funeral was one of torrential rains. Her cook, Kamande, helped people up through the downpour, everyone slipping through the mud and rain.[27] Accorded all the support of the bereaved, she was treated like Denys's widow. In death she was finally able to have her Englishman in a way that she never could in life. They had quarreled and brought their relationship to an end a year before Denys's death, though they remained friends;[28] unable to let her go completely, he had offered her a loan for the farm if she would return to run it (apparently she had left for Denmark), which she did.[29] Tanne herself had been unable to let go of Denys emotionally. Kamande remembered that time: "We were afraid she would lose her mind."[30]

In one of the great literary deceptions, she suggested in *Out of Africa* that the plane accident had been a veiled suicide—a kind of moody carelessness toward life—because of her decision to leave Africa:

> Denys, who held himself to be an exceptionally rational person, was subject to a special kind of moods and forebodings, and under their influence at times he became silent for days or for a week, though he did not know of it himself and was surprised when I asked him what was the matter with him. The last days before he started on this journey to the coast, he was in this manner absent-minded, as if sunk in contemplation, but when I spoke of it he laughed at me.

> I asked him to let me come with him, for I thought what a lovely thing it would be to see the Sea. . . . This is the only time that I have asked Denys to take me with him on his aeroplane that he would not do it.[31]

When Beryl Markham's book, *West With the Night* (signaling a shift in European understanding of the Africans), was released, she described how Denys had approached her to go up with him. With that one sentence, "He asked me to fly with him to Voi one day, and of course I said I would," she put the lie to Tanne's careful construction of Denys's death.[32] She added another view to the accident, explaining that Denys was an inexperienced pilot. Eventually she admitted that the final row between Denys and Tanne had been over her.[33]

Beryl's book was not known by Tanne's circle of friends back in Denmark and all her life she was able to maintain and preserve the memory of Denys in the manner that she preferred.

It may have been his casualness, finally, that caused Denys Finch Hatton's death, a casualness that would make him flash a light in the eyes of a lion not ten yards away. Perhaps it was the Peter Pan complex observed by friends, that of not wanting to grow older.[34] He was 44 when he died. His obituary noted that he had been a marvelous player at cricket. At his funeral lines from "The Rime of the Ancient Mariner" were read.

For years Tanne had been thinking of going back to Denmark, and the decline of her relationship with Denys, as well as the financial problems exacerbated by the Great Depression, had made her decide before the accident to return to her childhood home. As a way out of her financial troubles, Tanne could have sold her land in parcels and kept some of it, but she stubbornly refused.[35] The entire farm sold, she arranged for land for the Africans to settle on, but became upset when they did not like the arrangements, which involved being moved around.[36] When Chief Kinanjui died, so close after Denys's death, she was unable to cope and refused to allow him to be brought to her farm from the hospital, as his people requested.[37] With the chief's death one phase between the Africans and Europeans had come to a close; when the baroness had first arrived, any social conversation with Chief Kinanjui was taboo, but by the end, easy exchanges between Africans and Europeans were possible.

With Denys's death, Tanne's world was irretrievably marred. To remain in Africa with no hope of reuniting with Denys was inconceivable. To be in Africa as a single woman amid the memories of personal relationships which had caused her so much pain and brought so little in return was too difficult to bear. She wavered. Before Tanne finally left the farm at Ngong, Ingrid Lindstrom stayed with her for three days, not sleeping for those three nights, afraid because her Danish friend spent each long day wondering whether to go back home or commit suicide.[38]

Her fine crystal glasses were packed in sawdust, and all the crates filled. To her uncle she wrote that "It is really very sad to see it end this way, and even when one has feared it for a long time it still finally comes as something almost unnatural."[39]

After she left, the coffee plantation that had been occupied by some 2,000 people developed into a suburb of Nairobi known as Karen, a left-over reminder of her former ownership.[40]

III

THE AUTHOR

21.

Pellegrina

"I will not be one person again,
Marcus, I will be always many persons from now. Never again will I
have my heart and my whole life
bound up with one woman, to
suffer so much."

🐛 *She is a dark, long-haired beauty who, chameleonlike, attracts men by playing to their fantasies of a perfect love. She wears long feathers and fine silk wools, or shifts in mood to the simplicity of the linen hood worn by Italian women. Traces of a fire are left in a long, vertical scar along her neck. Once admired as an opera star, she abandoned the stage after this fire. There is one unusual feature to her: wherever she walks, she has no shadow. Men in faraway places remember her; once a man meets her, he can dream of no one else.*

While sailing a dhow under the stars from Lamu to Zanzibar, a redheaded Englishman recalls his love for her. He has met other men who over wine have revealed falling in love with Pellegrina, but each has loved the same woman under a different guise: as a mystic and revolutionary, a milliner, a prostitute in Rome. To her companion, Marcus, she confides: "I will not be one person again, Marcus, I will be always many persons from now. Never again will I have my heart and my whole life bound up with one woman, to suffer so much."[1] Swiftly, she flees from the men who seek her, and spreading out her arms, her cape flies up into the appearance of wings, as Pellegrina dies from exhaustion, triumphant. Her escape is final.

Pellegrina Leoni, a character from "The Dreamers," was the character Isak Dinesen would hold to and identify with most strongly; her most important tale, she felt, was "The Dreamers."[2] She was, she said, Pellegrina, and a picture of her near the end of her life shows her face hidden by the soft folds of a large hood.[3]

Isak Dinesen confided to a friend that like her character Pellegrina, after her return to Denmark she consciously sought to reject identity and the suffering that resulted from an attachment to the aspirations and accouterments of personality (i.e., personal relationships).[4] In "The Dreamers," Pellegrina is a female Don Juan who sets up a sweet yearning in men, who retains her freedom through a conscious lack of connection to others. Pellegrina took on the characteristics of the men in the baroness's life for whom domestic life and its attachments were impossible in a conventional sense; Pellegrina was a freeing of the female self for Isak Dinesen as she played in fiction the same tricks that her men had played on her in life. Pellegrina's abandoned men, Lincoln Forsner, an Englishman and dreamer, had Finch Hatton-like characteristics, and her Swedish Baron Guildenstern was consciously modeled on Bror.[5]

Ironically, as Isak Dinesen perceived her own personal movement to be away from identity, she moved instead more and more into a sharply defined identity, a self-stylizing that kept her at a distance from others. She became a great role player.[6] She adopted a shifting aesthetic pose as one way to control and dominate painful experiences. "Your own mask," she wrote, "would give you at least that release from self toward which all religions strive"; in her tales, the mask acts as release and protection, as an ironic incurring and deflecting, worn before realities both transparent and opaque.[7] Photographs from that period show a sharp break with the natural African look of the safari hunter under shade trees, an increasingly stylized appearance which contradicted her avowed conscious rejection of all personality roles; one stark photograph of her in black and white with hair slicked back suggests the striking pose of the androgynous dandy. Seeking for anonymity and detachment while moving sharply into a highly ritualized and dramatic existence, her life was exquisitely set in internal and external opposition.

After her return to her childhood home along the Strandvej with the gnarled "Blue Rain" branches clustering over the doorway, Tanne sank into a stupor which lasted several months, as reality became submerged within the outlines of dream; in *Seven Gothic Tales*, one character comments that "dreaming is the well-mannered people's way of committing suicide,"[8] of negating and reshaping personality—dream was the imagination playing with deep forces, proof of the creative instinct as supreme.[9]

After the rather exalted life Tanne had led at the foot of the Ngong Hills as head of a coffee plantation of 2,000 people, she was now faced with the problem of how to occupy herself. Used to running her farm with feudalistic authority, she recreated in entirely different circumstances and with diminished resources her own small fiefdom. This fiefdom became repeated in the simplest activities, as she played on the thick brown Oriental rug in the living room with Nils, the small son of her housekeeper, taking stuffed and china animals with names like Simba and with a ball played at "shooting" down the animals.[10]

Another time, Nils appeared in shining gold, dressed by Tanne to impress visitors.[11] He served as a mock page, very seriously handing around cigarettes and cigars to guests, pulling chairs out for the ladies, and solemnly toasting with red soda (everyone else had red wine). Finger bowls were expected at all meals.[12]

That letters from Africa addressed her as the "lioness" pleased her—though such names were not an uncommon flattery and courtesy by the Africans—and she appropriated the name to herself as proof of a former grand existence. Throughout the rest of her life in Denmark, the baroness—she insisted on retaining the use of the title—would have enthusiasms which held the possibility of returning her to Africa, or, if briefly, to adventure (she spoke of a desire to ride a motorcycle down Paris streets), but which were not informed by any real seriousness, becoming more a consoling imaginative ritual, as she performed gestures which gave the illusion that a return to her previous life of adventure was possible.[13] Enervated, she was too drained to make any of these plans come through.

In London, she tried becoming a war correspondent in Abyssinia to cover the war started by Mussolini, who had proclaimed that "though words are beautiful things, rifles, machine guns, plane and cannon are still more beautiful."[14] Women were not, she was told, accepted. With Baroness Moura Budberg, a Russian exile who was a friend of Maxim

Gorky, she found reason to go to Geneva for three weeks to listen to the speeches in the League of Nations. "We stayed," recalled Moura Budberg, "at a hotel that had a cabaret . . . and Tania, though she was in despair about the pending invasion, was avid to see and do everything. We listened to speeches all day and got intoxicated with dance music all evening."[15]

During a meeting with Albert Schweitzer, wanting to share in his humanitarian fame, she asked about starting her own hospital for the Africans. "But," said Tanne, "I soon realized that the expenses of the undertaking would by a long way exceed my means. . . . The images of an existence nine thousand feet up, under the long hill of Bardamat, among the Masai children, dissolved like other mirages above the grass."[16] The political moves evaporated, with no real substance behind them. It was her writing that would claim her the most consistently, if erratically, and it was here that she fashioned the grand gesture, a sweeping acknowledgement—and defiance—of fate.

In a spirit of frivolousness she had dismissed doing fine cooking or heading an asylum for the insane, deciding to make a serious commitment to writing. Placing a picture of Denys and blueprint of Africa on the desk in Ewald's room, she sat quietly as the white sails crossed the window, the sun gleaming metallically on the sound. The carriages swaying along the Strandvej of her childhood had long disappeared, as speeding motorcars raced to Elsinore, their horns blaring. Taking pen in hand, her glasses perched on her nose, the Masai spears hung in careful angles on the walls, she turned to writing in a recreation and restructuring of the self. Her mother acquiesced to her demands, giving her dominion over the house and cutting down on all visitors so that her daughter could work, patiently putting up with her imperious and bad-tempered manner. When the heavy French doors were left open, her mother reprimanded Tanne, provoking a sharp response: "In Kenya, my boys closed the doors after me."[17] Because this daughter was so much like her husband, the mother felt repeated in their relationship the nuances of her marriage to Wilhelm. Underneath it all, there was a deep sympathy and affection between them.

With an eye to profit, Tanne chose to write first in English, rather than turning to the mournful sounds of the Danish language; English would reach a wide audience abroad.[18] She knew English from her youth, from a bit of study at Oxford, and had spent her time in its midst in Africa (originally disdaining the British, Denys had swayed

To the Baroness of Blixen in rememberance of ...

Eugene Haynes and Isak Dinesen. Special courtesy
of Eugene Haynes

her in their direction), sometimes without speaking Danish for many months. She associated English with the classicism she had glimpsed through Denys. It kept her closer to the life she had known in Africa, at the same time that it removed her from the life she had returned to in Denmark.

When her manuscript *Seven Gothic Tales* was finally ready, publishers refused it.[19] She had chosen to write counter to the prevailing style of social realism, rightly knowing that she was best when working in the literary tradition of the *tale* which went back to Boccaccio and Chaucer. At the same time, her writing had the elegant sniff of the aristocrat and a disdain for the plain, while her rejection of current fictional modes recalled the spirit of the lonely adventurer. *Seven Gothic Tales* was baroque in style and was an artistic coalescence of the historical and cultural experiences which shaped Isak Dinesen. While it placed her firmly in the tradition of European romanticism in particular, a rebellious quality of the antiromantic ran through the tales.

Searching for a publisher, she decided to pack her valise and travel to England to see Lady Islington who could arrange for her to meet Constant Huntington of Putnam. At their luncheon meeting, Huntington listened politely, and after a few pleasantries, refused to read her manuscript, saying that there would be no market for a collection of short stories by an unknown author. Back home, upset and "wishing to be quite out of the world," her brother Tommy, anxious to help his sister, remembered Dorothy Canfield, a friend of the family and placed the manuscript in her hands when she visited Denmark; she in turn enthusiastically passed it on to her neighbor in Vermont, Robert Haas. He agreed to publish them, expecting only modest sales, unprepared for their success.[20] Worn out by the long food lines of the Great Depression, Americans, intrigued by distant aristocrats, were ready to be entertained by cataclysms of the Paris commune safely removed, the icy questions of *being* provocatively hidden behind a romantic veil of duels and masquerades, love entanglements and exotic countries.

In preparation for publication in Denmark, Tanne rewrote the tales into Danish, freely adding Danish references. When published at home, they were a failure. The claw of the Depression had laid hold of the Danes, with an unemployment rate reaching 40 percent, causing them, after too many years of knowing monarchy, to be affronted by the aristocratic hauteur of *Seven Gothic Tales*.[21] They were criticized as pastiche and having a false opaqueness; further, stolid Danes reacted against what was seen as perversity and decadence. Frederick Schyberg in *Berlingske Tidende* complained that

> there are no normal human beings in *Seven Gothic Tales*. The erotic life which unfolds in the tales is of the most highly peculiar kind. Men love their sisters, aunts their nieces, various characters are enamored of themselves, and young women cannot or will not bear children. . . . Augustus von Schimmelmann is separated from his wife because he is in love with her diamonds! Later an Italian smelling-bottle solves his complex. Morten de Coninck is in love with his ship, Fortuna, Baron von Brackel and Count Boris harbour feelings for a skull and an entire skeleton, respectively.[22]

But Tanne (who was always stung by criticism, bringing out old, yellowed copies written by unkind critics to show friends) had had her moment of triumph, inviting her brother and his wife for dinner, and in her chic evening dress made the grand announcement that her book had been chosen by the Book-of-the-Month Club.[23]

Seven Gothic Tales, completed within two years of Tanne's departure from Africa, was published in 1934 under the pseudonym Isak Dinesen; confused critics took her to be a man, and Constant Huntington wrote asking to have the tales by an unknown author for England. The *Tales* reflect the personal dilemma of identity which confronted the Danish author throughout her life (a dilemma reflected in her confusion, when it came time to sign a contract, over which one of her names to use) and is her imaginative resolution of the question "who am I," the circling literary glance of *Seven Gothic Tales* turning on an existentialist quest.[24] The answer resonates throughout in a romantic key, a revelation appearing in the aesthetic ideal of a *will to create* (in a neat sidestepping of the Nietzschean *will to to power*). The implications are clear: a possession of the self (i.e., through self-stylization) leads to possession of one's immediate reality, and by extension, the world. Like Yeats, Wilde, and Nietzsche, she was "stirred by the ultimate promise of art, the promise that one may achieve complete possession of oneself by becoming the author of one's own being."[25]

"Deluge at Norderney"—as do many of the tales—tells us more about the power of art. Calypso is a young girl whose uncle and guardian is interested in her only so long as he can disguise her as a boy, dressing her in soft, masculine cloth. Taking the knife to obliterate traces of the woman she is about to become, she steps before a mirror, catching a glimpse of nymphs and centaurs painted in an erotic revel. As she stares in the mirror, Calypso's reaction reminds us that art is capable of eliciting reflections that bring us into moments of instinctive recognition, fragile and intimate, yet filled with a "great harmony" that turns the self to great strength and power.

22.

An "African book"

"the most important book I have
ever published, and I believe that it
will take its place in the permanent
great literature of the world"

🐦 *Tanne had decided to settle in many kilometers from Rungstedlund at the local hotel in Skagen, a fishing village of sand dunes swept by the sea and a cold wind. Green and brown sails bobbed in the water, and fishing nets were set out to dry nearby as the moustached mail courier went about his route. At midday Tanne could be seen driving her blue car through the village, the small boys running alongside begging for a ride. As the afternoon darkness came on, she sat down to write her memoir of Africa, stopping to take tea with the neighbors and the hotel proprietor, Mrs. Ostergaard; the scowling schoolmaster made them laugh as he passed by.* [1]

On October 9, 1936—because of the painful memories of her African experience, she had not been able to write about her farm much before then—the newly acclaimed author wrote to her publisher, Robert Haas:

> Brøndums Hotel, Skagen
>
> Yes I mean to finish my African book and I have retired from the world
> to get it done, since in my brother's house it is very difficult for me to

get peace and quiet. If you can find a map of Denmark and will have a look at it you will see that the peninsula of Jutland to the North round (sic) into a point, and that the two Seas meet round it. I believe it is a unique thing in the world.[2]

The letter to her publisher suggested the importance she attached to being located exactly in place in a demand for self-clarity while she wrote her "African book."

Out of Africa, while appearing quite different from *Seven Gothic Tales* (the baroque style was replaced by the classic language of high tragedy), was actually a thematic extension of the artistic concerns she had raised earlier. Writing *Out of Africa*, she was able to realize the credo *Seven Gothic Tales* preaches: *Seven Gothic Tales*, written after Africa was lost to her, existentially questions personal being; the artistic response to "who am I" is suggested—"I am what I create myself to be."

On April 1, 1936, Tanne sent a peeved letter to Robert Haas:

Many thanks for your kind letter. I am writing my African book, but it is going very slowly,—first because I have had a small comedy acted at our Royal Theatre here in Copenhagen the day before yesterday, and the rehearsals have taken my time, secondly because I have not been well, I have got an inflammation of the jaw-bone, and shall have to go into hospital for a slight operation. All the same, my book is getting on, if only very slowly, and I am going to send you the second chapter of it in a fortnight. I believe myself that you will "see" it better, and like it better as it advances. But do not hurry me, I can not stand it. I am doing my best, and you will get it when it is ready.[3]

This letter was like so many letters that Tanne would send in response to Robert Haas's questions about how her writing was progressing.[4] He was always anxious to receive any work she might have for publication, but at best, Tanne was a slow writer. In Africa, her health had been broken by tropical disease and syphilis, and throughout her later life in Denmark illness of one sort or another would interfere with her writing. Here, Tanne talks about rehearsals for her marionette comedy, *The Revenge of Truth*, in addition to personal problems and illness (she told a neighbor that since her return to Denmark a third of her life was spent in illness), but there was an emotional exhaustion and loneliness that she attempted to alleviate by travels and a busy social life which interfered with her writing during her later years.[5]

By September 28, 1937, Tanne's publisher at Putnam's in London,

Constant Huntington, was able to write his opinion of *Out of Africa* to Robert Haas:

> Baroness Blixen's English style is based largely on the King James version of the Bible, and Shakespeare, Shelley and other classic English literature. There is also inevitably a slight foreign flavour which we have not tried to eliminate entirely. There are no colloquial English expressions and the style is quite as well adapted to America as England.[6]

The manuscript required considerable work, and Constant Huntington and Tanne corresponded almost daily for three months regarding necessary revisions. "Our method," wrote Huntington, "has been for me to call her attention to the need for change, and for her to provide the new version herself."[7] Tanne was a perfectionist and, noted Huntington, she attached importance to "matters of capitalisation . . . italics, punctuation, arrangement and form of quotations, etc, and actual changes in meaning from the original typescript."[8] A dispute between the two publishers arose when Tanne insisted that the English edition of *Out of Africa* be published in America. When asked by Putnam's to assume some of the editing costs, Robert Haas was disgruntled, pointing out that he had incurred considerable expense from the over 8,000 corrections his staff had already made in the manuscript.[9] Despite all of the editorial corrections necessary, Constant Huntington wrote Robert Haas that he considered *Out of Africa* "the most important book I have ever published, and I believe that it will take its place in the permanent great literature of the world."[10]

Tanne wanted *Out of Africa*, her second book, to be published in America under her own name, but Robert Haas discouraged the elimination of her pseudonym for reasons of publicity and reader recognition.[11] She wanted the book published simultaneously in England and America and was afraid that she might offend the American public when this became impossible. Robert Haas reassured her that "you are leaning backward, so to speak in your estimate of the amount of consideration due the American public. The fact is, as it seems to me, at least, that the American public knows absolutely nothing of when a particular book is published in England."[12]

The title presented another problem. Tanne wanted to call her book *An African Farm*, but was dissuaded by her publisher at Putnam's who thought it sounded too much like the title of Olive Schreiner's book, *The Story of an African Farm*—and indeed it was Schreiner's *African Farm* which provided an artistic lens for Isak Dinesen's literary vision, many of the ideas turning up in *Out of Africa*.[13] Claiming to have read Schreiner's story of a farm in South Africa when she was fifteen, Tanne noted that "out in Africa, the book was often in my mind; and, as I was riding on my farm, or camping, or away from it in the Masai reserve, I would think: 'This is like the place where Waldo sat and reflected upon life and death'; or: 'in such a morning did Lyndal and Waldo walk out together to feed the ostriches.'[14] Robert Haas suggested calling it *An African Pastorale* or *An African Dream*, while disliking her preference for *Ex Africa*. In correspondence it was referred to as *An African Tale* before being released under Tanne's title, *Out of Africa*.[15]

Tanne was afraid America might find the recollections of her African experiences dull and felt uneasy about her ex-husband's book, *African Hunter*, feeling that it might detract from her own book.[16] Because she did not want *Out of Africa* to be classed along with other travel and hunting books, particularly popular in the thirties, she refused to approve the use of woodcut illustrations then (presumably) used for such books. She liked the cover that was chosen, a green tapestry of jungle dotted with brightly colored animals reminiscent of a child's fantasy—there were pink and blue flowers, yellow elephants and a pink zebra, with the largest animal being a stork with pink wings whose yellow eye stared out at the reader. The cover suggested the imaginative style that would transform her African experience into fantasy, and Tanne was pleased with the choice.[17]

On February 6, 1938, Tanne wrote to Robert Haas that "Mr Huntington writes to me that the intellectual circles in England like it, but that 'the great governing class does not,' 'they think there is a lion in the streets.' "[18]

The irony was that a European feminine voice and sensibility had captured Africa, the Africa of wide, splendid spaces that present no stopping point for the human eye, a land so completely masculine in its beauty and its life, with its tribal chiefs and white hunters. Here was a land suffused in a dreaminess that suggested unbounded possibilities for being and action. Africa became a place of epic vistas where the possibility for heroic action and thought was played out against elemental forces, the Africa of paradise, delineated by the danger of finality, of tragedy and loss.

Self-mythology can be boring if it does not transcend its immediate self-interest, something *Out of Africa* does through a complex interplay of language that subtly engages all the senses. Her artistic triumph was in conveying a vision of nature that appears real and vital in its beauty, even as that beauty dissolves into a moving mirage on stage. *Out of Africa* is about the loss of that Africa of the imagination, the lyricism and rhythms of an Africa once known, then reinvented. Her artistic power is intensified by the evocation of that universal longing for a paradise won and lost—in an age that had lost its paradises once too often, a note of recognition was struck.

In America, *Out of Africa* was an immediate success, its choice by the Book-of-the-Month Club guaranteeing huge sales. There has been some wonder at the excitement Tanne felt when her book was chosen by the Book-of-the-Month Club, and it has been labeled a pathetic triumph.[19] It has also been suggested that perhaps she mistook it as a literary honor of high merit.[20] But there was another reason for the excitement. By April 15, 1938, Robert Haas of Harrison and Robert Haas, Inc. (later to become Random House) had sold 7,000 copies of *Out of Africa,* while the Book-of-the-Month Club had sold 92,000.[21] Such large numbers ensured substantial financial rewards and a wide audience. For Tanne, writing from a distant foreign country and whose first language was not English, this kind of recognition in America meant international acclaim. The Book-of-the-Month Club could mean the difference between obscurity and instant success.

23.

Occupation

1940: "The next two or three
years stand out by nothing but
their nothingness. . . . "

🐛 *Hitler sipped tea while watching Warsaw bombed in slow motion during a
screening at his home. He listened to Wagner operas with his advisers shortly before
Germany crossed the Polish border and World War II began. Creating a "cathedral of
ice," Albert Speer impressed the world with the military might of the Third Reich by
shining a galaxy of lights on German soldiers—"if you understand Wagner," Hitler
reportedly said, "you understand the Third Reich."[1]*

World War II crept slowly into Danish consciousness. The Danes
were completely unprepared to meet the Germans—when the first
German ship appeared on the Danish shore, the local police sent one of
their men out on his heavy-wheeled bicycle to investigate. When he
failed to return, another man was sent out and repeatedly throughout
the day different men followed, all of them disappearing.[2]

Germany, the old enemy of the Danes, occupied Denmark in April
1940, soon after the death of Tanne's mother; Tanne's brothers and
sister, protectively, took it as natural that she should have nearly all of

the inheritance.[3] Shaken by the loss of their mother, the Dinesen children broke out in family quarrels—for many years Tommy had found his sister's pride (and fame) made it almost impossible to disagree with her without angry retorts.[4] His sister's dislike of Elle's husband brought a further rift.[5] To reassure herself, the frail author had the fires set blazing in the thin iron stoves which cracked when heated; Old Pederson, who had lived at Rungstedlund since her childhood, gathered the wood at the back, offended when the other servants went out to gather more.[6]

The occupation was marked in the streets by a car covered with black cloth and skull and bones.[7] In Germany, the newspaper headlines proclaimed "Germany Saves Scandinavia." King Christian X had decided against resistance of a military sort, and that fall, in celebration of his birthday, the streets were packed with people in a show of strength, a small path cleared for cars and men on horseback. "The next two or three years stand out by nothing but their nothingness; they look, today," commented Tanne bleakly, "like the Coalsack in the firmament of time. The King in his proclamation had enjoined us to maintain an attitude of calm and dignity, a prize was set on lying dead, a penalty on being alive."[8] At first, because of the passive resistance of the Danes, the Allies believed that Denmark supported Germany.[9]

Upset at the restraint shown by their parents, a gang of boys in Aalborg began sabotage activities. Calling themselves the "Churchill-Club," they set fire to trains, destroyed telephone lines used by the Germans, and stole their weapons, then confused them by sending out false handbills signed in the enemy's name. Their activities made it into American comic strips, and the Allies gradually became aware that the Danes were not in complicity with the Germans. There were twenty-five sabotage strikes in 1940; by 1943 close to 1,000 were reported. Taking their impetus partly from the "Churchill-Club," an underground sprang up, weapons were illegally transported in baby carriages, bird feeders used as part of the underground letter route, "saboteur-nails" passed out to puncture the tires of pursuing cars, and instruction books printed up showing how to make explosives.

"As in the following months the Danish resistance movement fetched headway," recalled Tanne, "we all began to rise from our sham graves, drawing the air more freely and ceasing to gasp for breath."[10] Following the imposition of martial law, bloody fighting broke out, and scores of navy ships disappeared from the harbor, leaving German sailors stranded; railroads were blasted and German barracks and places of collaborators set on fire. Cartoons of Hitler being spanked by Stalin with a mallet were passed out, and illegal pamphlets of a pink sword slicing through a brown swastika circulated.

There were seven thousand Jews, and 94 percent were sent underground.[11]

Shortly before the occupation, Tanne had traveled to Berlin with a commission to report back as a war correspondent for the newspaper *Politiken;* her plans to continue on to Paris and London were stopped by the occupation. Another plan to travel to Mecca with Farah had fallen through.

On an unscheduled side trip she went to Bremen, where she experienced her first blackout, and made her way through the dark streets with an old porter clicking his tongue as he took her to register at police headquarters before going to her hotel. She was irritated by the food ration card which had been given to her to show at meals.[12]

For the first time since sailing to Africa in December 1913, she met with von Lettow-Vorbeck, now a general. He proudly took her to a park to view an elephant of red bricks with a medallion on its foot depicting his head. The English officers who had aimed at his gray hat in the African sand, he told her, after the war had sung to him the rousing "For he's a jolly good fellow." It would have been a fine thing, she told him, if they had met face to face while she was running transport for the opposite side in Africa.

In the streets of Bremen she heard the noise of factories and workshops at full capacity and saw the precision of the German language repeated in the marching soldiers of the Third Reich, the human soul transmuted by technology and the machine; it was the shaping of a triumphant will that was, decided Tanne, its great achievement. A German youth who told her that "The law is the will of our foremost leaders . . . [meant to] transform . . . [the people's] souls," had, said Tanne, "the last word."[13]

She ended by comparing the Third Reich to Islam, noting that Islam was greater because it served God, not a nation; Islam was made for an army on the march and its Paradise was a "fantasy" for warriors. She did not ignore the danger in the Third Reich, and pointed to the inhuman and fearful in a state that viewed the surroundings through mathematical lenses. But, a lover of paradox, she could not help saying that while the Germans stood in "a mighty shadow" whose reach was unknown, they were illuminated by their "own light."[14] After watching a propaganda film being made in Berlin's slushy streets, sand and fir trees piled high to look like the highlands of Scotland, she reduced the Third Reich to celluloid and "staged" them in her imagination: "Time and again . . . I have . . . seen the heroes of the Third Reich as they would appear in the makeup of film stars, in the wings."[15]

Her views and notes from that time were put aside with the occupation and forgotten until after the war when they were published as "Letters from a Land at War," in the fledgling journal, *Heretica*. The essay reveals that she was invited to meet the highest members of the Third Reich, indeed, said her secretary, Hitler himself. She accepted, then declined (later regretting her decision), aware of the political situation.[16] Her essay reflects an ambivalence about the Third Reich. She did not go as far as her idol, Pirandello, who offered his Nobel Prize medal to be melted down by Mussolini for his war arsenal. But her fascination with the military and codes of honor, and the sharpnesses honed on feudalism and the aristocratic elite brought out a certain admiration for the power of the Third Reich; in the same breath she defended the Marat de Sade, saying that "it does mean something when a man looks as if he had been painted by a great artist."[17]

Earlier, from Africa, Tanne had written her brother that "I come from Darwin's desert," as she equated human beings with cattle, appearing to laud eugenics, and the improvement of the human race in connection with patriotism, a glimmer of pre-Nazi thinking which D. H. Lawrence himself had suggested with his talk of northern races and blood ties.[18] This is not to say that Isak Dinesen was a Nazi, but rather that ideas such as evolution, progress, and the "cult of heroes" were in the air which Hitler took up and brutally exploited.[19] Those who looked down from an aristocratic pedestal were more likely to find themselves staring—comfortably or uncomfortably—at Hitler eye for eye.

Back in Denmark, away from the dirty, snow-covered streets of Berlin, the dangerous presence of a military enemy was felt by all Danes. With the battle so near, it was difficult not to suffer personally; German soldiers were everywhere and riled the Danish author by camping on her lawn. She reacted by working on a novel, *The Angelic Avengers:*

For my own part, in order to save my reason, I had recourse to the remedy which, for that same purpose, I had used in Africa in times of drought: I wrote a novel. I advised my friends to do the same, for it took one's mind off German soldiers drilling in gas-masks round one's house and setting up their barracks on one's land. When I started on the first page of the book, I had no idea whatever what was going to happen in it, it ran on upon its own and—as was probably inevitable under the circumstances—developed into a tale of darkness. But when in the summer of 1943 the German persecution of Danish Jews set in, and most homes along the coast of the Sound were housing Jewish fugitives of Copenhagen waiting to be got across to Sweden, I slackened in my work; it began to look crude and vulgar to me to compete with the surrounding world in creating horrors.[20]

In a letter to Robert Haas, Tanne wrote that the "German censorship was at its most severe" while she was working on her Victorian novel.[21] She noted the hidden references to the occupation of Denmark in *The Angelic Avengers;* the book had been inspired by Winston Churchill's comment that the Danes were like "the Gangster's canary birds."[22] Tanne was not alone in her veiled political rebellion against Germany; performances of the ballet at the Royal Theatre were attended by huge crowds who united in secret delight at the covert gibes against Germany.[23]

Her brother Tommy was actively engaged in the resistance movement, but his involvement was kept quiet and never discussed.[24] Later, his older sister liked to say her house was part of the underground, but in reality it was only almost used in this capacity once.[25] Despite their heated arguments, her brother Tommy rode over on his bike—often answering her unexpected calls—to keep Tanne company and commiserate with her about her financial problems. Because of the total isolation from the rest of the world during the occupation, Tanne was not able to easily attend to financial matters, and the resulting confusion caused her great difficulty with her taxes.[26] But she provided her brother with inspiration before he went back to the resistance movement, and he remembered feeling "a weight lifted for a little while from my shoulders when, during my visits to her, she showed me a glimpse of an entirely different universe, a world of visions and dreams, above space and time and this absurd, inhuman war."[27]

During the war, Tanne had become friends with one of her neighbors, the architect and historian Steen Eiler Rasmussen and his wife. Dressed casually, in a ragamuffin way, her body disappearing in old trousers and baggy sweater, she would cycle over to have tea and cakes with them.[28] Automobiles had replaced carriages along the Strandvej where Tanne and her sisters (her brother preferred sailing) first rode their bicycles back into the Deer Park, bodices neatly tucked into their long skirts as their father's brother, Uncle Lars, fumed at the audacity of young women and slapped his knee: "When I see a lady riding a bicycle it seems to me I damn well have the right to warm her bottom."[29]

Much of this time Tanne was very ill. Writing to her publisher the baroness attributed the development of her ulcers to the war; at the same time, she astonished him by asking for a fur coat and food packages containing things that were not easily available in Denmark.[30] He for his part thought of her as a "prickly pear."[31] But her neighbors saw none of her cantankerousness as she asked Rasmussen points of history.[32]

During one conversation, when asked by Rasmussen if she could repeat one thing in her life, what would it be, she replied, "to go on safari with Bror"; her ex-husband had died in a car crash, stirring old feelings and memories.[33]

Tanne was fascinated by the dollhouse Rasmussen had made for his daughters, a tiny replica of his own house. As the girls stared in astonishment, she told them how, after they were asleep, she would make herself small enough to enter the dollhouse. When they begged to know her secret formula, she replied, "Oh, a book has been written on that, but it has not yet been translated into Danish." The book was *Alice in Wonderland.* As the conversation continued and Tanne discovered that the dollhouse had no bathroom, she told Rasmussen's daughters that she had been in Rungstedlund with no bathroom before renovations. Then she had been without a bathroom in Skagen when she wrote *Out of Africa* and had so longed for one—and would not now long for a bathroom a third time in their dollhouse.

"She was very careful about gifts," recalled Rasmussen. One year she had given her mother a motorcar, and a doll was seated at the driver's wheel to show that Tanne would be on call as a chauffeur. To Rasmussen's daughters for Christmas she sent the gift of a tiny basin and miniature fixtures for a bathroom.[34]

Once she told Rasmussen about defying a German soldier. She had ignored the curfew to walk out in the dark night with a friend (Denmark was blacked out at night, the only light seen was from across the sound in Sweden). She denied feeling fear when a German soldier stopped them, even though she knew the possibility of being shot existed. In recalling the incident to her neighbor, she may have been thinking of the courage of Heloïse confronting the German soldiers in *Winter's Tales*.[35]

"The Heroine" is set in 1870, amid rumors of an impending war between France and Prussia. Called forward for interrogation, Heloïse pulls her skirt aside to avoid touching a German soldier. Offended, the soldier orders her to appear before him without her skirt, or she and the refugees with her will be executed. She refuses, and by her heroism, saves the people with her. Six years later, Frederick, one of the men accused of espionage, chances to see her perform in *Diana's Revenge*, causing a sensation as Diana by appearing on stage wearing nothing. "The Heroine" speaks for *Winter's Tales*: catastrophe is imaginatively posed, eliciting its own ironic resolution. The icy bitterness of winter is felt in Isak Dinesen's demands upon the individual faced with forces powerful enough to annihilate existence. What interests her is a grand defiance of that which seeks to disrupt a universal equilibrium—salvation is possible through the integrity of personal response. By insisting on defining one's being in an unrelentingly ideal way—an aristocratic way that at times goes beyond distinctions of class—significance is seized in a world that too easily diminishes the individual by an unpredictable grip.[36] Moral responsibility becomes ambiguous as strict observance of an idea, a code of honor, is expected, despite its effect upon human life; everything, even cruelty is excused, as the aristocratic response is exalted until it merges with the divine.

Winter's Tales, with characters perishing in rye fields and on ice floes, reflected the brutality of the war and her continuing despair. In "The Young Man with the Carnation," she revealed an unexpected problem:

> The idea of his fame augmented and intensified his despair. If in the past he had been unhappy, and had at times contemplated throwing himself in the river, it had at least been his own affair. Now he had had the glaring searchlight of renown set on him; a hundred eyes were watching him; and his failure, or suicide, would be the failure and the suicide of a world-famous author.[37]

But even here she objectified herself, her uneasiness at her fame as a writer becoming one of her character's problems and part of her role playing.

Once the tales were completed, it proved difficult to get them out of Denmark. Constant Huntington wrote to Robert Haas that "the British Legation in Stockholm, the Ministry of Information, and the

Red Cross have all been trying to help me get Baroness Blixen's stories from Stockholm."[38] Eventually by going across to Stockholm Tanne was able to have the manuscript sent out by the British Legation there.[39] At the same time, she let her publisher know that because of the political situation in Denmark, she would not be able to make any editorial corrections and that the manuscript would have to stand as it was.[40]

The Angelic Avengers appeared soon after, with a denial on Tanne's part of any political significance to the work, perhaps a result of her disappointment in her efforts at a first novel. Earlier mention of her work on a great novel appear in Tanne's correspondence with her American publisher—something The Angelic Avengers did not turn out to be.[41] She wanted to dissociate herself completely from it, calling the book "a highly illegitimate child," probably because it did not meet her aesthetic requirements, and would not consider publishing it except under the new pseudonym of Pierre Andrézel, "no doubt," said a critic, "a relative of an officer mentioned in Chateaubriand's Memoires."[42]

But it was the publishing figures for Winter's Tales which turned out to be "amazing," said Robert Haas, "for a book of this nature": the Book-of-the-Month Club had published 300,000 to start and Robert Haas 20,000.[43] Winter's Tales found its way into the popular reading of soldiers everywhere, having struck a responsive chord with its courage and cruelty; the narrator of "Alkmene" spoke for many when he said: "I saw and understood clearly that the forces amongst which I had been moving were mightier and more formidable than I had guessed, and that my own whole world might be about to sink under me."[44]

When the war finally ended, a new era in horror had been ushered in: Oppenheimer had made his Faustian pact with technological forces that reduced people to shades on stone. Hitler had exterminated 6 million Jews in the concentration camps, and almost as an afterthought, at least 9 million Slavs and Gypsies.[45] Another expert in horror, Joseph Stalin, the architect of the terror famine in Ukraine, would dominate the peace accords.

24.

Thorkild Bjørnvig,
Young Heretic

"It was like meeting a person of a
kind I had heard about in myth
and history. . . . "

 *After the surrender of Germany, Denmark—as Tanne had predicted—
experienced a resurgence of the arts, which indirectly provided occasion for intrigue in
the Danish author's later years.[1] Tanne collected a group of young, brilliant and
talented men around her, the Heretics and their friends.*

Her relationship with Thorkild Bjørnvig in particular would cause
gossip among the astonished Danes for many years to come.

Thorkild Bjørnvig rode his bicycle through the cold night to attend
a dinner and drink sherry at the Baroness von Blixen-Finecke's home.
He was exhilarated: the Baroness had written him that her niece, the
Countess Caritas Bernstorff-Gyldensteen, was "enchanted" by his
poems and wanted to make his acquaintance. Now seated at the dining
table next to the countess, he found her leaning over and whispering

that her aunt had insisted she read his poems before the dinner, but "I regret that I have not yet had time to read your poems. . . . Please, don't tell her that I haven't."[2]

The eye of the baroness had been caught by the dark-haired young man, who was, she observed a bit breathlessly, a "really beautiful poet." His solid bearing was pleasingly tempered by a boyish face which easily broke into a quick, infectious laugh. Contemplative, he had the sensitivity of mind and manner associated with romantic poets. For visits with the baroness he favored a loose sweater and tie with full trousers, which he wore modestly.

She adopted him as her protégé. They put their names to a written "pact" of friendship, inspired by the mystic and a "perfect trust"; the words of the marriage ritual, "Till death do us part," were used by the baroness to complete the pact.[3] While she smoked cigarettes and drank coffee, they talked about animals and vivisection, poetry, the cosmos and the war that had ended, the erotic principle and religion.[4] She confided to him her deep loneliness and mourned the loss of her steadfast servant, Farah. She was a severe master, insisting that he call up long passages of poetry from memory, and agreed to his request that she submit material to his new magazine, *Heretica*. "Write," she advised him, "because you owe the gods an answer."[5] Their meetings impressed him: "When I left her, whether in the intense light of the early spring evening or in rainy darkness along the seashore, I often felt intoxicated with a tremendous expectation of life greater than I had ever known before. It was like meeting a person of a kind I had heard about in myth and history."[6]

The *baronessen*—he addressed her in the third person—told him she was always available to him: he could reach her late into the night by throwing stones at her bedroom window. When he balked at her request to act as her escort to an embassy party or to carve their initials in a tree, she in a fury referred to the "white heat" of his "cowardice."[7] Dutifully, he carved the initials, and she stuck freesias in his hair, other times tugging playfully at his curls. She was sixty-four, he thirty-two when they met; inconveniently he had a wife and small son.

When she met his son, she kissed him ardently; the next day her protégé received a summons to Rungstedlund. Sitting near the fireplace, she explained that he should not worry, her kiss would not infect his son. When the young poet appeared confused, she told him about contracting syphilis as a young woman, a confidence which she used as a kind of secret rite in sealing her friendships, as a private initiation into a kind of sympathy and intimacy.[8] Using the old formal Danish she preferred, she concluded: "But it is no longer contagious; it is not harmful—to everyone except myself."[9]

Learning that he had gotten a concussion by hitting his head, she responded by claiming that at that exact moment she had lost patience with him and exclaimed: "May this blow strike the Magister on his head!"[10] Seemingly contrite, she invited him to come from the hospital to recover at Rungstedlund:

> Would you consider settling down here with the feeling that your stay is indefinite, as it sometimes was for guests on the old Russian estates? They might stay for a month, but it also happened that they stayed for ten years. That is the way you should feel about it, while you are here, and spend no thought on time."

He came, for three months, without his wife and child. She put him in the green room, with the flowered carpet and oaken furniture, where she stayed in the winter when the cold drafts drove her out of her own room.[12] Many days the baroness failed to appear, sometimes sending letters instead. Her housekeeper, Mrs. Carlsen, brought the young poet breakfast in bed; he read and wrote, and walked out alone by the woods and harbor.

She had invited Thorkild to stay, offering him the protection of the "lioness on the threshold."[13] She insisted on his going to bed by 9:00, unceremoniously escorting his wife out on one of her rare visits when she threatened to stay longer. Some evenings she played him records on Denys's old gramophone until he fell asleep. Their relationship, she told him dreamily, was a faint echo of the time she had been with Denys, in Africa. She ended up giving him the gramophone as a gift; another time she presented him with her father's coat, gotten in trade from the Indians in America. When she offered to leave him Rungstedlund after her death, he refused.

When he did the baroness's bidding by reluctantly going to Bonn on a study grant, she triumphantly played the "Marseillaise" on the old gramophone. Letters furiously exchanged between them repeatedly referred to their friendship "pact," and when it appeared that the Bonn trip was completely a waste to Thorkild's thinking, that he wanted to return to Denmark, the baroness tried to dissuade him, offering him in one letter a "Ritual for Choice."[14] The only good Thorkild was able to retrieve from the trip was a meeting with an Irishman who drank beer and often slept over, using some overcoats as a blanket and his briefcase as a pillow. After Thorkild wrote to the baroness that "In him," this redheaded bearded Irishman with freckles, could be seen that "the end has come long ago, so he laughs across the ruins, because he may as well laugh," she took a fancy to meeting the Irishman and in her large, spidery writing ordered Thorkild to bring him home.[15] When a junket to France undertaken at her urging—as part of his "education"—turned into failure, she chided: "So you thought you could go out and seek the holy grail with a perambulator, did you?"[16] She regarded his marriage as a hindrance to her plans for him, and to his destiny.

The baroness suspected her own predilection for megalomania, at times slipping into the role of the divine; quoting Heiberg, she reassured Thorkild, "Now if you have lost your faith in God believe in me, and I will give you shelter."[17] After rereading one letter in the privacy of her study, the baroness replaced the word God with "I."[18]

She spied on the young poet, going through his letters, and went into a rage when she discovered a letter sent to his wife by a friend ridiculing Thorkild's stays at Rungstedlund.[19] His wife Grete, losing in the fight over Thorkild's affections, went to the edge of suicide. With what Thorkild took to be the baroness's blessing—she was always looking to engage him in some great adventure—he fell in love with another woman.[20] He felt betrayed by the baroness as she treated the confidences of the lovers casually, telling others of their illicit romance.[21]

In a premonition of their final rupture, one day in front of the fireplace she unexpectedly turned to him and darkly asked: "Wouldn't you like to meet my good friend? Yes, my best friend, the Devil."[22] As she felt herself losing power over him, she called on the nether powers: during one conversation she stopped abruptly, silently pointing a revolver at the poet, then placed it on the table without a word. Her despair had turned the meeting sinister, as she sought control. Afterwards, they never spoke of it. Sensing the drawing to an end of their relationship, she cried to him in a dirge, "release me, release me."

She ended up fictionalizing their relationship in "Echoes," resurrecting Pellegrina, who meets the young boy Emanuele, a promising singer: "she sensed, as she had done before, the power of her beauty and her mind over a young male being, her heart cried out in triumph: 'I have got my talons in him. He will not escape me.'"[23] But he does.

On their last evening together six years after meeting, Thorkild felt that her exhortation—"Won't you get up on the broomstick with me?"—enacted itself out before his eyes.[24] He described a chilling Isak Dinesen greeting him in the white costume and mask of Pierrot, rather than the long elegant gown and jewels she usually wore.[25] The cigarette smoke drifted up around her chalk white face and dark red lips as she began a slow, sarcastic attack on their friends, and everything else, so that, finally, the "evening began," said Thorkild, "to resemble, most of all, a harsh satirical play." Despite himself, Thorkild was drawn into the vortex as he began "to laugh and let myself get carried along in a whirl of wild and hilarious and terrible irony; nobody looked normal, and nobody escaped. It was the perfect nihilism, or black mass."[26] The performance had its effect on Thorkild, who suffered from a stupor for days after, "a severe mental hangover." He never saw her again.

Pierrot had become for Isak Dinesen not the buffoonlike Pierrot of Tivoli, but a being whose sadness had crystallized into such an utter biting and ironic negation of the world that the spectre of nihilism was evoked—write of me the way you have written about Nietzsche,[27] "Darwin's child,"[28] she had told Thorkild Bjørnvig. Her Pierrot allowed for nothing sentimental, and was perceived as diabolically grinning in its white-facedness, at the same time that it lent her a mythic dimension. She had carried theatre to its penultimate in a private meeting, alienating through the sharpness of her performance. In her attempt to achieve the extraordinary among ordinary circumstances she overreached herself, plunging back into an even greater depth of loneliness.

25.

The Heretics

"my talent in life was one of
keeping a 'salon' "

🐝 *The Baroness Blixen invited the Heretics and their friends—wives and other
women were largely excluded—to her home for intimate dinners which might be
arranged around a special topic like Christianity.[1] Duck and pheasant were sent from
the large estates during hunting season, and new potatoes with parsley, hens and
horseradish, and Florentine cake were served to the guests. Fresh cod was bought even
during winter from the Rungsted fishermen who stood on the frozen sound at their
fishing holes as a ferry cut through the ice around them. In summer a bowl of strawberries, cherries, and raspberries stood on the table, and the air was filled with sweet
smelling bouquets of red cabbage, daisies, and gladiolas arranged by the elegant hostess.[2] The baroness wore long sleek gowns to these gatherings—one black dress with a
black hood she named "little Devil."[3] Her effect was one of contradiction, one Heretic
remembering an evening with her as "exhilarating," like an "evening at the theatre,"[4]
while another guest always left depressed.[5]*

The handsome young men who came to be identified as the
Heretics had reacted against World War II—political systems had

brought on the war, and the Heretics were suspicious of all systems. They were romantic, believing truth was found in the imagination and the creative act.[6] *Heretica*, the journal around which a literary movement sprang up, was one of the most significant in one hundred years. The influence of the Heretics—and those associated with them—upon Danish culture would be substantial, as they became the leaders of cultural life.

The impact that Isak Dinesen made on this group was enormous, as she validated and encouraged their perceptions of themselves as writers and artists. Her sympathy, support, and protection proved a heady experience for them, while her intellectual and literary achievements spurred them on in their own development.

Tanne would say: "Denys held that my talent in life was one of keeping a "salon," like those of Madame du Duffand or Mademoiselle de Lespinasse, and that my intercourse with the Natives fell under this definition."[7] Her relationship to the young Heretics had this same quality of the salon about it, a courtlike salon, tinged with eroticism and enhanced by the glamour of her international fame. She held court in the way she had in Africa—with unbridled authority and a great sweep of protectiveness. Her wit amused the Heretics, while her presence awed them: "Have you been to court?" became a common question among them.[8] When they failed to pay her proper homage, irritated, she called them "young puppies," and pointedly referred to the exalted place she had left to converse with them;[9] her literary reputation put her in contact with a wide range of luminaries, from the pope in Rome to the queen of Denmark, John Gielgud, Aldous Huxley (who was experimenting with drugs, to her disapproval) to Tennessee Williams (who fell asleep at their meeting).[10] Other times, someone out of favor would be left out of invitations until amends had been made.[11] New visitors to her door were carefully schooled by a servant to use the word baroness in addressing her.[12]

Conscious of herself as myth, Tanne convinced those around her that she had psychic powers and moved in the supernatural.[13] She appropriated an isolated independence that insisted on audacity, noting that before feminism there was a woman who "existed independently of a man and had her own center of gravity. She was a witch." On the power of the witch she cheekily continued: "One may suppose that for most men . . . a woman who can exist without a man certainly also can exist without God, or that a woman who does not want to be possessed by a man necessarily must be possessed by the devil."[14]

Witchcraft, recalled one friend, ran through their conversation like "a charming leitmotif."[15] When her brother shot a hyena in Africa, she told him, the tracks stopped abruptly; a woman's death was reported. Local belief told of old women becoming hyenas at night.

Denmark had lingered in pagan times and burned many witches, and once a year up and down the Strandvej bonfires burned in recollection of that time. Gustava Brandt, a boisterous and rakish poet—who, invited to a simple dinner at Rungstedlund, might show up in white tails and, like a character from one of her tales, a carnation—said to her, "if you had been a witch 200 years ago you would have been burned." Laughing, she replied in her deep, throaty voice, "yes, and you would have lit the pyre."[16] Gustava, mischievously, had thrown the household upside down by sending the baroness a bull calf on her birthday, boxed in a crate.[17]

With a deadpan mien, she told one story that had taken place in Africa. The Africans came to her: "We know you are a witch."

"Yes, yes, that's true."

"We know you are a very great witch."

"Yes, that's true."

They wanted her to kill the governor—"Are you sure, once a witch gives her word she can't go back on it." The next day the governor was reported dead. When friends asked how she had done it, Tanne replied, "As a witch I can't tell you."[18]

Another time Tanne called a friend to her bedside and told him of a woman who had complained to her about her husband's bad treatment of her. Tanne told the woman to go home and not worry, that everything would be all right. The woman called again, bringing asparagus as a gift and told Tanne's secretary to let the baroness know everything was all right, that fortune had changed and her husband was dead.[19]

By secretly spying, Tanne was able to convince the Heretics of her special powers of intuition, at the same time that she played with the young men as if they were characters she had created in one of her stories.

Ever the storyteller, Tanne—"a deep and dangerous little figure, consolidated, alert and ruthless"[20]—partly out of boredom, would manipulate and arrange the lives of the people she knew, in particular of the Heretics. If a marriage displeased her, she did not hesitate to intrude into the relationship destructively.[21] One friend, Aage Henriksen, noted his disillusionment at realizing that it was "your destiny to end up in one of her stories."[22] She was the all-powerful stage manager found in her tales, even having the portal outside her Rungstedlund home built to create the illusion of a stage. When the cedar trees outside died, she was consoled by realizing that the now wide-open expanse of lawn leading to her house conveyed the feeling of a stage.[23] When the baroness, unannounced, brought visitors to view Thorkild Bjørnvig at work in the green room, he noted feeling "as if [a] wall behind which I thought I was unseen and protected, suddenly turned out to be a stage curtain that had gone up."[24]

Ehrengard, a tale which Aage Henriksen suspected depicted his relationship to Isak Dinesen, is a masterpiece because it lyrically brings to fruition her aesthetic ideas.[25] At the same time, it is suggestive of the controlled relationship she had to the Heretics, and the way she perceived her artistic machinations.

When Isak Dinesen met Aage Henriksen in 1951 (for a time after their meeting he lived at Rungstedlund), he was in the early stages of beginning his career as the foremost scholar, critic, and philosopher in Denmark. He was writing a dissertation on Kierkegaard in which he argued that his novels created the fiction that a cosmic harmony existed, while at heart suspecting that it did not. Tanne, whose fiction had the same quality to it, was struck once again by Kierkegaard (she had read him in Africa) and they exchanged letters about his work, in particular the "Diary of the Seducer," which would influence her tale *Ehrengard.* A plan to use the title *Diary of a Seducer* for her romantic tale would fall through.[26]

Ehrengard is an adult fairy tale: Prince Lothar, after much hesitation (which threatens the lineage of the kingdom), marries a beautiful young woman, and a select circle learns that a child is expected long before the propriety of the kingdom demands. Cazotte, an artist and seducer, prepares to guard them and their secret at Rosenbad, a rococo hideaway he has specially prepared for them—and his own seduction of the lady-in-waiting, Ehrengard. Cazotte owes much of his conception to Kierkegaard, his temperament making him an aesthetic paradox.[27] He *observes,* while he seeks a reality that is lyrical, and possession of the beautiful. Beauty for him depends upon the yielding of reality to his overtures as he heightens the moment into a form which varies with the circumstance.[28] Through art (and careful calculation) Cazotte—as did Isak Dinesen—seeks to perfect reality by possessing it; the transformation that results is imbued with a poetic sensuousness.

In reading the tale, we can speculate about Isak Dinesen's views of her own manipulations as she interfered in the lives of those around her and sought, repeatedly, to control the Heretics, to seduce them (and others) through symbolic gestures, through a glance, request, or conspiracy—Cazotte himself aims to seduce Ehrengard spiritually, seeking his badge of victory in the *blush*.

Those who knew Isak Dinesen experienced her distaste for ordinary morality; her explanation for her own code (which did not shy away from the demoniac) might be said to lie in Cazotte's character: Cazotte's plans for the seduction of Ehrengard suggest the demoniac nature of the artist who must participate in all aspects of reality. If Cazotte can be suspected of evil, it is the demoniac evil of the artist who through his secret, unknown perceptions can deliver the known world away from those he comes in contact with; in striving for the imitation of a divine order, he ignores the possibility that he may bring about an unsettling and disturbing reversal of reality as it is understood by those around him, in particular in those seduced by him. Perceiving his relationship to Ehrengard through the erotic he seeks to possess life perfected through the expression of art; he recognizes the fleeting phenomenon of reality idealized.

This unsettling of people around her was a common trait of the baroness.

She had a way of pulling those around her off their feet and of intruding into the secrets of their lives that the Heretics and their friends rebelled against. Aage Henriksen, who visited Tanne for ten years, eventually fell away from her, as everyone did.[29] Their meetings, said Henriksen, "were quite ordinary," but then there were brief times that gave their meetings a sense of "sacred moments" during which was revealed the nature of life's deepest forces.[30] She tried to arrange love affairs for the married Aage Henriksen. He resisted, sending her a poem with a jade stone from one of his wife's necklaces, with her approval.[31] She did not give moral advice to the young men around her, but rather insisted that one's "passions were God in you."

At a last meeting with Aage Henriksen, she asked: "What do you really think of me?"

"You are greater than I am."

"Yes, that's true."

"Am I honest?"

"Am I honest?"

"No, but I did not demand that of you."

"Well, then, kiss me."

"No."

"Well, good-bye you stingy man."[32]

While the relationship with the Heretics was at times a tumultuous one (i.e., she withheld material from *Heretica* when the Heretics morally reprimanded her), their admiration and companionship sustained her in some very lonely years.

She had died many years earlier, she told them, and they were afraid she might not return from her walks to the edge of the sound.[33] They all tried, but failed to alleviate her despair.[34]

26.

A Grand Joke

"I am three thousand years old"

Tanne had met her secretary, Clara Svendsen, during the war, taken by her declaration that no human being meant as much to her as Byron; a Catholic, Clara had given the Danish writer an ivory crucifix belonging to her mother. When Tanne confided the details of her syphilis, Clara felt herself to be in the presence of a living martyr. Their relationship was a stormy one, with the illness-wracked baroness ordering Clara out of the house during arguments, which were witnessed by the Heretics or other visitors. But the baroness could be playful, participating in household games, dumping a glass of water on the head of an unsuspecting servant after a run through the house. Clara remained fiercely loyal, selling her watch to pay bills and standing in long lines during the war to buy cigarettes for her employer, taking on extra work after the war to make up for not always receiving her wages.[1]

Every summer for three months Eugene Haynes came to stay, bringing cigarettes for Tanne and bottles of whiskey for Clara. He stayed in Clara's thatched cottage in the village of Dragør, or with Tanne, who left a volume of Agatha Christie next to his bed each night.[2] When he first arrived, the Danish children, used to seeing only people of light coloring, followed him through the streets. He responded by telling them, "I plan to come here for many years and the novelty has to wear off."[3] Afterwards there was a knock on the door and flowers on the doorstep left by the children who never followed him again.

As a young boy, Eugene had worked as the stock boy in a St. Louis department store, Stix, Baer and Fuller, skimping on his lunch hour to play the cafeteria piano. Curious, Arthur Baer went out of his way to listen to his young employee, so impressed by what he heard that he sent Eugene to New York to study at Juilliard; because it was almost impossible for an eighteen-year-old black to cash out-of-town checks, Baer sent him cash weekly by registered mail. After hearing him play, the legendary Nadia Boulanger—before whom Stravinsky and Toscanini had bowed—accepted him as a student, saying sympathetically, "I know what you have to go through in America."[4] He played the concert halls of Europe, becoming part of the talented group of black expatriates like James Baldwin (whom he met in Paris) who had fled America. A concert in Carnegie Hall brought rave reviews, but no agent would handle him. In East St. Louis restaurants refused him entrance, calling to mind such performers as Billie Holiday, who sang in places that refused her entrance and insisted she use the back door.

When Eugene met Tanne in 1951 through a friend, Bent Mohn, he was awed, glad to have been prepared at soirées attended by Lillian Gish and Tallulah Bankhead. She suggested he call her Tania; he called her "lioness" and the last of the "femmes du monde." She in turn said that a bit of Africa had come to her, adding "Oh, how I miss the colors of Africa, the beautiful browns and beiges."[5]

One day after meeting him Tanne rang Eugene up and told him to meet her at the races: "Just ask for me when you get there." The stadium where the races were held turned out to be huge, and Eugene, exasperated, searched everywhere until he finally saw her. She responded: "Oh Eug-a-ne, how *clever* of you to find me."[6]

He escorted her to Paris; rumor had gotten about that the fabulously wealthy baroness was being escorted by an American musician, her lover. When *Last Tales* was published, with the story "Echoes," the literary world wondered who Emanuele was. Carl Van Vechten, his guardian in New York, asked Eugene if he was Emanuele.

"No," he replied.

"What a pity," answered Van Vechten.[7]

When Tanne gave an interview to *Life* magazine, saying she would not mind owning slaves, Eugene reprimanded her, noting that her fantasy—which had nothing to do with slavery as a harsh economic manifestation—would be misunderstood; she agreed with him.[8] But it was an idea which fascinated her. In "The Invincible Slave-owners," she was unrelenting in her depiction of the psychological masochism in a relationship that shifts its power and weakness in a reciprocal way; here is a story suggesting the form many of Tanne's own relationships took.

A beautiful young woman, Mizzi, dressed like a schoolgirl in white dress and pink sash—everyone thinks because of a cruel stepmother—attracts all of the young men to her, while her governess waits on her, somberly watching in her black silk dress and gold chain. One of Mizzi's admirers discovers that they are playacting in a cruel game of paradox:

> Very likely next year the parts would be interchanged; Lotti would be the slave-owner and Mizzi the slave. Lotti might then become an invalid lady of rank, in a bath-chair, since that role could be played without the jewels or feathers, the want of which Mizzi had deplored in the woods. And Mizzi would be the companion, demure in the plain attire of a nurse, patient under the whims of her mistress. It was good to think that they might still, then, in the forest, weep in each other's arms, and kiss like sisters.[9]

Even though the women are poor, they are seen through aristocratic eyes, as "partisans of an ideal, ever in flight from a blunt reality, the great, gentle ladies, who were incapable of living without slaves."[10]

But there was a mischievous side to Tanne which tempered her unrelenting attitude, a humor which was missed by the more serious minded of the Heretics, and her friends.[11] In a visit to Paris with Eugene and Bent Mohn, they went to the Left Bank, where a crowd regularly gathered to catch a glimpse of Sartre sitting in his favorite café; Tanne was interested in seeing Sartre, even though she had been disappointed when Sartre and his gloomy existentialism became popular after the war—the war had ended, and that, she felt, was cause for celebration.[12] Not knowing that Sartre no longer went to the café, Tanne stood with a crowd and waited, finally turning to the people around and announcing: "This is Bent Mohn, one of Denmark's most gifted and handsomest poets. You didn't meet Sartre, but the evening is not lost."[13]

"Bent," noted Eugene, "wrote poetry no more than that lamp."[14]

After a performance of the Mexican ballet in Paris, Tanne led a group of friends through the men's dressing room. She nodded, greeting the men in various stages of undress, some of them in the nude. Asked at a Parisian party what she would like, she replied a lot of old French countesses and lots of young men. Another time, she confused the young men around her by informing them that her foremost wish was to be "very young, very rich, and with the scent of a dog."[15]

In one infamous meeting with the young writers of Heretica, she astonished them by wearing her Pierrot costume. Frail, she stood before them in the white silky costume, the black skullcap and large plume of feathers rising above the deep lines creating a crepe mask of her face, accented by red painted lips and a flirtatious stare—a courtesan Pierrot, recalled one friend.[16] At her appearance, they fell into a stunned silence, moving away one by one. It was a grand joke they failed to understand.

Disappointed in their reactions, Tanne insisted on wearing the costume out to lunch with Knud Jensen, teasingly calling the eventual owner of the Louisiana Museum a member of the "cheese" family.[17] Then, still dressed as Pierrot, she posed for a photograph.

Beneath the veneer of mischief, Thorkild Bjørnvig understood her impulse to act Pierrot as an ironic negation of self, a playing out of the role of her character, Pellegrina.

Taking her impetus from a dislike for everything bourgeois, and in attempting to divert herself and others from the conventional, Tanne's impression on others could be grotesque, yet fascinating. The glamour of her international fame, her wit and intellect, together with her flair for the theatrical caused her finally to be experienced not as a human being, but as an intriguing cultural phenomenon.[18]

"I am," she liked to say, "three thousand years old"—three thousand years of history had gone into shaping her.

27.

"Amaze me?"

🐛 *With Clara, Tanne traveled to Rome in 1957, at the invitation of Eugene Walter. The year before, said Walter, "she wanted to see a typical mountain town" to use for a story she was writing.¹ He had taken her to lunch with the Duke and Duchess of Sermoneta in their "mediaeval garden at Ninfa."² Afterwards they had climbed the hills to Sermoneta, which became the setting for "Echoes." Tanne had agreed to return to Rome if Walter could promise her as good a time; in response, Walter decided to fete her return visit with a special Festival of the Two Monkeys, held on three successive evenings.*

The first evening they went over to the Isola Tiberina, in an apartment that had once served as a morgue; yellow roses decorated the stark, white room with low ceilings. One guest remembered that the room would be used by Antonioni in *L'Aventura*, and that "the couch and low coffee table by which the heiress and her lover meet in the film while her girl friend waits outside, are the same at which we sat and talked."[3] Prince Henry of Hess was among the guests, and artists milled around with their protégés.

The second evening of the festival was held in the Palazzo Caetani, and red roses were everywhere. A marionette play was performed, with one puppet dressed in imitation of Tanne, in a fox stole, real diamonds, and a green hat made of parrot feathers, loudly denouncing all "facts," delighting the famous author.[4] After the performance, the host's small daughter, dressed in gold leaves, led the baroness to a room which was, recalled one guest, "filled with tiny gifts for her: cups and saucers painted with butterflies, a crystal pendant from a dwelling of George Sand, candied violets in a cloisonné box."[5]

The last evening was arranged at the living quarters of the Princess Brianna Carafa d'Andria; bouquets of pink roses were brought in to match the rosé punch. An Italian pianist made some unexpected discoveries at the British Museum and played from the rare manuscripts of some Albinoni sonatas, the baroness's favorite French songs were sung by an American soprano, and the Afro-Cuban singer Wanai was there, the room filled with her Caribbean songs.[6]

Particularly in the last decade of Tanne's life, there came to be an implicit understanding between her and her friends, that might have been expressed as Diaghilev's remark to Cocteau, "Amaze me." Capable of the extravagant gesture, the Danish author elicited the same from others. In "Babette's Feast," a tale about the servant of two sisters who spends all of her lottery winnings on the ingredients for an extravagant French meal, such a gesture is meant to evoke immortality by being part of a grace and harmony which is the province of the great universal imagination. The tale reflects the attitude of the aristocrat who understands abundance and romanticizes poverty, making it possible to poeticize everyday experience by ignoring the practical; the tale becomes her aristocratic defiance of bourgeois limitations. (Originally written because she had been told that Americans liked food, Tanne submitted the story to Ladies' Home Journal, only to be told that her reference to esoteric foods was beyond the understanding of their ordinary reader.)[7]

Tanne had recently been quite ill, and a second spinal operation had been performed to sever nerves to ease her pain.[8] She ate little, causing a stir by only taking a bit of asparagus, oysters or grapes, and champagne. Her weight went to seventy-seven pounds, and she was diagnosed as having concentration camp symptoms of malnutrition, with what she said was a "terrible swelling of my feet, legs, and hands";[9] her repeated illness (her health had broken in Africa) from lingering vestiges of the syphilis, from much of her stomach being operated away for ulcers, and a disinterest in her own physical being,[10] all made it so she could not—or would not—eat more.[11] Forced to have blood transfusions and intravenous feedings, she gleefully reported after one transfusion that the vigor she felt meant the blood coursing through her veins must be from a young football player.[12] About her book *Anecdotes of Destiny,* just published, she said that "It is with this book as its author—it should be somewhat fatter to look like anything."[13]

She had another project in mind, a novel composed of about 200 tales, with the title *Albondocani,* taken from the masquerading Caliph Haroun al Rashid of the *Arabian Nights.* Some of it was used in her *Last Tales,* published a year later; her plan was to finish the book right before her death.[14] In *Last Tales* she had firmly decided that in a reality often experienced as precarious, salvation lies in the art of the story; the story is capable of transcending the immediate and particular to the infinite and eternal. To be more specific: when one's individual existence is questioned and its significance unclear, the *story* attests to the experiences and events that have contributed to a human life; the self creates by living through the dimensions that constitute a story, and through creating becomes part of the universal and divine. When the cardinal in "The Cardinal's First Tale," responds to a woman's silent question of who is he with a concommitant "who are you," he is asking for proof of her existence, and is implicitly soliciting proof for his own, and for all human existence. For Isak Dinesen, the "design" of the story, and by extension, the role of the storyteller, provided the grand gesture which could defy a shifting and disconcertingly pliable reality.

Often in pain, she would lie flat on the floor or in bed, dictating the tales to her secretary, Clara, moving forward through what she called "boar plowing," starting a page and then going back.[15] A skilled craftsman, some of the stories she went over fifteen times, giving great attention to the simplest words.[16] Occasionally she was sidetracked. Never frugal, she was interested in making money to ease her bills and had started catering to the magazine market with such stories as the curdling "Uncle Seneca."[17] But most of her tales were the kind that would cause Robert Langbaum to risk his literary reputation early in his career by undertaking an analysis of her work; his work did much to further her reputation in the States.[18]

By now she was so famous that writers tried to imitate her work, and when Kelvin Lindemann engineered the press releases to make it look as if the author of his book, *An Evening in the Cholera Year*, was the baroness, she became upset enough to threaten to stop all writing.

In the end, she vanquished Lindemann.

Dressed in a great big bearskin of a coat, the baroness stepped out of a cab with Clara and Eugene Walter. The driver, puzzled, remained behind the wheel on the small bridge spanning the Tiber. Traffic was stopped up for at least two blocks behind, and Italian curses filled the air. The trio held on to an edge of Lindemann's book, and, oblivious to the commotion around them, recited:

> Rat shit,
> Bat shit,
> Three-toed sloth shit,
> Tiber and Oblivion
> Receive this book and its author![19]

The "magic" had its effect: soon after Lindemann died.

That same year, 1957, Tanne received a call in the middle of the night that told her the Nobel Prize was to be awarded to her; the next day she learned that the prize was not hers because of political considerations.[20] Three years earlier when Hemingway had won the Nobel Prize he had not forgotten Blix's wife and listed her with several others that should have won the award instead.

28.

America, 1959

"a hunter beckoning with a riding
crop, or as of an actor in the role
of Prospero motioning this or that
airy creature into existence, or
perhaps back out of existence"

*Invited by the Encyclopedia Britannica to come to America in 1959 to make a film
telling one of her tales, Tanne decided to make the trip. A cartoon in the* New Yorker
*heralded her, two beatniks walking down the street discussed her upcoming appearance
at the YMHA.*

To her appearance at the YMHA Tanne was escorted by the young
poet, William Jay Smith. She looked ravished, her face accented by eyes
darkened with kohl and lips painted red; in the streets of New York
people turned round to stare at her.[1] The sense of dramatic presence
she had finely honed in Africa was evident, despite her physical weakness. When she first saw the audience, recalled Glenway Wescott, she
turned and stretched "her fine-boned arm in a gesture of some
singularity—as of a hunter beckoning with a riding crop, or as of an
actor in the role of Prospero motioning this or that airy creature into
existence, or perhaps back out of existence—we all spontaneously
stood up and acclaimed her."[2] When she left the auditorium, Tanne

was in a wheelchair and dressed all in black, holding roses in her arms.[3] At the end of March the papers announced her third appearance, by demand.

Carson McCullers, who saw Tanne give a speech at the American Academy and National Institute of Arts and Letters (to which Tanne had been elected), commented that "She was very, very frail and old but as she talked her face was lit like a candle in an old church. My heart trembled when I saw her fragility."[4] At her request, McCullers arranged a meeting with Marilyn Monroe at her country home, and the Danish author was entertained by the breathy actress telling of drying noodles with a hair dryer, her husband Arthur Miller listening at her side.[5] Marilyn Monroe had caught the attention of Tanne because of her popularity in Denmark; Monroe fascinated the feminists with her self-creation, with her development of female vulnerability and sexuality until it had become a power in male relationships.[6] Not forgetting her own similar creation, when she heard Maria Callas on the stage, she exclaimed, "I have created her as Pellegrina, she is truly Pellegrina."[7]

New York's socialites vied among themselves to fete the famous author, and Eugene Haynes arranged for Tanne to be hosted at the first party given, by Carl Van Vechten.[8] At the different gatherings, Tanne met Marianne Moore and e. e. cummings, and the Sidney Lumets entertained her in their penthouse. After Tanne—who was only sampling an occasional oyster and asparagus—ate a hearty soup at one of the parties, Clara and Eugene were afraid she would keel over.[9]

Parmenia Migel had befriended Tanne after asking to do some translations of her work; now Migel and her family looked after the famous Danish visitor. A force in the ballet world, Migel would end up entertaining Paloma Picasso and acquiring the Stravinsky-Diaghilev papers. Her observation about Tanne was that she "always liked a surplus, an excess, the feeling that more power was hidden than was visible on the surface";[10] she had taken Tanne to French restaurants where the baroness would order a huge, expensive feast, then eat nothing.[11] The Danish writer was urging Parmenia Migel to write her biography.

Because Tanne had specifically asked to meet Nobel Prize winner Pearl Buck, Parmenia Migel arranged a meeting between the two. Pearl Buck arrived dressed in a grayish-blue suit and flowered hat. The baroness made her entrance to the meeting late, dressed in a black hat made of black ostrich feathers, long black gloves, black silk stockings, and holding a long black cigarette holder, which she lit, but didn't smoke. Then the baroness began to talk, without a pause. When it was time to leave, she gave a slight nod to Pearl Buck; downstairs in the taxi she turned to her companion and asked: "Tell me, was that Pearl Buck?" When she was remonstrated with "You know it was," she replied: "Yes, yes. I suppose it was. She didn't say anything."[12] After the baroness left, Buck had said nothing, except to comment on the arrangement of the blue lilies downstairs.

The time she met Tchelitchew—himself acting out a forlorn Pierrot—bets were taken on who would outtalk the other; but he dominated.[13] Tchelitchew had repeatedly drawn the angular lines of Sitwell's face and the baroness asked that he do her portrait, but was refused. Edith Sitwell had spread word that she was reincarnated as Queen Elizabeth; privately, the baroness regretted that in Denmark it wasn't possible to be reincarnated as Queen Elizabeth, and that the Danes paid her little respect.[14]

For a while she stayed at the Cosmopolitan Club in New York, irritated by the uniformity of the women. A letter had been misplaced there, sent to her by Tommy telling her that their sister Ellen was dying.

There was film talk about *Out of Africa;* Truman Capote started the rumor that Greta Garbo was coming out of retirement to play Isak Dinesen. After meeting Truman Capote, Tanne had agreed to write an introduction to his stories; he called her book on Africa one of the most beautiful of the century. But Tanne came to feel betrayed by him and Avedon after the famous photographer took a harsh picture of her.

When Tanne asked to go to Harlem to hear jazz, Eugene Haynes discouraged her, noting that the Harlem she wanted to see was a "storybook Harlem" that didn't exist.[15]

All of the meetings, appearances, and festivities took their toll on the emaciated Tanne, who ended up in the hospital from malnutrition and exhaustion.

29.

Finale

🐛 *Back in Denmark after her success in America, Tanne now had great difficulty walking, slowly making her way down the stairs to sip tea and take a little to eat, sitting with Clara in front of the fire. Tanne would delay returning to her room saying, "I must smoke one more cigarette," which became many more; the smoking may have contributed to the mask of lines on her face (as did the African sun and syphilis).[1] The appearance she made as an old woman disturbed her, and she had complained to Parmenia Migel about her reflection in the mirror.[2] But in her art she converted her personal distress, saying that "In the faces of . . . old women a hundred delicate wrinkles screwed up cheeks and chin into a baroque, beaming mask— and they were no longer scars left by the warfare of life, but the traces of many laughters."[3]*

Back home, the attempt to please her continued.

A rose appeared on her doorstep every day from a secret admirer. The admirer—Bent Mohn—arranged for a muscular sailor named Leif to carry her up the stairs to a party. "I chose him for the sake of contrast," recalled Bent, "big and strong, and had him waiting in the street when . . . Tanne arrived in a cab. In order, I guess, both to show his strength and because it is really easier, the sailor chose to run up the stairs."[4]

Tanne responded with delight: "I was sitting on his arm like a small bird on a branch."[5]

To Viggo Kjær Peterson, a new young friend, she confided that care would have to be taken so he wouldn't break away from her like all the others.[6] Her demands with the Heretics had been so overwhelming at times—she would expect someone to travel with her to Italy or France on one day's notice—that her publisher Ole Wivel, himself a leader of the Heretica movement, would lie on the floor of his home to escape her when he spied her frail but overbearing figure through the window.[7]

At a visit Viggo and Tanne made to the small, intimate Royal Museum (where the mad Danish king had distractedly walked the stage), she positioned herself in a chair, flirtatious, so he could be seen from every angle, "like on a stage," remembered Viggo.[8] During a discussion about whether life could be expected after death, they wondered how she could best let him know if indeed there was; she concluded that being too weak to move a table, she would have to send a different, easier, signal back.[9]

With Tommy she had visited her old military friend, von Lettow-Vorbeck (who had opposed Hitler), and listened to him replay World War I; with a few strategic changes, he gave the victory to Germany. The year before she died, the baroness sent him flowers and a kiss on his birthday; the next kiss, replied the ninety-year-old general, she would have to claim in person.

A project that had preoccupied her was raising enough money to turn Rungstedlund into a bird sanctuary, to keep the cement pavements from running over it. In one of her popular radio talks she asked everyone to send 1 krone as part of her campaign to raise money for the sanctuary; to her relief, the campaign proved successful.

On the side of the desk in her study hung a framed map of her African farm and the Ngong Hills, and the few letters from Denys were in her desk. Every night she went to her study to look at the map and to stare at the photograph of Denys; until her death she would perform this same nightly ritual, looking south, in the direction of Africa.[10] In her will she left 100 shillings to each of the Africans from her farm still alive.

Epilogue

In Shadows on the Grass, *her sequel to* Out of Africa, *we have the closest version of how Tanne viewed the place of death in her life:*

> At times I believe that my feet have been set upon a road which I shall go on following, and that slowly the centre of gravity of my being will shift over from the world of day, from the domain of organizing and regulating universal powers, into the world of Imagination. Already now I feel, as when at the age of twenty I was going to a ball in the evening, that day is a space of time without meaning, and that it is with the coming of dusk, with the lighting of the first star and the first candle, that things will become what they really are, and will come forth to meet me.

> The unruly river, which has bounced along wildly, sung out loudly and raged against her banks, will widen and calm down, will in the end fall silently into the ocean of dreams, and silently experience the supreme triumph of Unconditional Surrender.[1]

Death became a final and transcendent equilibrium, an imaginative surrender.

Isak Dinesen—known to Danes as Karen Blixen—died of starvation in the late summer of 1962, September 7, almost to the day that Mama had died so many years earlier. Her international reputation as a writer was assured; the myth she had created—personality observed as "play or theater"—continued to absorb people as if she were alive.[2] Despite a life of emotional upheaval and personal tragedy, shortly before her death she could tell her brother Tommy that she had been blessed by a happy life. As early as Africa, she had said that even if she died on a dung heap, she would believe in the beauty of life.[3]

Her own life, she later added, might "perhaps have some interest as a document to clarify the principles underlying the ditches and the trip around the lake and that produced this particular stork."[4]

Notes

Chapter 1

1. Isak Dinesen, *Out of Africa* (New York: Vintage Books, 1972), 11.

2. See Bror von Blixen-Finecke, *African Hunter*, F. H. Lyon, trans. (New York: Alfred A. Knopf, 1938).

3. *Out of Africa*, 11.

4. Elspeth Huxley, *White Man's Country*, (London: Chatto and Windus, 1935, new ed. 1953), 1:61

5. Ibid., 1:4–5.

6. Ibid, 1:254.

7. See Elspeth Huxley, *Mottled Lizard* (London: Chatto and Windus, 1962).

8. *White Man's Country*, 1:256.

9. Errol Trzebinski interview, Mombasa and London, 1983.

10. David Kronberg interview, Boston, 1985. While ill, Lord Delamere read books on science and Darwin. He was mesmerized by science, early on ordering an x-ray machine when it was still considered a hoax. See *White Man's Country*, vol. 1.

11. Isak Dinesen, *Letters from Africa*, Frans Lasson, ed., Anne Born, trans. (Chicago: University of Chicago Press, 1978), 171.

12. Isak Dinesen, *Seven Gothic Tales* (New York: Vintage Books, 1972).

13. Ingrid Lindstrom interview, Mombasa, 1983.

14. *White Man's Country*, 1:10.

15. See Charles Miller, *The Lunatic Express* (New York: Ballantine Books, 1973).

16. White Man's Country, 1:26.

17. Ulf Aschan, *The Man Whom Women Loved* (New York: St. Martin's Press, 1987), 36.

18. *Letters from Africa*, 1.

19. Karen Blixen Archives, noted by Judith Thurman, *Isak Dinesen: The Life of a Storyteller* (New York: St. Martin's Press, 1982).

20. *Out of Africa*, 23.

21. *Letters from Africa*, 2.

22. Isak Dinesen, *Daguerreotypes and Other Essays* (Chicago: University of Chicago Press, 1979), 93.

23. *Letters from Africa*, 2.

24. *Daguerreotypes*, 93.

25. Ibid., 92.

26. *Out of Africa*, 11.

27. Parmenia Migel Ekstrom interview, New York, 1981.

28. *Letters from Africa*, 1.

29. Ole Wivel interview, Copenhagen, 1980 and 1981.

Chapter 2

1. Thomas Dinesen, *Boganis* (Copenhagen: Gyldendal, 1972), 26.
2. Isak Dinesen, *Last Tales* (New York: Vintage Books, 1975), 249.
3. Martin Green, *Dreams of Adventure, Deeds of Empire* (New York: Basic Books, 1979), 328.
4. The facts of the Dinesen family history are drawn primarily from Thomas Dinesen's *Boganis*. He would write that fourteen of his ancestors had fallen in the battle at Ditmarksen in 1500, and that as early as 1286 an ancestor, Stig Andersen, had been part of the group of men who had murdered the notorious womanizer, King Erik Glipping. The incidents surrounding the king's death are part of folklore, and contemporary Danish authors are still producing fictionalized versions of what really happened (Helle Bering-Jensen interview, Medford, Mass. 1982). Dinesen's "The Fish" is her own imaginative version of the events leading to his death.
5. Isak Dinesen's sister, for example, in World War II exclaimed at the stunning beauty of the lights of combat against the night sky (Viggo Kjær Petersen interview, Copenhagen, 1981, and Minneapolis, Minn., 1985).
6. See *Letters from Africa.*
7. *Out of Africa,* 18.
8. *Boganis,* 18.
9. See "Copenhagen Season," in *Last Tales,* 257.
10. See *Boganis.*
11. It is here worth noting an editorial correction to "Sorrow-acre" which Clara Selborn (formerly Svendsen), Isak Dinesen's secretary, drew to my attention in a letter dated August 1982:

"The section between the red brackets was *added* when Karen Blixen *rewrote* SORROW-ACRE in *Danish*—then introduced into the British edition—but it never was included in the American edition and is also lacking in the edition at present distributed in Great Britain by University of Chicago Press because that is a reprint from the American edition."

In addition, she notes: "If you ever come across the anthology where J. Billeskov Jansen says in his introduction that *Sorrow-Acre* was shortened from the English version, you'll know that it's the other way about." (Isak Dinesen would at times want to include something new in a tale, running into difficulties because of publication deadlines.)

Editorial correction to "Sorrow-acre":

'You are young' said the old Lord. "A new age will undoubtedly applaud you. I am old-fashioned, I have been quoting to you texts a thousand years old. We do not, perhaps, quite understand one another.

['But if, to your ears, my orthodoxy does now sound antiquated, remember that within a hundred years both mine and your own speech will sound antiquated to the generations then discoursing upon word and life. Have patience, let me explain myself to you.

'Believe me, I have the public welfare as much at heart as you yourself. But should we, in our concern for *le bien commun,* gaze only at those human beings who happen to be about us today, and look neither before or after? When we consider the matter rightly we will find the past generations to be in majority—Well,' he interrupted himself, as Adam made a gesture of impatience, 'let them rest, as they deserve to. But the coming generations, you will agree, must be ever in majority. And when we speak of the welfare of the many we must needs let them have the last word. King Pharaoh, I have been told, made a hundred thousands of his subjects slave for him, and suffere (sic) great hardships, in order to build him a pyramid. He might at the same cost, have distributed bread and wine amongst his people, have fed and clothed them, and have been blessed by them. Still even so things would have been with them, today, what they are now: they would all be dead and gone. And a hundred generations have, since the days of King Pharaoh, lifted their eyes to the pyramids with pride and joy, and acclaimed them their own. A great deed, my nephew,—be it even brought forth with tears, aye with blood,—is a fund of resource, a treasure for the coming generations to live on, it is, within hard times and the hour of need, bread to the people.

'But the true insight into these matters,' the old Lord went on, 'you will never find, and can never reasonably expect to find, with the common people, to whom the chief concern in life is their daily bread, and who are living, mentally as well as physically, from hand to mouth. Nay, my nephew, it is our affair and our responsibility, we, who have inherited from the past and who know that we are to live on, in name and blood, through the coming centuries. These humble peasants, whose life is one with the life of the earth, and of whom you have spoken with so much fervency, what good are we to them but this: that they may trust us to look after le bien commun, not at the moment only, but in the future? And see you now, my good nephew, you and I may find it a little difficult to see eye to eye.]

But with my own people I am, I believe, in good understanding.

12. Aage Henriksen interview, Humlebæk, Denmark, 1980 and 1981, and Minneapolis, Minn., 1985.

13. "The Aristocrat," from the private papers of Aage Henriksen.

14. Dagmar Alvilde came from a military family that liked to give the impression it was noble by using "von" before the name of Haffner (a tenacity inherited by her granddaughter who would hold on to the title of baroness long after her marriage to Baron Blixen-Finecke had ended). Her mother, Anne Margrethe Kaasbøl, had been born to wealthy parents but became an orphan when her mother died, the father too insane to take care of her. Her life took a fatal turn when as a fifteen-year-old girl she was sent to the home of a clergyman; John Wolfgang, the clergyman's brother-in-law, used his nineteen-year edge over Anne Margrethe to seduce her. He moved her to a small farm and kept her as his mistress while he prospered, becoming the owner of a large estate and moving up in military rank to lieutenant-general. In the church book where important parish events are recorded, is found:

Dagmar v. Haffner
Father: General v. Haffner
Mother: Miss Anne Margrethe Kaasbøl

A heavy line is drawn through the name Miss Anne Margrethe Kaasbøl and firmly written instead is "Generlinde v. Haffner." On Dagmar Alvilde's christening day, Johan had finally married the woman who had stoically borne him three children out of wedlock, the woman he had seduced eight years earlier. Two sons born before the marriage became generals, while a daughter born later became the temperamental Countess Frijs. Johan Wolfgang for his part never became entirely reconciled to his wife, leaving her penniless when he died. Despite this unfortunate history, Thomas Dinesen always maintained that his older sister Tanne inherited her famous unbending will from this great-grandmother, Anne Margrethe. (See *Boganis;* also, a private letter to Parmenia Migel Ekstrom, January 18, 1968.)

15. "The Aristocrat."

16. *Last Tales,* 255.

17. In the center of town was the intimate Royal Court Theatre where the short frail Christian VII had strutted about in Voltaire's *Zaire,* convinced in his madness that his subjects would believe he was as powerful as the role of Orosmane he acted; his antics were not lost on later generations—in Tanne's early notebooks neatly typed out in French would be the play *Zaire.* (Karen Blixen Archives, Royal Library, Copenhagen, Denmark; information about Christian VII provided by Kirstian Vang in an interview at the Royal Court Theatre, Copenhagen, Denmark, 1980.)

Isak Dinesen was fully conscious of the significance of Christian VII's desire to play a role for which he was completely inadequate. In "Converse at Night in Copenhagen," she refers to the king's plight: "The Soudane Orosmane himself can here—as he has never before been able to, as, alas, he will never be able to again—sink his lofty burden of grief, incomprehensible to the common mortal, into human hearts, into the hearts of a poet and a whore" (*Last Tales,* 323–24).

18. All of the artists had sailed out with flowers and flags to greet Thorvaldsen when the sculptor returned from Rome, sparking a renaissance of the arts. (Reported by Hans Christian Andersen, *The Story of My Life* [Boston: Houghton, Osgood & Co., 1880] and by August Bournonville, *My Theatre Life,* Patricia McAndrew, trans. [Middletown, Conn.: Wesleyan University Press, 1979].)

19. See *Boganis,* ch. 5.

20. Anne Kopp interview, Folehave, Denmark, 1981.

21. *Last Tales,* 262.

22. Parmenia Migel Ekstrom interview, 1981.

23. *Boganis,* 42.

24. Ibid.

25. *Last Tales,* 271–72.

26. See *Letters from Africa.*

27. *Last Tales,* 260.

28. Isak Dinesen, *Ehrengard* (New York: Vintage Books, 1975), 16.

29. *Last Tales,* 263.

Chapter 3

1. Visit to Rungstedlund.

2. See Wilhelm Dinesen, *Paris under Communen* (Copenhagen: Gyldendal, 1968).

3. In "Copenhagen Season," this rumor became a fiction, Tanne imagining her father deeply longing for his cousin, stopped by her noble breeding, while the character of the cousin desires, aristocraticlike, "a greater audience" to applaud her actions and appearance. Tanne's brother Thomas would respond that the story reflected more his sister's character than the father's (*The Life of a Storyteller,* 403–4).

4. Critics and biographers have described Wilhelm Dinesen as going to America out of his own personal feelings of sadness and disillusionment. While this is in part true, he nevertheless was very much part of a national political disenchantment that manifested itself by large groups of Danes leaving for America—much as his daughter followed the stream of Europeans to Africa.

This interest in emigrating reflected the political and economic changes that Denmark had undergone in a little over 100 years and marked the change in attitude of Europe toward individual human rights. As late as the mid-1700s Frederick V (who, it was said, had been raised with a twin boy from among the common people) had sent out a "general order regarding emigration to foreign colonies in America," warning anyone who offered "flattering temptations and malicious seductions" for people to emigrate. Not only was Denmark anxious to keep its people at home (except for an occasional criminal sent abroad), much of Europe felt similarly.

By the end of the eighteenth century, however, Locke's writings on the "natural rights" of human beings and such legislation as "the French Declaration of the Rights of Man in 1789" which allowed for freedom of individual movement combined to provide a more tolerant attitude in Europe toward emigration to the new country. This greater tolerance was not tested or acted upon by the Danes until 1869 and again in 1872-73 when the first waves of Danish emigration to America took place. Having lost 40 percent of its status as a major European power by the end of the war of 1864, a psychic paralysis followed in its people, with a despairing lack of all faith in the future. The decision to seek out new and strange lands that offered the promise of something better was a way to once again establish control in a world that had shattered around them. (See Kristian Hvidt, *Flight to America: The Social Background of 300,000 Danish Immigrants* [New York: Academic America Press, 1975].)

5. This idea was confirmed in an interview with Thorkild Bjørnvig, Samsø, Denmark, 1980 and 1981.

6. See *Letters from Africa.*

7. Wilhelm Dinesen, "A Dane's Views on Frontier Culture: 'Notes on a Stay in the United States,' 1872-1874, by Wilhelm Dinesen," Donald K. Watkins, trans. *Nebraska History* 55 (Summer 1974): 264-89.

8. "Notes on a Stay," 273.

9. See Richard B. Vowles, "Boganis, Father of Osceola; or Wilhelm Dinesen in America 1872-1874," *Scandinavian Studies* 48 (Autumn 1976): 369-83.

10. Watkins, 277-78.

11. Ibid.

12. T. E. Lawrence, *Seven Pillars of Wisdom* (New York: Penguin Books, 1979), 30.

13. Aage Henriksen interview.

14. Parmenia Migel, *Titania: The Biography of Isak Dinesen* (New York: Random House, 1967), 8.

15. Clara Selborn interview, Dragør, Rungstedlund, and Copenhagen, 1980 and 1981.

16. See Wilhelm Dinesen, *Boganis: Letters from the Hunt,* Lise Lange Striar and Myles Striar, trans. (Boston: Rowan Tree Press, 1987).

Chapter 4

1. Mary Bess Westenholz, "Erindringer om Mama og hendes Slægt," *Blixeniana* (Copenhagen: Rungstedlund Foundation, 1979), 86.

2. Steen Eiler Rasmussen interview, Rungsted, Denmark, 1981.

3. Frans Lasson interview, Copenhagen, 1981.

4. See *Boganis.*

5. Ole Wivel reported that Tanne felt her family did not want her to exist (Ole Wivel interview).

6. Thomas Dinesen, *My Sister, Isak Dinesen,* Joan Tate, trans. (London: Michael Joseph, 1975), 14.

7. The facts in this chapter for the history of the Westenholz women are taken primarily from the family history written by Mary Bess Westenholz, "Erindringer om Mama og hendes Slægt."

8. This and several other incidents are reported differently by Judith Thurman, *The Life of a Storyteller;* see *Blixeniana,* 1984, for suggested corrections.

9. See *Letters from Africa.* In *Seven Gothic Tales,* Isak Dinesen argued for a "moral infinity."

The women, Victorian in their attitudes (as Thomas Dinesen notes in *Boganis*) were, as Hans Andersen points out in his article, "About Mama and Moster Bess" (*Blixeniana,* 1979) more interested in ideals than in instincts; he reports that her daughter, Bess Westenholz, said she had no interest in a girl behaving in a natural way, but rather in a mannered, "polite" way.

10. See *Letters from Africa.*

11. *Ehrengard,* 44–45.

12. Ibid., 44.

13. Ole Wivel interview.

14. *Titania,* 32.

15. Letter from Thomas Dinesen to Parmenia Migel Ekstrom, January 18, 1968 (Parmenia Migel Ekstrom private papers); Thomas Dinesen in his letter endorsed Parmenia Migel's biography of his sister, while noting that *Moster* Bess, "although she certainly was deeply religious, the word 'church' meant nothing to her, and she never tried to gain proselytes for her faith."

16. It seems quite likely that the peculiar situation created by women running ahead of their men, helped to deprive her of the only role then accorded any respect to women, that of wife and mother. Family references to Aunt Bess suggest that she deeply regretted her spinsterhood, and the traditional role of wife and mother became all the more appealing to her, an idea against which Tanne would continually set herself.

17. It was also Aunt Bess who wrote to Tanne telling her that she was clearly the most beautiful woman in the world (along with one other woman). Tanne reacted by calling it a silly remark, though she must have been charmed by it. The remark shows the affection with which her aunt viewed her. (See Anders Westenholz, *The Power of Aries,* Lise Kure-Jensen, trans. [Baton Rouge: Louisiana State University Press, 1987].)

18. *Letters from Africa,* 261–62. For a feminist reading of Isak Dinesen's tales, see Sara Stambaugh, *The Witch and the Goddess in the Stories of Isak Dinesen* (Michigan: UMI Research Press, 1988); and Marianne Juhl and Bo Jakon Jørgensen, *Diana's Revenge,* Anne Born, trans. (Odense: Odense University Press, 1985).

19. Miss Nat-og-dag (Danish for night-and-day), a spinster who believes

she has been a great courtesan, is given the enviable authority of madness in "The Deluge at Norderney" and freed from the limited status of being an unmarried woman; another woman character, George Sand-like, rides freely disguised as a man through "The Roads Round Pisa"; the six-foot Athena in "The Monkey" wears a "big cloak" that blows out about her "like a pair of large wings," and "safe in her great strength," she asserts her disinterest in marriage to the handsome, if somewhat shorter and scandalous, Prince Charming sent to woo her; while Pellegrina, a female Don Juan, looks "Like some big bird which runs to catch the wind and get on the wing" as she embraces her destiny.

20. See *Seven Gothic Tales*.

21. Karen Blixen Archives, Royal Library, Copenhagen.

Chapter 5

1. See *Boganis*.

2. *Last Tales*, 253.

3. The history of Regnar Westenholz is taken primarily from "Om Mama"; see also Frans Lasson and Clara Svendsen, eds., *The Life and Destiny of Isak Dinesen* (Chicago: University of Chicago Press, 1976).

4. "Om Mama," 67.

5. Helle Bering-Jensen interview.

6. Clara Selborn interview. Isak Dinesen's fascination with Hitler can better be understood when it is remembered that such people as the Windsors met with him before the horrors of his regime were apparent.

7. "Om Mama," 198.

8. There is nothing like the love of a "homely woman," Wilhelm Dinesen would jot in his hunting journal (see *Letters from the Hunt*).

9. Two hundred eighty-three letters were sent, *Boganis*, 33.

10. *Boganis*, 40.

11. Ibid.

12. See *Letters from Africa*.

13. *Boganis*, 44–45.

14. Ibid.

15. Clara Selborn interview.

16. See *Boganis*.

17. Ole Wivel interview.

18. Ibid.

Chapter 6

1. Clara Selborn interview.

2. *Daguerreotypes*, 199–200.

3. Clara Selborn interview.

4. In "Carnival," Isak Dinesen succeeded in a tour de force by "masquerading" with language so that the identities of various characters dressed for a masquerade were linguistically disguised; in a lifting from the masqueraders of Danish history, a female character appeared as "a sort of macabre dandy," Søren Kierkegaard.

5. Few people thought the upper and lower classes would choose to pursue courtships and business in the same place. But they did, attesting to recent shifting class lines. Edmund Gosse wrote:

> life unfolds in a specifically Danish manner of far-reaching democracy. Here in Tivoli, you may see a working man stopping the foreign minister to ask for a light for his cigar, there a tradesman and family are standing next to a foreign ambassador, enjoying the same spectacle.
> From Edmund Gosse's *Two Visits to Denmark*, cited in *The Story of Tivoli* (Copenhagen: Tivoli Gardens, 1981), 36.

6. Allan Frederiche, the Danish ballet historian, and Niels Larson, the director of the Pantomime Theatre at Tivoli Gardens, provided the main historical background for the *commedia dell'arte* tradition in Denmark (interviews, Copenhagen, 1980). Additional information was provided on Tivoli by two booklets put out by Tivoli Gardens, *The Story of Tivoli* and *The Pantomime Theatre* (Copenhagen, 1981).

7. See *The Story of Tivoli*.

8. See *Boganis*.

9. Helle Bering-Jensen interview.

10. Wilhelm Dinesen was defeated for his first bid to Parliament in 1887; he was first elected in 1892 (see *Boganis*).

11. From "Wilhelm Dinesen," by Georg Brandes.

12. *Daguerreotypes*, 50.

13. *Boganis*, 65.

14. See *The Life of a Storyteller*.

15. It was through his books that Isak Dinesen would come to learn about her father (Ole Wivel interview); themes, for example, from *Letters from the Hunt* are apparent in her work.

16. *Last Tales*, 271.

17. David Kronberg interview.

18. Ole Wivel interview.

19. Jonna Dinesen interview, Leerbæk, Denmark, 1980 and Folehave, Denmark, 1981.

20. *Daguerreotypes*, 19.

21. Ibid., 19–20.

22. Karl Marx, "The Communist Manifesto," in *A World of Ideas*, Lee Jacobus, ed. (New York: St. Martin's Press, 1983), 115.

23. See *The Life of a Storyteller*.

24. Clara Selborn interview.

25. Richard Ellmann, *Yeats, The Man and the Masks* (New York: E. P. Dutton, 1947), 71.

26. See, for example, Mark Twain's *The Mysterious Stranger* and Melville's "The Encantadas."

27. *Winter's Tales*, 53.

Chapter 7

1. See *Titania*.

2. *Daguerreotypes*, 2.

3. Ibid.

4. Ibid.

5. See "Copenhagen Season."

6. Rungsted officially became an inn in 1520 when "Christian VI gave Villum Carram a charter for 'the new Rungsti Inn, with all the acreage and meadows belonging to it, together with one hundred wagon-loads of wood to be picked up from the ground and free feeding in the forest for his own swine, on the condition that he keep a hostel for Danes and foreigners, so that traveling men have nothing to complain about.!' " (*Daguerreotypes*, 200.)

7. Isak Dinesen told the history of Rungsted Inn in a radio address printed in "Rungstedlund" (*Daguerreotypes*, 195–218); she would ride over on her bicycle to ask for the finer points of history from Steen Eiler Rasmussen (interview, 1981).

8. P. O. Olesen, director of the Hunting Museum, interview, Rungsted, Denmark, 1980.

9. Kristian Vang, interview at the Royal Court Theatre, Copenhagen, 1980.

10. Thorkild Bjørnvig interview, Samsø, Denmark, 1980 and 1981.

11. *Daguerreotypes*, 205.

12. Taken from Isak Dinesen's introduction to Hans Christian Andersen, *Thumbelina and Other Fairy Tales* (New York: Macmillan, 1962).

13. *The Life of a Storyteller*, 40.

14. Karen Blixen Archives. Her favorite childhood play, later mentioned in *Seven Gothic Tales* as an inside joke, was "The Revenge of Truth," written when Tanne was about fifteen years old and shows an innocent adolescent curiosity about the intimate relations between men and women. The earlier versions of the play, before it was revised for later performance in Denmark, one copy in English, a more hefty one in German, has an Ionesco-like repetition of some of the conversation. There is already, importantly, a certain nihilistic edge to the conversation—and, at the same time, an interest in personal style.

In a conversation between two characters, Sabine and Fortunio, Fortunio notes his interest in books written by the Vacuumists, those who see absurdity in the world. Sabine replies that all other books convey such a meaningless reality even more strongly. But in the real world, continues Sabine, away from books one's experience can be a different one, if only human beings know to design their worlds properly. With money enough to build a glass enclosure and sit dressed in an elegant gown on the lake floor, fish staring through, one might experience, even knowing that crimes had been committed, a calmness. One might have been pregnant with many lovers, asphyxiated them and the babies, and still keep one's slender look. (Significantly, Isak Dinesen returned to work on this conversation—translating it into English—in the last year of her life.)

Various versions to be found in Karen Blixen Archives, Royal Library, Copenhagen

15. "Next to one cast list there are the names of the actors who will play them, and it sets the precedent. Ea is always Columbine; Elle is Harlequin; and Tanne, Pierrot. The Pierrot is foolish and proud. He has a minor and comic part." (*The Life of a Storyteller*, 42.)

Contrary to the previous observation in *The Life of a Storyteller*, Tanne's interest in Pierrot was more for his tragic sadness, his unrequited yearning. (In an interview, Ole Wivel made clear that Dinesen preferred the elegant French Pierrot to the overridingly foolish Pierrot in Tivoli.)

16. Niels Larson interview; also, the facts of Tivoli's development are here taken from *The Story of Tivoli* and *The Pantomime Theatre.*

17. Niels Larson interview.

18. Frederik Böök, *Hans Christian Andersen: A Biography* (Norman: University of Oklahoma Press, 1962), 42.

19. Martin Green interview, Medford, Mass., 1981.

20. Niels Larson interview; *Theater Life*, 186.

21. Clara Selborn interview.

22. Information about Christian VII and his impact upon the Danish imagination was obtained primarily from the director of the Royal Court Theatre, Karen Neiiendam (interview, Copenhagen, 1980) and from Kristian Vang, and P. O. Olesen of the Hunting Museum in Rungsted. Another important source was John Brown, *Memoirs of the Courts of Sweden and Denmark During the Reigns of Christian VII and Gustavius III and IV of Sweden* (Paris and Boston: Grolier Society, 1900). Missing gaps were supplied by Palle Lauring, *A History of the Kingdom of Denmark*, David Hohnen, trans. (Copenhagen: Høst and Son, 1960).

23. Aage Henriksen interview.

24. In later years, when Dinesen had lost everything that had meant anything to her in Africa, she would turn to the past to relieve her pain, "the sins of people in power . . . beginning to look romantic, like passions and crimes on the stage" (*Seven Gothic Tales*, 359). She would exploit her fascination with the romantic elements of theatre and drama, disguise and mystery, recalling Queen Mathilda's unfortunate plight in "The Poet." In a literary tour de force, she brought Johannes Ewald and Christian VII together in "Converse at Night in Copenhagen."

25. *Last Tales*, 315.

26. Even after he was married to the English princess Caroline Mathilda, the king was said to frequent brothels in disguise, once being mistaken for a woman. Attracted by acting, King Christian VII took pleasure in masquerades and would attend masked balls at the palace with his mistress, a former young harlot.

27. *Last Tales*, 336.

28. See *Memoirs of the Courts.*

29. *Seven Gothic Tales*, 358. Once embraced by the people for her innocence, the queen was now mocked for her lack of modesty and decorum. Finding himself in a position of advantage, Struensee quickly gained control of Christian VII, and without knowing Danish managed to issue 1,069 orders within ten months. He abolished press censorship and ruled the country until one January night after a masked ball. A rebellion was inspired by the queen-dowager, Juliana Maria, and a group of conspirators frightened the king into signing papers for the doctor's arrest. This series of events led to the Danish Revolution in 1772. The English Caroline Mathilda was exiled, Struensee beheaded, and relations between England and Denmark became strained.

30. See *The Life of a Storyteller.*

31. Clara Selborn interview.

32. Jonna Dinesen interview.

33. *Titania*, 16.

34. Noted in *The Life of a Storyteller*, Karen Blixen Archives.

35. See *Daguerreotypes.*

36. *The Life of a Storyteller*, 40.

37. Ibid.

38. Jonna Dinesen interview.

39. *Out of Africa*, 252–53

40. Ibid.

41. See *Letters from Africa*.

Chapter 8

1. Isak Dinesen, *Carnival* (Chicago: University of Chicago Press, 1977), 13.

2. Ole Wivel interview.

3. *Titania*, 26.

4. *Letters from the Hunt*, 130.

5. Ibid., 78.

6. See *Boganis*.

7. See "Om Mama."

8. *Letters from Africa*, 427.

9. Ibid.

10. *The Life and Destiny of Isak Dinesen*, 32.

11. *The Life of a Storyteller*, 27.

12. *Titania*, 14.

13. See *Letters from Africa*.

14. Clara Selborn interview.

15. *My Sister, Isak Dinesen*, 32.

16. Ibid., 24.

17. *Titania*, 30.

18. Viggo Kjær Petersen interview, Copenhagen, 1981.

19. In seeking for balance in a precarious reality, like her characters Jonathan and Calypso in "The Deluge at Norderney," Dinesen moved between being and nonbeing. Later in her life she shifted slightly, dividing the possible human energies "between force and being." Force, the force of action, of movement (a masculine concept) was dismissed by her, and being (which she attributed to and saw as the prerogative of women) was embraced. She felt, however, an ambivalence toward a clear presentation of the created self—in "The Deluge at Norderney" Jonathan and Calypso are given separate fates, one existing as a powerful personality and one not, each finding their being (and nonbeing) burdensome. Finally, however, Dinesen, who saw the creation of self as a peculiarly female responsibility, understood that dress and costuming, role playing, was the one area women could transgress boundaries in claiming, perfectly and ideally, their own being.

20. *Titania*, 21.

21. Thorkild Bjørnvig interview.

22. *Life and Destiny*, 66.

23. *Letters from Africa*, 427.

24. See *Boganis*.

25. *Letters from Africa*, 211.

26. Isak Dinesen, *On Modern Marriage and Other Observations* (New York: St. Martin's Press, 1986), 20.

27. Thomas Dinesen reported to Donald Hannah that as a young woman Tanne was filled with "feelings of frustration . . . [because s]he was trying, he thought, to keep up with a social set without having the financial means of

really doing so, and to mix in the exclusive world of the Danish nobility of the time without having any definite place in its hierarchy" (Donald Hannah, *"Isak Dinesen" and Karen Blixen: The Mask and the Reality* [New York: Random House, 1971], 22).

Chapter 9

1. A remark made to Cocteau.
2. Arnold Haskell, in collaboration with Walter Nouvel, *Diaghileff, His Artistic and Private Life* (London: Victor Gollancz, 1935), 53.
3. Parmenia Migel Ekstrom, in an interview, was adamant that Tanne had seen Diaghilev. Clara Selborn, in a separate interview, said it was fairly certain that Denys Finch Hatton would have seen Diaghilev and conveyed a sense of the Ballets Russes to Tanne, probably even urging her to see them on one of her trips to Europe.
4. *Blixeniana*, 1983, p. 187; also contained in the Karen Blixen Archives. The facts of Tanne's Paris stay are taken primarily from this diary, 1910.
5. *Blixeniana*, 1983, 187.
6. Ibid.
7. Karen Blixen Archives.
8. *Blixeniana*, 1983, 188.
9. Ibid., 191.
10. Clara Selborn interview.
11. *Blixeniana*, 1983, 191.
12. Ibid., 213.
13. *The Life of a Storyteller*, 97.
14. *Letters from Africa*, 53.

Chapter 10

1. *African Hunter*, 3.
2. *"Isak Dinesen" and Karen Blixen*, 25–26.
3. Beryl Markham, *West with the Night* (Boston: Houghton Mifflin, 1942), 209.
4. Parmenia Migel Ekstrom interview.
5. *Letters from Africa*, 418.
6. *Winter's Tales*, 107.
7. Ole Wivel suggested in an interview the problems that the Dinesen women, in particular Tanne and her sisters, must have had in marrying, their strong personalities overwhelming the sons of the local farmers.
8. Ole Wivel interview.
9. See *Letters from Africa*.
10. Anders Westenholz has said that "The father's unhappy love for Agnes came to live on in his daughter's infatuation with the aristocracy" (*Power of Aries*).
11. *Life and Destiny*, 66.
12. *Letters from Africa*, 287.
13. Clara Selborn interview.

14. *African Hunter*, 5–6.
15. Ibid., 5–7.

Chapter 11

1. *Seven Gothic Tales*, 271.
2. *Lunatic Express*, 14.
3. Ibid., 16–17.
4. The facts on Great Britain moving into East Africa were obtained primarily from *The Lunatic Express, White Man's Country* (vols. 1 and 2), and Ronald Robinson, John Gallagher, and Alice Denny, *Africa and the Victorians* (New York: St. Martin's Press, 1961).
5. *African Hunter*, 8.
6. *Lunatic Express*, 17.
7. *Letters from Africa*, 2.
8. *Daguerreotypes*, 92.
9. *Lunatic Express*, 48.
10. See *Lunatic Express*.
11. Information provided at Fort Jesus.
12. Ibid.
13. *Seven Gothic Tales*, 271.
14. Prince Wilhelm of Sweden, *Episoder* (Stockholm: Norstedt, 1951).
15. Ibid.
16. Ibid., 151.
17. *Letters from Africa*, 2.
18. See *Episoder*.
19. Charles William Hobley, *Kenya, From Chartered Company to Crown Colony* (London: H. F. & G. Witherby, 1929), 23.
20. See John Henry Patterson, *The Man-eaters of Tsavo* (New York: Macmillan, 1927; orig. printed, 1907).
21. *Lunatic Express*, 382.
22. See introduction to *Kenya, From Chartered Company to Crown Colony*.
23. *Lunatic Express*, 310.
24. See *Silence Will Speak*.

Chapter 12

1. *Letters from Africa*, 2.
2. Ibid.
3. Ibid., 3.
4. The facts of the train from Mombasa to Nairobi are taken primarily from *The Lunatic Express*; additional background was provided by *The Man-eaters of Tsavo*.
5. The preferred spelling for the Gikuyu tribe is with a "G" (interviews with Mbaire Mutuguti and Kahoya Mbugua, Cambridge, Mass., 1986 and 1987).
6. *Lunatic Express*, 42–43.
7. *White Man's Country*, 2: 248.

8. *Silence Will Speak,* 84.
9. Ibid.
10. *The Leader,* April 4, 1914.
11. *Letters from Africa,* 3.
12. Ibid.
13. *Letters from Africa,* 10.
14. Ibid., 9. Ole Wivel noted in an interview that he always felt Tanne's experience as a farmer at the back of their conversations.

Chapter 13

1. See *Letters from Africa, White Man's Country,* vols. 1 and 2, and *Silence Will Speak* for more information.
2. See Jomo Kenyatta, *Facing Mt. Kenya* (New York: Vintage Books, 1965).
3. See *The Leader,* a continuing dispute in letters to the editor.
4. *Lunatic Express,* 88.
5. Ibid., 61.
6. See *Lunatic Express.*
7. See Elspeth Huxley, *The Flame Trees of Thika* (New York: Penguin Books, 1983).
8. *Letters from Africa,* 9.
9. *White Man's Country* 1: 25.
10. Ibid., 1: 251–52.
11. Ibid.
12. Peter Beard interview, near the Ngong Hills, 1983.
13. See Carlos Baker, *Ernest Hemingway, A Life Story* (New York: Scribner's, 1969).
14. *West with the Night,* 201.
15. Kamande Gatura (known as Kamante in *Out of Africa*) interview, near the Ngong Hills, 1983.
16. See *West with the Night.*
17. Ibid., 201.
18. Ibid., 219.
19. Ibid., 212.
20. Ibid., 219.
21. Ibid., 257.

Chapter 14

1. *Letters from Africa,* 6.
2. *Winter's Tales,* 107.
3. *West with the Night,* 209.
4. Ibid.
5. Ingrid Lindstrom interview, Mombasa, 1983.
6. See *African Hunter.*
7. *Letters from Africa,* 22.
8. Ulf Aschan interview, Nairobi, 1983.
9. Isak Dinesen, *Shadows on the Grass* (New York: Vintage Books, 1974), 54.
10. *Letters from Africa,* 22.

11. *The Leader*, August 8, 1914, 28.

12. Ibid., 10.

13. Ibid., 20.

14. Ibid., 27.

15. André Gide, *Journals 1889–1949*, Justin O'Brien, trans. (New York: Penguin Books, 1978), 213.

16. *The Leader*, October 17, 1914, 2.

17. See *Letters from Africa*. Uncle Aage Westenholz reported back to Denmark that: "In the afternoon, two young Englishmen were here, one the son of a Lord, the other probably of equally prominent family—Tanne's acquaintances belong by and large to the Peerage . . . ' she despises the English middle class. I have a degree of sympathy with these people, though; it is a class of people on their way downward, who realize this themselves . . . hunters and warriors who have to yield to industry and modern agricultural society; this is why they seek the uncivilized environment here" (*Power of Aries*, 18).

18. *The Leader*, November 21, 1914, 13.

19. Ibid., 8.

20. Ingrid Lindstrom interview; in the same letter to *The Leader* (May 25, 1918) defending himself against pro-German charges, Bror defended his wife, saying, "With your knowledge of the Dinesens and their anti-German feelings you can understand it has been very hard on my wife being looked upon as pro-German."

21. *The Leader*, November 21, 1914, 9.

22. See *White Man's Country*, vol. 2.

23. *Silence Will Speak*, 109.

24. See *Silence Will Speak*.

25. *White Man's Country*, 2: 8.

26. Ibid., 2: 9.

27. A. Davies and H. G. Robinson, *Chronicles of Kenya* (London: Cecil Palmer, 1928), 100–101; cited in *Silence Will Speak*, 103.

28. *White Man's Country*, 2: 5.

29. Ibid.

30. *White Man's Country*, 2: 7.

31. *Letters from Africa*.

32. *White Man's Country*, 2: 6.

33. *Letters from Africa*, 13.

34. Ibid., 41.

35. See *Letters from Africa*.

36. Ibid., 58.

37. *Daguerreotypes*, 94.

38. *Letters from Africa*, 41.

39. *Daguerreotypes*, 95.

40. *African Hunter*, 92.

41. *Winter's Tales*, 109.

42. Ibid., 111.

Chapter 15

1. Franz Kafka, *The Diaries of Franz Kafka, 1914–1923*, Max Brod, ed., Martin Greenberg, trans. (New York: Schocken Books, 1949), 77.

2. Many people reported hearing this story from Isak Dinesen, including Thorkild Bjørnvig and Aage Henriksen (interviews).

3. *Letters from Africa*, 247 (a quote from Sophus Claussen).

4. There is some controversy over this fact; people loyal to Bror Blixen feel that she contracted the disease from somewhere else, using as proof that Cockie Birkbeck, Bror's second wife, never contracted syphilis (Cockie Hoogterp (Birkbeck) interview, England, 1983; Ulf Aschan [Bror's godson] interview, Nairobi, 1983). But this is not complete proof: Denys Finch Hatton, as far as has been reported, never contracted syphilis from Isak Dinesen in their subsequent relationship. And shortly after her marriage there is nothing to contradict that Tanne was anything but loyal and traditional (and Victorian) in her intimate relationships, despite her later assumed poses.

5. Ann Hablanian interview, Cambridge, Mass., 1985.

6. P. O. Olesen interview, 1980.

7. Errol Trzebinski interview, Mombasa and London, 1983.

8. Thorkild Bjørnvig interview.

9. *Last Tales*, 79.

10. Ibid., 98.

11. Ibid.

12. Kamande Gatura, *Longing for Darkness*, Peter Beard, ed. (New York: Harcourt Brace Jovanovich, 1975), introduction.

13. *Last Tales*, 90.

14. Ibid., 26.

15. *Letters from Africa*, 246.

16. In *Seven Gothic Tales*, Isak Dinesen mentions "moral infinity."

17. See *The Life of a Storyteller*.

18. Errol Trzebinski interview.

19. Mbaire Mutuguti and Kahoya Mbugua interviews.

20. Ole Wivel interview.

21. Frans Lasson introduction to *Letters from Africa*.

22. Ann Hablanian interview.

23. *Letters from Africa*, 63.

24. Clara Selborn interview.

25. *Shadows on the Grass*, 125.

26. *Out of Africa*, 173.

Chapter 16

1. "The board of directors consisted of: Ingeborg Dinesen . . . ; Royal Hunt Master Caspar von Folsach; Lieutenant Colonel Torben Gent; Attorney at Law Thorkil Knudtzon; Viggo de Neergaard; Count Clarence von Rosen; Georg Sass; Chairman of the Board Aage Westenholz . . . ; and in Nairobi, Managing Director Bror Frederick von Blixen-Finecke" (*Power of Aries*, 12).

2. *The Leader*, August 8, 1914, p. 20.

3. Martin Green, *Dreams of Adventure, Deeds of Empire* (New York: Basic Books, 1979), 329.

4. *Letters from Africa*, 357.

5. See *Dreams of Adventure*.

6. Karen Blixen Archives.

7. Eugene Haynes interview, Jefferson City, Mo., 1983.

8. Lady Altrincham interview, England, 1983.

9. *Letters from Africa*, 24.

10. Elspeth Huxley and Lady Altrincham interviews.

11. See *Titania*.

12. See Thorkild Bjørnvig, *The Pact: My Friendship with Isak Dinesen*, Ingvar Schousboe and William Jay Smith, trans. (Baton Rouge: Louisiana State University Press, 1974).

13. *Out of Africa*, 22–23.

14. Kamande Gatura interview.

15. See *Letters from Africa*.

16. See Ngũgĩ wa Thiong'o, *Writers in Politics: Essays* (London: Heinemann, 1981).

17. Attack, for example, by Ngugi; praise from Kamande Gatura (interview) and Kenyatta (see *Life and Destiny*).

18. *Out of Africa*, 120–21.

19. Ibid., 202.

20. Olive Schreiner, *The Story of An African Farm* (Introduction by Isak Dinesen) (New York: Limited Editions Club, 1961), vii–ix. In her introduction to Olive Schreiner, Isak Dinesen could be writing about *Out of Africa*:

> The young authoress is grave, then, and her noble young characters are grave with her, they all of them have the tragic mind. In this they are well in accord with the world of the continent which forms the stage for their activities, for Africa is a tragic country. The idea of the happy end, which our own modern literature claims, neither in life nor in fiction is popular in the African world, not for want of human feeling, but because there it seems somewhat far-fetched. The African landscape has a tragic note in it. Even the big game of Africa seem to move in the tragic sphere more than their brothers of other continents. . . . All African Natives have a strong feeling of tragedy. From the introduction to *The Story of An African Farm*, vii–ix.

21. This sense of Africa as dreamy and beckoning echoes the best of some of Prescott's histories.

Chapter 17

1. *Silence Will Speak*, 11.

2. See *Letters from Africa*.

3. *White Man's Country*, 2: 43.

4. *The Leader*, December 21, 1918, 31.

5. See *Letters from Africa*.

6. Ibid., 100.

7. Ibid.

8. Ibid., 41.

9. *West with the Night*, 158.

10. Ibid.

11. *Silence Will Speak*, 42.

12. Ibid., 31.

13. Ibid., 42.

14. See *Silence Will Speak*.

15. *West with the Night*, 195.
16. *Silence Will Speak*, 70.
17. In correspondence (received 1987), Ian Jack has pointed out that undergraduates at Oxford like to tell stories about each other which are not necessarily true; particularly interesting in the stories told about Denys Finch Hatton are the qualities of his personality they illuminate.
18. *Silence Will Speak*, 33.
19. See Martin Green, *Children of the Sun* (New York: Basic Books, 1976).
20. *Silence Will Speak*, 74–75.
21. *Out of Africa*, 215.
22. Errol Trzebinski interview.
23. *Out of Africa*, 346.
24. See *Titania*.
25. *Letters from Africa*, 347.
26. Ibid., 166.
27. Ibid., 347–48.
28. Ole Wivel interview.

Chapter 18

1. *Letters from Africa*, 99.
2. See *Titania*.
3. *Letters from Africa*, 433.
4. See *The Power of Aries*.
5. Kamande Gatura interview.
6. *Out of Africa*, 8; Ingrid Lindstrom interview.
7. *Power of Aries*, 14–15.
8. Ingrid Lindstrom interview.
9. *Letters from Africa*, 191; referred to as Old Knudsen. in *Out of Africa*.
10. Ibid., 201.
11. Ibid., 202.
12. *Power of Aries*, 16.
13. Ibid.
14. *Power of Aries*, 17.
15. Ibid., 20.
16. Ibid., 21.
17. Ibid., 25.
18. Ibid., 22.
19. See *Letters from Africa*.
20. *Power of Aries*, 23; Aage Westenholz would go through the inheritance of one child of his trying to maintain the farm, and have his credit cut off from one bank.
21. Several people reported her regrets on this financial connection to the family (i.e., interview with Clara Selborn and Aage Henriksen).
22. *Letters from Africa*, 108.
23. Ibid., 120.
24. See *Letters from Africa*.
25. A visit to Kenya confirms this hypnotic quality of the landscape.
26. Cockie Hoogterp (Birkbeck) interview, England, 1983. It might be worth noting here that Cockie Birkbeck reported Bror Blixen never remarried

after his second marriage to her, merely letting people believe he had done so.

27. Cockie Hoogterp interview.

28. Anonymous correspondence, 1986.

29. Cockie Hoogterp interview.

30. Ibid.

31. See *Letters from Africa*.

32. *Power of Aries*, 25.

33. Errol Trzebinski interview.

34. *Power of Aries*, 26.

35. Lady Altrincham (married to Governor Grigg of Kenya) interview.

36. Much has been said about the lack of conventional morality in B.E.A. at this time. But, in fact, certain strict social mores applied among the European immigrants who carried with them Victorian attitudes. A sexual relationship outside of marriage was as often as not kept secret, and a hostess might pretend to be oblivious to any "illicit" amorous affairs among the guests within her home (Errol Trzebinski interview).

37. See *Letters from Africa*.

38. See *My Sister, Isak Dinesen*.

39. See *Letters from Africa* and *My Sister, Isak Dinesen*. Like Bror, Denys would be away from the farm for long periods, arriving for brief stays there to a gracious home, fine food, and a lovely woman who looked to his every word without the responsibility that usually entailed (Errol Trzebinski interview, reporting on the words of Denys Finch Hatton's nephew).

40. See *The Life of a Storyteller*.

41. Lady Erskine interview, Nairobi, 1983.

42. *The Life of a Storyteller*, 208.

43. Ibid.

44. Ibid., 209.

45. See *Letters from Africa*.

46. Notebooks in Karen Blixen Archives.

47. *Letters from Africa*, 159.

48. Ibid., 156.

49. Ibid., 158.

50. *Seven Gothic Tales*, 274.

51. *Letters from Africa*, 244.

52. Thorkild Bjørnvig, *The Pact*. Transl. William Jay Smith (Baton Rouge: Louisiana State Univ. Press, 1983).

53. *Letters from Africa*, 276.

54. Ibid., 284.

Chapter 19

1. See *Letters from Africa*.

2. See *West with the Night*.

3. Mary S. Lovell notes: "It is claimed by several informants that the Africans she would have accompanied on the hunting expeditions were members of the Kipsigis tribe, and not the more colourful warrior Nandis. . . . However, the aristocratic Nandi are a more colourful and widely known race, and perhaps Beryl was merely indulging in a little poetic licence" (*Straight On Till Morning* [New York: St. Martin's Press, 1987], 34).

4. *Letters from Africa*, 79.

5. See James Fox, "The Beryl Markham Mystery," *Vanity Fair* (October 1984).

6. Ibid., 113.

7. See Fox.

8. *West with the Night*, 4.

9. Fox, 111.

10. Cockie Hoogterp interview; James Fox interview with Beryl Markham ("The Beryl Markham Mystery"); many of the facts for Beryl Markham's life are taken from *West with the Night* and the Fox interview in *Vanity Fair*, as well as interviews with Errol Trzebinski and Cockie Hoogterp; see also *Straight On Till Morning* and James Fox, *White Mischief* (New York: Random House, 1984).

11. Mary Lovell confirms the truth of this story in *Straight On Till Morning*. As this book goes to press, Errol Trzebinski has written to tell me that in her forthcoming Beryl Markham biography she has concluded that "the complexities of the arrival of a royal heir which indeed match the question of paternity of Beryl's own son Gervase, when he was born in London in 1929," was used as the basis for Isak Dinesen's tale *Ehrengard*.

12. Thurman's interview with Beryl Markham, cited in *The Life of a Storyteller*.

13. *Letters from Africa*, 174.

14. Lovell reports that Tanne and Beryl became friends, Tanne sympathizing with her over her unhappy marriages. Errol Trzebinski, on the other hand, quotes Beryl Markham as saying that "Tania overlooked me, perhaps I was too young—perhaps she thought me foolish; she was rather remote and set herself apart" (*Silence Will Speak*, 211).

15. Fox, 112.

16. Rose Cartwright interview, Nairobi, 1983.

17. Fox, 112.

18. Elspeth Huxley reports this anecdote in her introduction to *Out of Africa*.

19. See *White Mischief*.

20. Ibid., 67; Beryl Markham in *West with the Night* reports that she was the first to scout elephant from a plane.

21. See *White Mischief*.

22. *Letters from Africa*, 344.

23. Lady Altrincham interview.

24. *Letters from Africa*, 343.

25. Errol Trzebinski interview.

26. *On Marriage*, 64.

27. *Out of Africa*, 211.

28. *On Marriage*, 37.

29. Facts of Rose Cartwright's life are taken from an interview with her in Nairobi, 1983.

30. See *Silence Will Speak*.

31. Ibid.

32. *On Marriage*, 27.

33. See *Silence Will Speak*.

34. Ibid., 120.

35. Many people mentioned this in interviews as a fact, both in Denmark and Kenya; Parmenia Migel in an interview took this as accepted fact, while

Errol Trzebinski and Judith Thurman dismissed it (Thurman interview, New York, 1980, cited as proof Beryl Markham's deep laugh when confronted with the question of Denys Finch Hatton's sexual preferences).

36. *Carnival*, 63

> "When I am gone," he finished, "and when you two are left to your-selves, and believe that you are following the command of your own young blood only, you will still be doing nothing, nothing at all, but what I have willed you to. You will be conforming to the plot of my story. For tonight this room, this bed, you yourselves with this same young hot blood in you—it is all nothing but a story turned, at my work, into reality."

Ancedotes of Destiny, 215.

Martin Green notes the *commedia* sensibility of the 1920s: "Indeed, some-thing like a Commedia influence could be seen in society as a whole, in the styles of clothes and make-up of the 1920's" (*Transatlantic Patterns* [New York: Basic Books, 1977], 91).

37. Ibid., 62. The *commedia dell'arte* influences in Dinesen's work occur on different levels: on the *actual* level, as images of the *commedia* are incorporated into a story, as in "Anna," where the pantomime theatre and the Chinese lamps of Tivoli are found; on the *imitative* level, as, for example, when life becomes the movement of the pantomime; on the *metaphorical* level, as in "Con-verse at Night in Copenhagen," when nature becomes a "moon-mask [as it] came in sight right up in the sky" (*Last Tales*, 315); on the *symbolic* level (obviously), as in "Anna," where we are taken to Bergamo, the origin of the *commedia*, and the link is made between the origins of the pantomime tradition and the garden of Eden (*Carnival*, 186); and on the *metaphysical* level, as, for example, universal powers are hinted at and translated into puppetry (which is an extension of the *commedia*) in "The Immortal Story":

> "And because you can walk and move without pain, you believe that you are walking and moving according to your own will. But it is not so. You walk and move at my bidding. You are, in reality, two young, strong and lusty jumping-jacks within this old hand of mine."

> "So," he went on, "so are, as I have told you, the poor jumping-jacks in the hands of the rich, the fools of this earth in the hands of the shrewd. They dance and drop as these hands pull the strings.

38. Errol Trzebinski and Judith Thurman note this possessiveness, as do friends.

39. See *Letters from Africa*.

40. *Carnival*, 64.

41. See *Letters from Africa*.

42. *Out of Africa*, 45.

43. Aage Henriksen, in "Karen Blixen and Marionettes," provides an elo-quent argument on the use of marionettes in Isak Dinesen's tales (*Isak Dinesen/Karen Blixen: The Work and the Life* [New York: St. Martin's Press, 1988]).

44. Ole Wivel has noted that Tanne felt her family did not want her to exist (interview).

Chapter 20

1. Clara Selborn interview.
2. *Letters from Africa*, 334.
3. Ingrid Lindstrom interview.
4. *Letters from Africa*, 335.
5. Ibid., 334.
6. Ibid., 332.
7. See *Titania*.
8. See *Letters from Africa*.
9. Ibid., 340.
10. Ingrid Lindstrom interview.
11. Ibid.
12. Ibid.
13. Ibid.
14. Many people mentioned this in interviews, including Ingrid Lindstrom and Rose Cartwright.
15. Lady Altrincham interview. Tanne, in a letter to Aage Westenholz, wrote that "since Bror and his wife were guests of Government House, I didn't go to any festivities there or anyplace else during the Prince of Wales's visit. It bothered me somewhat because everything in the country revolved around this event and it would have been fun to be part of, and it bothered me that my people who had felt that they were at the center of events were to become so bitterly disappointed" (*Power of Aries*, 77).
16. *African Standard*, October 6, 1928.
17. Lady Altrincham interview. In a letter to Aage Westenholz, Tanne wrote that a furor had ensued when the Prince of Wales had sent a telegram accepting her invitation to stay at the farm instead of Government House: "I found that everyone who had anything to do with Government House, including Bror, who had been invited to stay there, . . . was in a state of the wildest panic and beseeched me not to mention the Prince's telegram to a living soul because it would be considered a major scandal if he were to stay anywhere but at Government House, where they expected him and planned a party for him, and since they hoped to talk him out of coming to Ngong. I said that it was none of my business of course and that, naturally, the Prince was welcome in my house should he wish to come" (*Power of Aries*, 76). Finch Hatton sent a telegram stating that the prince had been won over—"Conventional arrangement being made" (Ibid., 76–77).
18. Lady Altrincham interview.
19. Ulf Aschan interview.
20. Lady Altrincham commented on her appearance (interview); photographs attest to this change.
21. See *West with the Night*.
22. See *Silence Will Speak*.
23. *West with the Night*, 194.
24. Ibid., 196.
25. *Straight On Till Morning*, 109.
26. *Out of Africa*, 352.
27. Kamande Gatura interview.
28. Rose Cartwright interview.
29. *Power of Aries*, 33.

30. Kamande Gatura interview.
31. *Out of Africa*, 346–47.
32. *West with the Night*, 193.
33. See Fox interview.
34. See *Silence Will Speak*.
35. Ingrid Lindstrom interview.
36. Rose Cartwright interview.
37. See *Out of Africa*.
38. Ingrid Lindstrom interview.
39. *Power of Aries*, 35.
40. That the suburb is called Karen has been taken to be an honor among some, but it really remains more as a designation that was never changed (Mbaire Mutuguti interview).

Chapter 21

1. *Seven Gothic Tales*, 345.
2. Thorkild Bjørnvig interview. Bjørnvig said that Dinesen agreed "her most important story was 'The Dreamers.' She said that she no longer wanted to be Pellegrina. After she left Africa she renounced identity. She found that was liberating. I couldn't renounce my identity, though she would have liked me to. . . . She wanted fame and didn't want fame. [Her attitude toward identity] . . . was a contradiction." Jonna Dinesen agreed in an interview that there was a major change in Dinesen after her return from Africa, particularly after she became successful as a writer. According to Dinesen's sister-in-law, as fame and glamour claimed her many of her humane qualities became submerged; one cannot help but feel that Thomas Dinesen felt the same way.
3. Thorkild Bjørnvig interview.
4. Ibid.
5. Clara Selborn interview.
6. Bernard McCabe, *The Tablet* (London) (May 1968), 987.
7. *Carnival*, 67.
8. *Seven Gothic Tales*, 277.
9. *Shadows on the Grass*, 110.
10. Clara Svendsen, *Notater om Karen Blixen* (Copenhagen: Gyldendal, 1974).
11. See *Isak Dinesen: A Memorial*.
12. See *Notater om Karen Blixen*.
13. Birgit Bjørnvig interview, Samsø, Denmark, 1981 and 1982.
14. *Titania*, 102.
15. *Titania*, 104.
16. *Shadows on the Grass*, 117–18.
17. *Titania*, 91.
18. To an outsider, the sounds of the Danish language are melancholy.
19. For facts on Tanne's search for a publisher, see *My Sister, Isak Dinesen, Titania*, and *The Life of a Storyteller*.
20. See Columbia collection; also Dorothy Commins, *What is an Editor?* (Chicago: University of Chicago Press, 1978).
21. See *The Life of a Storyteller*.
22. Ibid., 269.
23. Viggo Kjær Petersen interview.

24. Clara Selborn interview.

25. Stephen Donadio, *Nietzsche, Henry James and the Artistic Will* (New York: Oxford University Press, 1978), 61.

Chapter 22

1. *Titania,* 108–9.
2. Columbia collection.
3. Ibid.
4. See ibid.; also, *What is an Editor?*
5. Steen Eiler Rasmussen interview.
6. Columbia collection.
7. Ibid.
8. Ibid.
9. Ibid.
10. Ibid.
11. Ibid.
12. Ibid.
13. Ibid.
14. See Isak Dinesen's introduction to Olive Schreiner's *The Story of An African Farm.*
15. Columbia collection.
16. Ibid.
17. Ibid.
18. Ibid.
19. See Hannah Arendt in the introduction to *Daguerreotypes; The Life of a Storyteller.*
20. See *The Life of a Storyteller.*
21. Columbia collection.

Chapter 23

1. See Albert Speer, *Inside the Third Reich,* Richard and Clara Winston, trans. (New York: Avon Books, 1971).
2. Helle Bering-Jensen interview.
3. To Parmenia Migel Ekstrom, Thomas Dinesen wrote: "Tanne and I sometimes had very angry scenes. This did not, however, start with the death of my mother and the question of the inheritance,—my sister Ellen, my brother Anders and I myself took it as a matter of course that Tanne should have almost all the inheritance as long as she lived" (from the private papers of Parmenia Migel Ekstrom).
4. Thomas Dinesen recalled: "But when Tanne became really world-famous, her pride . . . would brook no criticism, and I very often found it difficult to defend any point of view different from hers" (from the private papers of Parmenia Migel Ekstrom).
5. *Titania,* 116.
6. See *Notater om Karen Blixen.*
7. Information on the occupation was obtained from the Danish Resistance Museum, Copenhagen.

8. *Shadows on the Grass*, 130–31.

9. Helle Bering-Jensen interview.

10. *Shadows on the Grass*, 130–31.

11. See Aage Bertelsen, *October '43*, Milly Lindholm and Willy Agtby, trans. (New York: G. P. Putnam's Sons, 1954).

12. See "Letters from a Land at War," in *Daguerreotypes*.

13. *Daguerreotypes*, 116.

14. Ibid., 111.

15. Ibid., 123.

16. Clara Selborn interview.

17. *Daguerreotypes*, 133.

18. See *On Marriage*.

19. See Speer.

20. *Shadows on the Grass*, 131–32.

21. Columbia collection.

22. Ibid.

23. Allan Frederiche interview.

24. Clara Selborn interview; Jonna Dinesen interview.

25. Clara Selborn interview.

26. Columbia collection.

27. See *My Sister, Isak Dinesen*.

28. Steen Eiler Rasmussen interview.

29. See *Daguerreotypes*.

30. Columbia collection.

31. Ibid.

32. Steen Eiler Rasmussen interview.

33. Ibid.

34. Ibid.

35. Ibid.

36. Nevertheless, in her own life she was considered a snob. Thomas Dinesen wrote that, "three or four years before she died, [she] asked me: 'Tell me, why *do* you not want to belong to the upper class?' Whom do you consider form (sic) the upper class?' 'The estate-owning nobility!' " (from the private papers of Parmenia Migel Ekstrom).

37. *Winter's Tales*, 5.

38. Columbia collection.

39. Clara Selborn interview.

40. Columbia collection.

41. Ibid.

42. *Titania*, 132.

43. Columbia collection.

44. *Winter's Tales*, 218.

45. See Bohdan Wytwycky, *The Other Holocaust: Many Circles of Hell* (Washington, D.C.: The Novak Report, 1980).

Chapter 24

1. Ole Wivel interview.

2. See *The Pact*.

3. Ibid., 32–33.

4. Ibid., 24.

5. Ibid., 38.

6. Ibid., 25.

7. Ibid., 54.

8. Along with Thorkild Bjørnvig, several people suggested this, including Aage Henriksen and Clara Selborn (interviews).

9. *The Pact*, 27.

10. Aage Henriksen, *Isak Dinesen/Karen Blixen, The Work and the Life* (New York: St. Martin's Press, 1988), recalls an experience reminiscent of this involving Isak Dinesen boring her finger into his neck, and his head feeling the effects of this for a long time after.

11. *The Pact*, 44.

12. See *Notater om Karen Blixen*.

13. *The Pact*, 43.

14. While in Africa, Aage Westenholz extracted a pledge from Tanne regarding Bror, not allowing him on the farm without serious consequences; the idea of a "pact" may have had one of its seeds there.

15. *The Pact*, 90.

16. Ibid., 63.

17. Ibid., 27. This inclination to act as a protective power, developed in Africa, was also mentioned by Eugene Haynes (interview, Missouri, 1983).

18. *The Pact*, 101. As early as *Out of Africa*, we see this sense of self as divine.

19. This trait of Tanne's was mentioned by others, including Aage Henriksen and Knud Jensen (interview, Copenhagen, 1981).

20. This aspect of Tanne was also mentioned by Aage Henriksen (interview), who writes about it more fully in *Isak Dinesen/Karen Blixen*.

21. Tanne's relationship with Thorkild Bjørnvig was in many ways a prototype (in a more minor key) of her relationship with others.

22. *The Pact*, 62.

23. *Last Tales*, 172.

24. *The Pact*, 62.

25. Many people commented on her striking appearance dressed up, and her sexual power then (Ole Wivel interview).

26. *The Pact*, 144.

27. Ibid., 168.

28. Will Durant, *The Story of Philosophy* (Garden City Publishing, N.Y.: 1938), 435.

Chapter 25

1. See *The Pact*.

2. See *Notater om Karen Blixen*. This mixing of vegetables and flowers may have been influenced by one of H. C. Andersen's stories.

3. See Caroline Carlsen in *Blixeniana*.

4. Ole Wivel interview.

5. Aage Henriksen interview.

6. One of the Heretics, Ole Wivel, has said: "*Heretica* had no school of thought but believed in many different things. The Heretics were different in their tastes but common in what they disliked—Marxism and Christianity, every system, they denied systems. Poetry, art is the experience you do and all

answers were false to them except those from the creative process—the poem, the painting were supposed to be the important thing. You find out the truth when you write. That was why the Heretics were very strong after the war. They could never join a political party. There are so many things that are all brought out in art—'I am the road, truth and the life.' The truth was astonishing even to yourself" (interview). It was a renegade movement, coming from the university at Aarhus, located on the "dark side of Jutland" (Birgit Bjørnvig interview), rather than the more socially acceptable University of Copenhagen. Hendrik Rosenmeier (interview, Copenhagen, 1980) had an interesting comment to make about the Heretics, noting that they were the first in Denmark to understand T. S. Eliot (i.e., modernism).

7. Knud Jensen emphasized Tanne's desire to be at the center of a "salon" (interview).

8. Eugene Haynes interview.

9. Ibid.

10. See *Titania*.

11. Eugene Haynes interview.

12. Birgit Bjørnvig interview.

13. Knud Jensen interview.

14. In her tales, Tanne's female characters at times gain authority through their alignment with the netherworld. Miss Nat-og-dag's talent lies in the instinctive ability to understand the power of masquerade as a method for transfiguring the undesirable, in a conscious and unconscious control through her *will to create*. In earlier versions of the tale, Miss Nat-og-dag is referred to as a witch—women of power, even with the power of madness, are often aligned with the potency of the witch's brew (Karen Blixen Archives). In "The Monkey," the prioress is liberated through the possession of unknown powers; in earlier versions of the tale she too is referred to as a witch (Karen Blixen Archives).

15. Eugene Haynes interview. The people around Tanne (in particular the Heretics) viewed her as having the psychic powers of a witch. In many different ways (sometimes out of fun), she contributed to this supernatural view of herself. With Eugene Haynes, for example, she referred to their special kinship—he was, she said, a witch, as she herself was one (Eugene Haynes interview). She had learned the power of witchcraft in Africa, as an imaginative force.

16. Eugene Haynes interview.

17. See *Notater om Karen Blixen*.

18. Eugene Haynes interview.

19. Clara Selborn interview.

20. *Winter's Tales*, 94.

21. Knud Jensen interview.

22. Aage Henriksen interview.

23. Steen Eiler Rasmussen interview.

24. *The Pact*, 104.

25. Aage Henriksen interview. Some of the ideas here appeared in a longer version in "Isak Dinesen: The Aesthetics of *Ehrengard*" (pp. 46–54), in *Karen Blixen/Isak Dinesen: Tradition, Modernity, and Other Ambiguities*; A University of Minnesota International Symposium, Conference Proceedings, April 17–20, 1985.

26. In a letter to Aage Henriksen, dated July 18, 1953, she wrote: "I do not

know whether I should have a bad conscience with regard to your manuscript,—I've kept it much too long, and I will send it back to you immediately,
or can you pick it up when you come here? I have read it to the best of my
ability and for this purpose I have borrowed Brandt's 'The Young Søren Kierkegaard,' which I have not read before. The result of it all has been a very
strange feeling of personal relationship to S. K. This you would probably consider cheeky by nature and only command or hide my cheekiness because I
happen to be such a good pupil. If you were to come here I would deliberately
run the risk of trying to explain to you what exactly I mean. All this,—
obviously written in great haste, because Pastor Ryhede is again hovering in
the background—all this is what my lyrical friends, who hate and fear the
story, call 'Teasing.' But I reckon that you will not let yourself be teased."

In a letter Dinesen wrote to Aage Henriksen on October 14, 1954, she
suggested the points at which she imaginatively departed from Kierkegaard's
"Diary of the Seducer": "Very much occupied by your book I have read Søren
Kierkegaard again that is to say—the Diary of the Seducer, I have not come
further in this round [of reading Kierkegaard's novels]. And in order to make a
story of it—(and because I, as you know, think that Cordelia must be permitted
to exist and be a human being, and that Johannes may stand and fall with her in
such a way that if she is not a human being then he is not a human being either
and if she is not a heroine in a story then he is no hero,)—I have imagined or
the imagination has appeared with me: I am no Cordelia, or this time Cordelia
is speaking. Johannes is dead, Cordelia is old, she has inherited from her aunt
and does now possess her own house. Then comes a young devoted nephew,
"student and poet," and brings her without an inkling of connection the diary
of the seducer which has just been published (historically incorrect). She reads
it and recognizes the letters, the conversations, the situation. And with the
weight of the many years she is older now than he was when the diary was
written, she now thinks (many different things, but among other things), If I
had known this at the very last as she's comparing her sorrow to his: "oh most
unhappy! Could I have saved you? Could I have made more of you than I did?"
An echo reaches Johannes' spirit and he thinks . . . ?" (The punctuation in
this correspondence has been left as it appears in the original letters; from the
private papers of Aage Henriksen; see *Blixeniana*.) Dinesen's cheeky quarrel
with Kierkegaard is clear as she imagines a possible reversal of events based
upon dissipating the air of innocence surrounding Johannes's victim, Cordelia.
As the tale unfolds, Ehrengard emerges not as a version of the passively diminished Cordelia, a weakened "valkyrie" (*Either/Or*, 1: 419), but is instead elevated to a powerful "young Walkyrie" (*Ehrengard*, 27–28). (Aage Henriksen
ended by dedicating his dissertation to Dinesen.)

The manner in which the correspondence between the countess and
Cazotte suggested itself to Dinesen can be seen in her October 14, 1954, letter
to Aage Henriksen. Dinesen was familiar with *Les Liaisons Dangereuses* by
Choderlos de Laclos (it is mentioned in "Carnival") and no doubt the structure
of his novel of seduction and erotic intrigue (presented through letters)
inspired the form of the correspondence between Cazotte and Countess von
Gassner.

27. Robert Langbaum, *Isak Dinesen's Art: The Gayety of Vision*, notes:
"*Ehrengard* takes off from the novel, 'Diary of the seducer'. . . . Isak Dinesen
actually proposed Kierkegaard's title for her story, when the *Ladies' Home
Journal* suggested a change in the title for its abbreviated version which came

out in December 1962 as 'The Secret of Rosenbad.' . . . *Ehrengard* is . . . an answer to Kierkegaard, in that Isak Dinesen wants us to consider the seducer a scoundrel or at least to see the esthetic life as a dead end. But Isak Dinesen sees in the seducer's desire to bring the girl to fulfillment—to bring her woman-hood to birth, in Kierkegaard's metaphor—an emblem of the artist's desire at just the point where it meets with God's. Far from being a dead end then, the esthetic life is for Isak Dinesen continuous with that spiritual or religious life which Kierkegaard is at such pains to distinguish from it" (274–75).

Aage Henriksen, one of the Heretics, noted in a personal interview, August 1981, that Cazotte had his antecedent in a French history of erotica of the eighteenth century. It seems likely that the name Cazotte was taken from the author Jacques Cazotte who lived in eighteenth-century France. Cazotte was known for his interest in music, the supernatural, and the fantastical. He fre-quented Parisian salons, meeting many leading figures of the day, pursuing some of his friendships through correspondence. As was the vogue at the time, he wrote fairy tales (the French tales at the time attacked the unbridled imagination—see Edward Pease Shaw, *Jacques Cazotte* [Cambridge: Harvard University Press, 1942], 26). One of his tales, "Ollivier," had a character named *Enguerrand* (suggesting Dinesen's name for her tale, *Ehrengard*), while his famous tale "Le Diable amoureux" was about the devil's attempt to seduce a Spanish man while disguised as a woman (*Jacques Cazotte*, 58). Dinesen, an admirer of E. T. A. Hoffmann, may have been led to Jacques Cazotte through Hoffmann's tale "Elementargeist," where "Le Diable amoureux" is discussed by two characters.

Cazotte owes much of his "poetic" conception to Kierkegaard; his temper-ament is an aesthetic replica of Kierkegaard's seducer:

> his poetic temperament which, we might say, is not rich enough, or, perhaps, not poor enough, to distinguish poetry and reality from one another. The poetical was the *more* he himself brought with him. This *more* was the poetical he enjoyed in the poetic situation of reality; he withdrew this again in the form of poetic reflection. This offered him a second enjoyment, and his whole life was motivated by enjoyment. In the first instance he enjoyed the aesthetic personally, in the second instance he enjoyed egoistically and personally what in part was that with which he himself had impregnated reality; in the second instance his personality was effaced, and he enjoyed the situation, and himself in the situation. In the first instance he constantly needed reality as occa-sion, as factor; in the second instance, reality was submerged in the poetic.

Either/Or, 1: 301.

28. Through the letters to the Countess von Gassner, we learn of the importance of the sensuous to Cazotte's conception of art:

> You call an artist a seducer and are not aware that you are paying him the highest of compliments. The whole attitude of the artist towards the Universe is that of a seducer.
>
> For what does seduction mean but the ability to make, with infinite trouble, patience and perseverence, the object upon which you concen-trate your mind give forth, voluntarily and enraptured, its very core and essence? Aye, and to reach, in the process, a higher beauty than it could ever, under any other circumstances, have attained? I have

seduced an old earthenware pot and two lemons into yielding their inmost being to me, to become phenomena of overwhelming loveliness and delight.

Ehrengard, 12.

29. When she met Viggo Kjær Petersen, Tanne had looked at him carefully, saying "I will have to be careful with you." They remained friends until her death (Viggo Kjær Petersen interview).

30. Aage Henriksen interview.

31. See *Isak Dinesen/Karen Blixen*.

32. Aage Henriksen interview. This conversation is recalled slightly differently in *Isak Dinesen/Karen Blixen*.

33. See *Isak Dinesen/Karen Blixen*.

34. There was a cold core to Isak Dinesen that no one could reach, recalled Aage Henriksen (interview).

Chapter 26

1. See *Notater om Karen Blixen*.
2. Eugene Haynes interview.
3. Ibid.
4. Ibid.
5. Ibid.
6. Ibid.
7. Ibid.
8. Ibid.
9. *Winter's Tales*, 151.
10. Ibid.
11. Viggo Kjær Petersen interview.
12. Ole Wivel interview.
13. Eugene Haynes interview.
14. Ibid.
15. Ibid.
16. See *Isak Dinesen/Karen Blixen*.
17. Viggo Kjær Petersen interview.
18. Ole Wivel interview.

Chapter 27

1. Houghton Library.
2. Ibid.
3. Ibid.
4. Ibid.
5. Ibid.
6. Ibid.
7. See *Notater om Karen Blixen*.
8. Columbia collection.
9. Library of Congress.
10. Aage Henriksen interview.

11. Ole Wivel interview.
12. Aage Henriksen interview.
13. *Titania*, 216.
14. Ibid., 217.
15. Clara Selborn interview.
16. Ibid.
17. Columbia Library.
18. Robert Langbaum interview.
19. See *Titania*.
20. Thorkild Bjørnvig and Birgit Bjørnvig interview.

Chapter 28

1. Parmenia Migel Ekstrom interview.
2. *Titania*, 223–24.
3. Ibid., 224–25.
4. Ibid., 222.
5. See *Notater om Karen Blixen*.
6. Feminists like Simone de Beauvoir and Gloria Steinem have been fascinated by such women as Bridget Bardot and Marilyn Monroe, respectively.
7. Eugene Haynes interview.
8. Ibid.
9. Ibid.
10. *Titania*, 239.
11. Parmenia Migel Ekstrom interview.
12. Ibid.
13. Ibid.
14. Aage Henriksen interview.
15. Eugene Haynes interview.

Chapter 29

1. Clara Selborn interview.
2. Parmenia Migel Ekstrom interview.
3. *Shadows on the Grass*, 102.
4. *Titania*, 238.
5. Ibid., 239.
6. Viggo Kjær Petersen interview.
7. Ole Wivel interview.
8. Viggo Kjær Petersen interview.
9. Ibid.
10. *Titania*, 180.

Epilogue

1. *Shadows on the Grass*, 112.
2. *Letters from Africa*, 252. In Africa, Tanne had written: "I have so often felt, when I heard that someone had died,—at that moment one feels that they

have ceased to exist at a single, isolated point in their existence, but their life, their personality becomes a completed reality, and they are equally alive in every phase of it, something in the same way as when one is watching a play at the theater."

3. *Letters from Africa*, 76.
4. Ibid., 288–89.

A Selected List of Secondary Sources

Abrams, M. H. *Natural Supernaturalism*. New York: W. W. Norton, 1971.

Altick, Richard D. *Victorian People and Ideas*. New York: W. W. Norton, 1973.

Andersen, Hans Christian. *The Story of My Life*. Boston: Houghton, Osgood & Co., 1880.

The Arabian Nights Entertainments. New York: Harper & Bros., 1915.

Barthes, Roland. *Mythologies*. Translated by Annette Lavers. New York: Hill & Wang, 1979.

Bate, Walter Jackson, ed. *Criticism: The Major Texts*. New York, 1952; 2d ed., New York: Harcourt Brace Jovanovich, 1970.

Beaton, Cecil. *Cecil Beaton's Diaries*. Boston: Little, Brown & Co., 1961.

Beaumont, Cyril W. *The History of Harlequin*. London: C. W. Beaumont, 1926.

Bornstein, George. *Transformations of Romanticism in Yeats, Eliot, and Stevens*. Chicago: University of Chicago Press, 1976.

Brandes, Georg. *Creative Spirits of the Nineteenth Century*. New York: Thomas Y. Cromwell, 1923.

———. *Naturalism in 19th Century English Literature*. Great Britain: Russell & Russell, 1957.

Bronsted, Johannes. *The Vikings*. Translated by Kalle Skov. New York, 1960; reprint New York: Penguin Books, 1978.

Carr, Virginia Spencer. *The Lonely Hunter*. New York: Anchor Books, 1976.

Chalmers, Patrick R. *Sport and Travel in East Africa (From the Diaries of the Prince of Wales)*. London: Philip Allan, 1934.

Chisholm, Anne. *Nancy Cunard*. New York: Penguin Books, 1981.

Crosland, Margaret. *Colette*. New York: Dell, 1975.

Croxal, T. H. *Glimpses and Impressions of Kierkegaard*. London: James Nesbet, 1959.

Dinesen, Thomas. *Merry Hell! A Dane with the Canadians*. Translated from *No Man's Land* by Thomas Dinesen. London: Jarrold, 1931.

Fog, Mogens. "Karen Blixen's sygdomhistoire." *Blixeniana* (1978): 139–46.

Gilbert, Sandra M., and Susan Gubar. *The Madwoman in the Attic*. New Haven: Yale University Press, 1979.

Githii, Ethel. *Literary Imperialism in Kenya: Elements of Imperial Sensibility in the African Works of Isak Dinesen and Elspeth Huxley*. Dissertation, Tufts University, 1980.

Givner, Joan. *Katherine Anne Porter*. New York: Simon & Schuster, 1982.

Green, Martin. *Re-appraisals: Some Commonsense Readings in American Literature*. London: Hugh Evelyn, 1963.

Gubar, Susan. "Blessings in Disguise: Cross Dressing as Re-Dressing for Female Modernists." *The Massachusetts Review* 22 (Autumn 1981): 477–508.

Haecker, Theodore. *Kierkegaard the Cripple*. Translated by C. Van O. Bruyn. London: Harvil Press, 1948.

Harvey, William J., and Christian Reppien. *Denmark and the Danes*. New York: Kennikat Press, 1970.

Henriksen, Aage. *Karen Blixen og Marionetterne*. Copenhagen: Wivel, 1952.

Henriksen, Liselotte. *Karen Blixen, En Bibliografi/ Isak Dinesen, A Bibliography.* Copenhagen: Gyldendal, 1977.

Hoffmann, E. T. A. *Tales of Hoffmann.* Edited by Christopher Lazare. New York: A. A. Wyn, 1946.

Holberg, Ludvig. *Selected Essays of Ludvig Holberg.* Translated by P. M. Mitchell. Conn.: Greenwood Press, 1976.

Huxley, Elspeth. *Forks and Hope: An African Notebook.* London: Chatto and Windus, 1964.

Huxley, Julian. *Memories.* London: George Allen & Unwin, 1970.

JanMohamed, Abdul. *Manichean Aesthetics: The Politics of Literature in Colonial Africa.* Amherst: University of Massachusetts Press, 1983.

Johannesson, Eric O. "Isak Dinesen, Soeren Kierkegaard, and the Present Age." *Books Abroad* 36 (Winter 1962): 20-24.

_____. *The World of Isak Dinesen.* Seattle: University of Washington Press, 1961.

Jorgensen, Aage, ed. *Isak Dinesen, Storyteller.* Copenhagen: Boghandel, 1972.

Karen Blixen/Isak Dinesen: Tradition, Modernity, and Other Ambiguities. A University of Minnesota International Symposium, Conference Proceedings, April 17-20, 1985.

Kierkegaard, Søren. *Crisis in the Life of an Actress.* London: Collins, 1967.

Kleist, Heinrich von. *The Marquise of O—and Other Stories.* Translated by David Luke and Nigel Reeves. New York: Penguin Books, 1980.

Kochno, Boris. *Diaghilev and the Ballets Russes.* Translated by Adrienne Foulke. New York: Harper & Row, 1970.

Laclos, Choderlos de. *Les Liaisons Dangereuses.* Paris: Editions de la Renaissance, 1966.

Lawson, Joan. *Ballet Stories.* New York: Mayflower Books, 1979.

Mack, John E. *A Prince of Our Disorder.* Boston: Little, Brown & Co., 1976.

Mann, Thomas. *Stories of Three Decades.* Translated by H. T. Lowe-Porter. New York: Alfred A. Knopf, 1936.

Marker, Frederick J. *Hans Christian Andersen and the Romantic Theatre.* Toronto: University of Toronto Press, 1971.

Marx, Leonie. "Literary Experimentation in a Time of Transition: The Danish Short Story After 1945." *Scandinavian Studies* 49 (Spring 1977): 131-37.

Mitchell, P. M. *A History of Danish Literature.* Copenhagen: Gyldendal, 1957.

Moers, Ellen. *The Dandy.* New York: Viking Press, 1960.

Niklaus, Thelma. *Harlequin, or The Rise and Fall of a Bergamask Rogue.* New York: George Braziller, 1956.

Pearson, John. *The Sitwells.* New York: Harcourt Brace Jovanovich, 1978.

Poe, Edgar Allen. *Eighteen Best Stories By Edgar Allen Poe.* Edited by Vincent Price and Chandler Brossard. New York: Dell, 1965.

Powys, Llewelyn. *Black Laughter.* New York: Blue Ribbon Books, 1924.

Prescott, William H. *The History of the Conquest of Peru.* Great Britain: J. M Dent & Sons, 1968.

Robson-Scott, W. D. *The Literary Background of the Gothic Revival.* Oxford: Clarendon Press, 1965.

Salter, Elizabeth. *The Last Years of a Rebel.* London: Bodley Head, 1967.

Sand, George. *My Convent Life.* Translated from *Histoire de Ma Vie* by Maria Ellery McCay. Chicago: Academy Press Limited, 1977.

_____. *My Life.* Translated by Dan Hofstadter. New York: Harper and Row, 1979.

Sartre, Jean-Paul. *Sartre on Theater.* New York: Random House, 1976.

Shakespeare, William. *The Tempest*. Edited by Robert Langbaum. New York: New American Library, 1964.

———. *The Winter's Tale*. Edited by Frank Kermode. New York: New American Library, 1963.

Shaw, Edward Pease. *Jacques Cazotte*. Cambridge: Harvard University Press, 1942.

Sitwell, Edith. *Taken Care Of, The Autobiography of Edith Sitwell*. New York: Atheneum, 1965.

Spencer, Charles. *The World of Serge Diaghilev*. New York: Viking, 1979.

Spink, Reginald. *Hans Christian Andersen and His World*. London: Thames and Hudson, 1972.

Thompson, Josiah. *Kierkegaard*. New York: Alfred A. Knopf, 1973.

Todorov, Tzvetan. *The Fantastic*. Translated by Richard Howard. New York: Cornell University Press, 1975.

Trzebinski, Errol. *The Kenya Pioneers*. New York: Norton, 1986.

Tyler, Parker. *The Divine Comedy of Pavel Tchelitchew*. New York: Fleet, 1967.

Walter, Eugene. "Isak Dinesen" interview. *Paris Review* (Autumn 1956): 14 43–59.

Whissen, Thomas R. *Isak Dinesen's Aesthetics*. New York: Fleet, 1973.

Index

A Note about the Author

Olga Pelensky was born in Austria, and raised in Chicago. She is a poet and an artist whose paintings have been on exhibit in Chicago, Boston, and Tennessee. Her writing has appeared in *The Washington Post*, *The Boston Globe*, *The Christian Science Monitor*, *The Philadelphia Inquirer*, and *The Miami Herald*, among other places. For this biography she travelled to Kenya, Denmark, and England. She teaches at Boston University and is working on a biography of Lillian Hellman.